SOCIAL AND GENDER BOUNDARIES IN THE UNITED STATES

Edited by
Sucheng Chan

With the assistance of Jenni Currie

Mellen Studies in Sociology
Volume 1

The Edwin Mellen Press
Lewiston/Queenston/Lampeter

Library of Congress Cataloging-in-Publication Data

Social and Gender Boundaries in the United States.

   (Mellen studies in sociology ; v. 1)
   1. United States--Social conditions. 2. Minorities--
United States--Social Conditions. 3. Women--United
States--Social Conditions. 4. Social classes--United
States. I. Chan, Sucheng. II. Series.
HN57.S59 1988   306'.0973   88-32573
ISBN 0-88946-631-9

This is volume 1 in the continuing series
Mellen Studies in Sociology
Volume 1 ISBN 0-88946-631-9
MSS Series ISBN 0-88946-630-0

The Edwin Mellen Press
P.O.Box 450
Lewiston, N.Y.
U.S.A.

The Edwin Mellen Press
Box 67
Queenston, Ontario
CANADA   L0S 1L0

The Edwin Mellen Press
Mellen House
Lampeter, Dyfed
Wales, U.K.
SA48 7DY

Printed in the United States of America

CONTENTS

Acknowledgements

The essays in this volume are based on papers presented at a Conference on the Comparative Study of Race, Ethnicity, Gender, and Class held at the University of California, Santa Cruz, on May 30-31, 1986. I wish to thank Professor Frank C. Child, then Dean of Social Sciences, for supporting my efforts with a grant that not only covered all conference expenses, but also paid for part of the salary of Jenni Currie, my editorial assistant. I also wish to thank the Committee on Research and Oakes College, both of the University of California, Santa Cruz, for paying the rest of Ms. Currie's wages. Without her superb assistance, it would have taken me at least a year longer to get these papers to the publisher.

New Studies in
Ethnicity, Gender, and Political Inequality

Sucheng Chan

Race, ethnicity, gender, and class have been four of the most important axes along which hierarchical relationships have been defined in American society. In recent years, scholars have begun to move away from analyses focusing on only one of these factors to studies that examine the "intersection" of race and class, of ethnicity and class, of ethnicity and gender, of gender and class, or some other combination that determines the relative position of individuals as well as of groups in the social structure. However, despite many sophisticated discussions, few authors, in my view, have shown convincingly how such "intersections" in fact occur. Some argue that one factor creates a structure of superordination and subordination that "parallels" the stratification pattern molded by another factor, leading to a "dual system" of inequality, others assert that one factor (usually ethnicity or gender) can be "subsumed" under a more overarching one (usually class), but few have chronicled how these various hierarchies evolved over time.

One reason it has been difficult to construct a general theory that takes race, ethnicity, gender, and class simultaneously into account is that theories of each phenomenon have been built upon the study of different populations. Theories of race have developed mainly out of empirical studies of blacks; those about ethnicity are derived primarily from works on European immigrants; theories of gender have depended heavily on writings about the experiences of white women, while theories of class, particularly those of the Marxian variety, explicate the situation of industrial workers who, until recent decades, were mainly white. A more general theory that attempts to combine all the relevant concerns will likely be either unwieldy and confused or so abstractly elegant that it is not particularly useful in guiding empirical research.

None of the authors in this volume claims to break new theoretical ground by offering what the existing literature has not yet provided. However, their studies taken together suggest hypotheses that should be explored in order to modify existing theories so that they can account for the experiences of people of color more accurately. In this introduction, I shall draw selectively upon the material contained in these studies, rather than provide summaries of them, as is often done in the introductions to similar anthologies. Some findings or conclusions that I shall highlight may not be the same ones that their authors deem most significant. Furthermore, because my approach is analytical, I shall write about some of the studies at greater length than about others. Before discussing the essays themselves, I shall classify--in all too cursory, schematic, and simplistic a manner--existing theories of ethnicity, gender, and inequality, *not* for the purpose of reviewing the relevant literature but simply to locate the studies in this volume within the broad landscape of academic discourse.[1]

Ethnicity

Theories of ethnicity propounded by American scholars, based as they are on the historical experience of European immigrants, are either explicitly or implicitly linked to theories of international migrations, particularly the trans-Atlantic migration. Alejandro Portes and Robert Bach pointed out in their comparative study of Cuban and Mexican immigrants that theories of immigration fall broadly into two groups, each based on a different view of society.[2] One is favored by those social scientists who regard society as an equilibrium-restoring system based on consensus, in which different parts of the system adapt to social change through the creation of a new equilibrium.[3] Such scholars depict migration as a phenomenon governed by certain push and pull factors, with people flowing from underdeveloped areas with low wages to industrializing or industrialized areas with higher wages. The immigrants supplement the domestic work force and can advance up the socioeconomic ladder of the receiving societies once they acquire education, vocational and professional skills, and greater familiarity with the culture of the host societies. In the United States, ethnic self-consciousness is considered a temporary phenomenon that will fade over time; as immigrants begin to adopt Anglo-American values and norms, they will find acceptance and be treated equally in the"melting pot." This analysis of assimilation relies heavily on two images: "uprooting" as depicted by Oscar Handlin and a "race relations cycle," which is evolutionary, linear, and unidirectional, as discussed by Robert Park.[4]

A different kind of theory assumes society is divided into segments that are often in conflict with each other.[5] According to the "conflict" theorists, who place more emphasis on the coercive aspects of immigration, many immigrants, instead of migrating voluntarily, are induced--often by deceptive means--to go to the receiving countries to serve as a subordinate labor force. These newcomers can be controlled and exploited easily by employers who consider them racially "inferior." Members of such immigrant/ethnic groups cannot get integrated readily into the host societies even if they want to, because innumerable obstacles are placed in their way. These hurdles are "structural," because they are embedded in the way society is organized and have little to do with the innate qualities of individuals.

In the eyes of the "conflict" theorists, it is precisely because such immigrants can be set apart socially that employers desire their labor. Their presence enables a capitalist economy to develop two sectors of production as well as two labor markets. The primary production sector is dominated by oligopolies, while the secondary sector is filled with small, competitive firms. The labor market is similarly divided, with the cleavage drawn largely along racial, ethnic, and gender lines. In the United States, "old stock" male Americans of northwestern European origins historically have cornered the bulk of the better paid, unionized, and consequently more secure jobs in the primary labor market, while southeastern European immigrants (at least in the early years of their settlement), Asian, Mexican and other Latin American immigrants, blacks, and women of all ethnic origins have filled the ranks of the secondary labor market, where the jobs are low paid, where working conditions are poor, and job security is virtually nil. According to this line of analysis, some members of these minority groups, denied ascent up the socioeconomic ladder, create self-employment in ethnic enclaves--one of the few channels of upward mobility open to them. Living and working in their own ghettos, they tend to retain strong ethnic bonds--"primordial" ties that help them to survive in a hostile environment.

Proponents of both kinds of theory agree that various minority groups and women have occupied different rungs of the income and status ladders, but they offer opposing explanations for why such inequality exists. When talking about nonwhite groups or about women of all ethnic backgrounds, "consensus" theorists either explicitly or implicitly attribute the lowly status of such groups to their inherent--indeed biological--"deficiencies." "Consensus" theorists thus tend to blame the victims for their plight. "Conflict" theorists, on the other hand, argue that American society is stratified along racial, ethnic, gender, and class lines because those in power have consciously created mechanisms to preserve their own privilege and to exploit the labor of others. Though "conflict" theorists do not hold the subordinate groups responsible for their exploitation and oppression, their analysis nonetheless also poses problems when applied to minority groups: it tends to depict people as pawns controlled almost entirely by external forces. Minority individuals are seldom credited with the ability to play a role in the making of their own history.

There is, in addition to the two identified by Portes and Bach, a third school of thought which attempts to reconcile the dichotomy between "consensus" and "conflict" theories. Both sociologists and historians have written in this vein. The best known representative of the sociological approach is the now-famous treatise by Milton Gordon published in 1964, in which he identifies seven "types" or "stages" of assimilation: behavioral/cultural (also known as acculturation), structural, marital (also known as amalgamation), identificational, attitude receptional, behavior receptional, and civic.[6] Gordon proposes that the different types of assimilation may occur at varying speeds and to different degrees. His scheme makes it possible to look at ethnicity and the process by which it changes (assimilation) as complex, rather than simple phenomena. More importantly, it recognizes that the responsibility for assimilation lies with both the members of the immigrant/ethnic/minority group *and* with members of the dominant society. That is to say, behavioral/cultural and identificational assimilation are two types of assimilation that depend largely on the learning ability and volition of the immigrant/ethnic/minority groups themselves; structural, attitudinal receptional, and behavior receptional assimilation will occur only if the host society is receptive and does not erect barriers to block the immigrant/ethnic/minority groups' attempts; while marital and civic assimilation require the joint efforts of the immigrant/ethnic/minority groups and the society at large.

In the last two decades, historians have also produced very fine studies of immigrants as they lived in their homelands before emigration and after their settlement in the United States.[7] Such works depict the subjective experiences of individuals as they moved from one environment to another, as well as the various ecological settings in which they found themselves. Combining qualitative and quantitative sources of information, these studies are at once more sophisticated than the early filio-pietistic accounts of immigrant life and more readable than sociological studies, and provide the basis for testing and even generating theories of how migration affects social stratification.

In general, the essays in this volume fall under the third rubric. Although every essay deals with ethnicity in some sense, I shall select five of them--those by Ramón Gutiérrez, Gilbert Gonzalez, Gini Matute-Bianchi, Gene Levine, and Karen Leonard--for my discussion of ethnicity. As a group, they underscore four points: 1) conceptions of ethnicity grow out of social interaction; 2) ethnic identities change over time in response to historical events; 3) the same ethnic labels may mean different things to different people or vary in meaning among the same individuals in successive periods; and 4) unequal power relationships in small settings, such as within families, as well as in large ones, such as within the international political arena, shape the outcome of ethnic interactions. Thus, ethnicity has social, historical, cultural, and political dimensions, and because it does, ethnic groups are internally differentiated. Gutiérrez examines how various ethnic labels came to be used in the Southwest; Gonzalez, by focusing on how modifications in ethnic behavior are externally imposed, is concerned with the political dimension of ethnicity (although he himself does not so call it); Matute-Bianchi outlines the internal differentiation within a student population in terms of each subgroup's perception of itself and of the larger society; Levine compares two groups and discovers that structural assimilation can be further divided into economic and social facets; and Leonard examines how one immigrant changed his sense of self over time, as he related to individuals who were emotionally important to him and responded to larger political and historical changes.

Gender

Like theories of ethnicity, theories of gender are of several varieties. Alison Jaggar groups the theories into four categories, divided according to various views of human nature: liberal feminist, radical feminist, Marxist feminist, and socialist feminist.[8] Because each theory identifies a different cause of women's exploitation, each proposes a different strategy for achieving their liberation. Since Aida Hurtado has reviewed these theoretical positions at some length in her essay in this volume and commented on the problems they pose for women of color, I shall not elaborate on Jaggar's scheme any further, except to note that liberal feminism is a form of "consensus" theory, whereas radical, Marxist, and socialist feminism are basically "conflict" theories.

Joan Scott has divided theories of gender differently--on the basis of the main issues with which various authors are concerned.[9] She distinguishes three kinds of analysis: theories that dissect how patriarchy subordinates females, Marxist theories that argue that women suffer because they are exploited workers in a capitalist system, and psychoanalytic approaches of two kinds--an Anglo-American school, whose adherents analyze how individuals are objectified and a French school, whose proponents examine how language shapes female identity. As an historian, Scott finds each of these approaches wanting. Theories of patriarchy, in her view, have two weaknesses. First, while asserting the primacy of patriarchy, they do not show how gender inequality is related to other kinds of stratification. Second, by resting their case ultimately on biological/physical differences, the analysts of patriarchy ignore the social and cultural meaning given the human body. Marxist theories are problematic because gender is treated as a subordinate aspect of economic inequality and has no "independent analytic status of its own." Object-relations theories, for their part, are concerned primarily with small social groups and do not show how they are connected to larger social, economic, and political systems. Theories of language, on the other hand, tend to universalize the "subjectively originating antagonism between males and females" and are insensitive to historical change and cultural relativism. To overcome such difficulties, Scott proposes an historically-informed approach that rests on two propositions: "gender is a constitutive element of social relations based on perceived differences between the sexes, and gender is a primary way of signifying relationships of power."[10]

Scott then identifies four "constitutive elements" of social relations--symbols, norms, politics, and subjective identity--and notes that a "question for historical research is, in fact, what the relationships among the four aspects are." That is to say, instead of positing *a priori* logical or causal connections among them, as social scientists often do, she believes that historians must discover the actual linkages through research. Her second proposition, that "gender is a primary field within which or by means of which power is articulated," if followed, will close the conceptual gap between the "public" and the "private" spheres--a distinction that underpins theories of patriarchy--so that gender becomes a key phenomenon one would examine, along with traditionally-defined politics, diplomacy, and war, if one wishes to understand the overall distribution of power, be it at the subnational, national, or international levels.

Six essays in this volume touch upon gender issues, but in three of them, the analysis of gender is secondary, so I shall discuss only the works of Stephanie Reynolds, Aida Hurtado, and Alvina Quintana in the section on gender. Hurtado argues that we must examine "the dissimilar way in which sexist oppression is imposed on each group [white women and women of color] and the different relationship each group has to white men" if we are to understand why women of color have not hopped onto the white feminist bandwagon in droves. Reynolds and Quintana demonstrate how cultural expressivity and gender inequality are linked. Reynolds offers a detailed comparative ethnographic analysis of women's dance behavior and the manner in which women serve as conservators of culture, especially when their society is dominated by another, while Quintana maps the terrain of Chicana literature.

The three essays on gender in this volume do not fit easily within the existing schools of feminist theory, but concerned as they are with representation and expression, they highlight the symbolic aspect of gender interaction and of power distribution that Scott delineated. Collectively, they make the following points: 1) observable changes in gender relations within an immigrant/ethnic/minority group are some of the most salient indicators that the group is changing its sense of ethnicity; 2) women can play diametrically opposite roles in cultural/ethnic transformation--sometimes they act as the motive force for change while at other times they serve as traditional culture's main conservators; 3) because of their gender-based ability to undermine external efforts to "deculturalize" their people, the female members of subjugated groups must often choose between the obligation to uphold their ancestral culture and the desire to free themselves from sexist oppression; 4) the mechanisms used to subordinate white middle-class women (on whose experiences white feminist theories are based) are not the same as the ones employed to reduce women of color to a marginal existence, so before existing feminist theories can be applied to the latter's experience, they must be enlarged to account for a more complex and broader range of phenomena; and 5) as is true for white feminists, feminists of color consider the reappropriation of language--and consequently of history, culture, and psychology--to be one of the most important means available to them for achieving gender equality.

Political Inequality

Since the essays on political inequality do not directly address race or class as analytical categories, I shall not discuss theories of race and class except to note that the former, because they are concerned primarily with explaining racism, can be divided into three groups according to where each locates the origins of racism, while the latter fall generally either into a Marxist or a Weberian mode, with many complicated permutations for the Marxist one.

Writers who trace the evolution of "race" as an idea show how it developed to justify specific historical events, such as the enslavement of Africans by Europeans and the latter's efforts at colonizing much of the rest of the world.[11] Another group of scholars argues that racial inequality exists because certain people gain economically by exploiting the labor of others.[12] A third school of thought focuses on the psychological rewards that whites enjoy by denigrating people of color.[13]

As for theories of class, Karl Marx, as is well known, saw an individual's relationship to economic production--specifically the ownership, or lack thereof, of property capable of creating other material goods--as the primary determinant of one's class position.[14] Unlike Marx, Max Weber believed that class was only one of the three main bases of group solidarity, the other two being "status groups" and political parties. While Weber conceived of classes as expressions of economic, particularly property, relationships, he defined "status situation" as

> every typical component of the life fate of men that is determined by a specific, positive or negative, social estimation of *honor* . . . In content, status honor is normally expressed by the fact that a specific *style of life* can be expected from all those who wish to belong to the circle. Linked with this expectation are restrictions on 'social' intercourse (that is, intercourse which is not subservient to economic . . . purposes). . . . Stratification by status goes hand in hand with a monopolization of ideal and material goods or opportunities."

Parties, on the other hand, "reside in the sphere of power." Weber's formulation of political parties is intimately tied to his discussions of the modern bureaucratic state. In his understanding, although parties

> *may* represent interests determined through class situation or status situation . . . they need be neither purely class or purely status parties.[15]

The three essays in this volume that examine racial politics do not fall readily into the three approaches to understanding racism mentioned above. Rather, their authors see race relations as a changing phenomenon shaped by a continual struggle for power between whites and people of color. Unlike the existing literature which, by concentrating on how racism benefits its perpetrators, is primarily about the white side of the racial equation, the essays by Michael Fitzgerald, Michael Omi, and Isidro Ortiz and Maguerite Marin examine the calculations and actions of whites *and* people of color. By giving equal consideration to both, Fitzgerald, Omi, and Oritz and Marin have rescued people of color from the objectification they have suffered at the hands of scholars and have restored to them their rightful role as subjects of history. These essays highlight how the relative distribution of rewards and privileges in a society always results from struggles between or among different groups. That being the case, the stratification system in a plural society is inherently unstable, but it is this very instability that gives the members of subordinated groups some hope that improvements in their lot may be possible.

The Studies in this Volume

In "Changing Ethnic and Class Boundaries in America's Hispanic Past," Ramón Gutiérrez documents how ethnic labels used by different subgroups within the Spanish/Mexican population in the American Southwest have changed over time. At important historical junctures, these subgroups have felt the need to set themselves apart from others. In the history of Spanish America, three turning points stand out: the Spanish conquest and colonization of the Southwest, the American conquest of the region from Mexico, and large-scale Mexican immigration into the area after the turn of the present century.

According to Gutiérrez, at the time the Spaniards first arrived in the New World, they did not yet have a strong sense of national identity and thought of themselves mainly in religious and regional terms. Only in the process of colonizing the indigenous Indian population did the Spaniards begin to view themselves as a cohesive group. Beneath their developing sense of commonality, however, were finely nuanced status gradations based upon an individual's "purity of blood" or race, religion, citizenship, legitimacy of birth, wealth, and occupation--all of which, together, determined what Gutiérrez calls an individual's "total social personality." Purity of blood, religion, and citizenship mattered because in Spanish history these concerns were intertwined. The Islamic "Moors" had occupied the Iberian peninsula for centuries, and Spanish national identity was forged in the process of ousting them from Spain. The Moors, the Sephardic Jews who had settled in the Iberian peninsula in their diaspora, Africans whom Spanish traders encountered in their travels, and North American Indians whom Spanish soldiers, priests, and colonizers subjugated, were all dark-skinned, non-Christian, and alien. The Spanish defined themselves in terms of the opposite characteristics: fair-skinned, Christian, and Spanish. Legitimacy of birth was also important because the Christian notion of holy marriage upheld a patriarchal system. Finally, wealth and occupation indicated the material resources one commanded and one's station in life. Gutiérrez's account suggests that in studying complexly defined and internally differentiated ethnic groups, where so many diffferent factors interact to define an individual's or a group's identity and social standing, the Weberian notion of class may be more appropriate than the Marxist one.

The entry of the Americans created the second occasion when individuals of Spanish-Indian ancestry felt compelled to differentiate among themselves as well as between themselves and other groups. Because Mexico as a nation had existed for only a quarter century at the time of the American conquest, the people in the Southwest had not yet developed a strong sense of Mexican identity and still referred to themselves by regional categories. The Americans, however, called them all Mexicans. The nomenclature was not neutral, as Americans also held people of color in contempt, and Mexicans, in their eyes, were definitely nonwhite, even though the 1848 Treaty of Guadalupe-Hidalgo, which concluded the Mexican-American War (1846-1848), classified them as whites. To avoid potential castigation, the long-time residents of the Southwest insisted they were *Californios, Tejanos,* or *Neuvo Mexicanos,* depending on which state they lived in. Gutiérrez points out that by using such labels, these people were trying to emphasize their Spanish ancestry and to minimize or even disavow their Indian heritage.

The third period of internal differentiation began as an increasing number of lower-class Mexicans immigrated into the Southwest in the early twentieth century. At that point, the "old stock" Spanish-ancestry population further stressed their Spanishness in order to distinguish themselves from the new immigrants. As Gutiérrez reads the evidence, on this occasion the ethnic labels became infused with connotations of class. Terms such as *Chicano, pocho,* and *surumato* evolved to draw horizontal lines of demarcation among those of Mexican ancestry. Though originally a term of class-conscious denigration, *Chicano* eventually took on political meaning in the 1960s, when young activists used it both to affirm their pride in their working-class origins and to repudiate the social snobbery it signified within the Mexican American community.

Unlike theories that deal abstractly with the "intersection" of race and class, or ethnicity and class, without showing how such "intersections" take place, Gutiérrez's fine-grained historical analysis shows us how a group divides itself and is divided by others into segments both within itself and vis-à-vis the larger society through social interaction over time. Such an approach illuminates the manner in which ethnicity is both subjectively perceived and objectively ascribed. It also reminds us that ethnicity is always Janus-faced: an ethnic identity is simultaneously an affirmation ("I am X") and a denial ("I am not Y"). And finally, as Gutiérrez's explication of the term *Chicano* shows, the formation or selection of an ethnic identity often, though not always, involves a conscious political choice.

While key historical events set the larger contexts within which ethnic identities are forged, how identities are transmitted at the individual level from one generation to the next can best be understood by looking at socialization processes. Some instruments used to socialize young as well as new adult members of a group are internally created while others are externally imposed. In "The Americanization of Mexican Women and Their Families during the Era of De Jure School Segregation, 1900-1950," Gilbert Gonzalez analyzes one such externally imposed mechanism of cultural transmission: Americanization programs which were used at once to "deculturalize" Mexican Americans and to render them more desirable as workers. These programs were gender-specific in their conception and implementation, so Gonzalez's discussion of them illustrates how ethnicity and gender interfaced in one specific historical setting.

The creators of the Americanization programs, through which foreigners would be--it was hoped--made into Americans, believed that children's consciousness can be molded through schooling. Therefore, Americanization teachers could function as agents of social and cultural change. The goal of the programs was to "separate" Mexican children from their homes, the source of Mexican culture and identity, in order to give them a new and better "model" of home. The programs specifically focused on girls and women because their advocates believed that to change them was doubly efficacious: not only would they themselves reform their personal habits and values, but they would also, in the process of caring for their husbands and raising their children, introduce a different lifestyle into the Mexican American community. The core instruction in the programs involved home economics--cooking, sewing, cleaning, caring for husbands and children, teaching the menfolk responsibility and punctuality, and other similarly good, white American middle-class habits.

The programs, according to Gonzalez, did not serve the needs of Mexican immigrants well, because they contained two contradictions and the policy behind them was "schizophrenic." First, while attempting to wipe out certain "Mexican" cultural traits which were deemed "undesirable," they unwittingly upheld the patriarchal Mexican American family and its attendant norms of social behavior by perpetuating the sexual division of labor and the separation of the public sphere of work from the private sphere of homelife. Second, though the programs tried to inculcate "desirable" white American middle-class virtues, those who paid for them--state agencies, local school districts, and employers of Mexican American workers--wanted, at the same time, to ensure that Mexican immigrants remained a cheap, docile labor force. Since the Mexican immigrants' peasant background, inability to speak proper English, and lack of knowledge of American society made them easier to exploit, the "American" traits that the programs intended to impart were very selective indeed, and focused mainly on personal habits. Though Gonzalez does not state so explicitly, his discussion implies that characteristics associated with "rugged individualism"--independence, the courage to question and challenge authority, and the willingness to move on when a particular social environment becomes too restrictive--were definitely not aspects of "American" culture the "Mexicans" were supposed to learn through the Americanization programs.

This study of externally-determined, selective assimilation illustrates how members of a majority group may preach assimilation, but in reality will use the "ethnic" traits of a minority group to keep the latter in its lowly position, all the while criticizing them for their "un-American" backwardness. The Americanization teachers were certainly very much impressed with their own importance as agents of social change. As one stated, she felt she and her colleagues had "been the sources of the greatest improvement in human living" in the labor camps where Mexican immigrant workers and their families lived. That they had such a missionary attitude should not be surprising: after all, to "civilize the natives"--whether at home or abroad--was not only the white man's, but also the white woman's, burden.

Gonzalez's study suggests that ethnicity and gender are linked because women are considered to be repositories of culture, and their socially constructed gender roles are regarded as vehicles for cultural change, by virtue of their "natural" responsibilities in childbearing and childrearing. In short, gender-specific behavior is the fulcrum upon which ethnic transformation turns.

Gonzalez does not discuss the outcome of the Americanization efforts; neither does he examine how Mexican girls and women viewed and reacted to them. Gini Matute-Bianchi, writing about students in a high school in a different setting at a much later point in time, sketches several possible outcomes of the interaction between the Mexican-ancestry population and the American schooling system in her essay, "An Ethnographic Study of Mexican-Descent Students in a California High School." She classifies the students she observed into five subgroups: recent Mexican immigrants, the Mexican-oriented, Mexican Americans, *Chicanos,* and *cholos.* She examines the scholastic performance of each and discovers that the better students belong largely to the Mexican-oriented and the Mexican American subgroups, while the recent immigrants fare reasonably well, and the *Chicanos* and *cholos* do not do well at all.

Matute-Bianchi argues that the reasons for the lackluster performance of some of the recent immigrants, on the one hand, and the *Chicanos* and *cholos,* on the other hand, differ: the former, as a result of their limited English fluency and lack of familiarity with American culture, suffer from what she calls primary cultural differences, which existed prior to the students' arrival in the United States; the latter are hampered by secondary cultural differences, which developed after the subordinate group was "involuntarily incorporated" into American society. Matute-Bianchi claims that overcoming primary cultural differences does not threaten the immigrant students' Mexican ethnic identity. Such students are eager to learn the white American's ways so that they can do well in school, get good jobs, and become "successful" adults. As innocent recent immigrants, they are motivated by the American dream of achieving upward mobility through education and hard work.

Efforts to transcend secondary cultural differences, in contrast, subject the *Chicano* and *cholo* students to "derision, condescension, and mockery," because their peers consider being a "good" student to be a form of assimilation, which, in their eyes, is a betrayal of their ethnicity. Students who think this way do not believe the American dream will work for them; they see evidence all around them of family members and friends trapped in cycles of poverty from which there seems to be no escape, no matter how hard they strive. These students, who are American-born for the most part, do not have the same naive belief that working hard will pay off. To them, being a "good" student constitutes a loss, whereas being a "poor" student is an act of defiance, a stance taken in opposition to the dominant culture. Therefore, in Matute-Bianchi's view, the refusal of the *Chicano* and *cholo* students to conform to the behavior that teachers expect from good or successful students is, in fact, one means that an oppressed group uses "to resist structured inequality." Seen in this light, the students' behavior is a result of conscious choices they have made, given their own assessment of their life chances.

Matute-Bianchi's ethnographic approach allows her to get beneath the surface to explore the subjective consciousness of her informants, particularly the symbolic content of their ethnic identities. Like Gutiérrez, she demonstrates that ethnic labels convey profound meaning--meaning which is situationally determined. I think Matute-Bianchi's analysis can be carried further. There are two intriguing findings she does not elucidate. First, she does not explain why *some* American-born students (the Mexican Americans) do assimilate and behave in a manner conducive to scholastic success, while others (the *Chicanos* and *cholos)* do not. Since all three subgroups are American-born, their different behavior cannot be explained by their differential degree of "assimilation." Second, it is obvious the divergent behavior and performance of the five subgroups of students cannot be attributed to objective class differences, for all five come from families in which most of the wage-earners are farmworkers, cannery workers, and common laborers. To make further sense of her data, I believe we need to consider two propositions: members of a dominant group tend to allow subordinate groups (regardless of whether that subordination is based on race, ethnicity, gender, or class) to behave only in limited ways, and class position is not the same as class aspirations.

One of Matute-Bianchi's findings that requires further analysis is the fact that her data on teacher perceptions and attitudes point to a paradox that Gonzalez has already alluded to: although individuals from minority groups are encouraged to assimilate--indeed, in some instances, coerced into doing so--members of the dominant group often find only certain forms of behavior on the part of subordinate individuals acceptable. That is to say, there are specific kinds of positively-valued behavior that members of a dominant culture reserve for themselves. Others are not allowed to adopt similar manners. For example, when members of subordinate groups act with self-confidence--supposedly a desirable trait and an indicator of leadership--they are often accused of being "uppity." Why? Because they have "overstepped their bounds" and violated the sense of propriety or etiquette held by members of the dominant group, who feel threatened when "inferior" beings act assertively.

As I read Matute-Bianchi's evidence, the teachers in her study like the courteous behavior of the recent-immigrant students precisely because the deferential stance that students in Mexico are taught to assume towards their teachers is congruent with the behavior that white Americans expect from nonwhite minority groups and from women. Even though teachers in the United States are supposed to delight in students who are creative, who ask lots of questions, and who challenge received wisdom, they nonetheless also like their classrooms to be controllable. Recent-immigrant students who behave ever so politely and who are always eager to learn are a relief to teachers who have other students who are rowdy. Thus, Mexican (and Asian) immigrant students who are courteous to their teachers "stroke" the latter's egos in at least two ways: their respect is at once a sign of appreciation for their teachers *qua* teachers and an acknowledgement of their own "inferior" ethnic/racial status vis-à-vis whites. Because such behavior is "appropriate," it is more often than not rewarded. Like the Americanization teachers Gonzalez described, the teachers Matute-Bianchi observed are willing to "help" the well-behaved students because the latter fulfill the former's desire to have their status in life affirmed. In this instance, certain aspects of "ethnicity" (deferential behavior learned in another country) are valued because they shore up deeply-rooted concepts of racial hierarchy in American society. The *Chicano* and *cholo* students--especially the latter, who "act like gang members"--in contrast, offend their teachers because they are "smart-mouthed," "street tough," and "more Americanized." Not only are they sassy towards authority figures, but they also seem contemptuous of their assimilated Mexican American peers, whom they call "Wannabees"--"want to be white/Anglo." Their use of such slurs is clearly a not-so-veiled insult to all "Anglos."

What differentiates the recent immigrants, the Mexican-oriented, and the Mexican Americans, on the one hand, from *Chicanos* and *cholos*, on the other hand, is that the former wish to escape the class standing into which they were born and to join the amorphous American middle class. Said one student, "I've got to do well in school so that I don't have to face this [working in a cannery as her parents do] in my future." Students with such aspirations are willing either to give up their ethnicity altogether (as some Mexican American students have done) or they feel that doing well in school does not threaten their cultural identity (as is true of the recent-immigrant and Mexican-oriented students). The *Chicano* and *cholo* students, however, have decided that any aspiration for upward social mobility through education is unrealizable, so they do not strive for it. Instead, they hang on adamently to what they do have--a lower-class lifestyle that undergirds both their ethnic and their class identities. Thus, the class aspirations of the recent immigrants, the Mexican-oriented, and the Mexican Americans, are not the same as their objective class positions, whereas class aspiration and class position coincide for the *Chicanos* and *cholos*. What needs to be explored in the future is the historical process by which two dichotomous subcultures--one assimilationist and the other oppositional--developed among the American-born within the Mexican American community.

The short report by Gene Levine, "Assimilation in Comparative Perspective: Jewish and Japanese Americans," compares selected findings from two large surveys he has undertaken and illuminates in yet another way the different manner in which various groups have dealt with their ethnic identity. Both Japanese Americans and Jewish Americans, by all common socioeconomic indicators, such as educational attainment and income level, have become "successful." Levine finds that in terms of educational attainment and income, Jewish Americans have done better than Japanese Americans, but in terms of social integration into white/gentile American society, Japanese Americans have moved farther along, at least in Los Angeles: two out of three Japanese Americans count at least one white person among their best friends, while only four out of ten Jewish Americans count one gentile among their closest acquaintances; Japanese Americans are more likely to work with whites and to socialize with the latter outside of work than are Jewish Americans to work and socialize with gentiles; Japanese Americans belong to majority-group associations more frequently than Jewish Americans do; a larger percentage of Japanese Americans in Los Angeles live in white neighborhoods than do Jewish Americans among gentiles; and Japanese Americans worry less about interracial marriage (and the consequent erosion of the biological basis of their ethnicity) than do Jewish Americans.

High educational/economic attainment and social integration are both manifestations of what Milton Gordon calls structural assimilation. It would be interesting to know how the divergent historical experiences of Japanese and Jewish Americans have led them down different paths of structural assimilation. For example, to what extent and in what ways did the internment of persons of Japanese ancestry during World War II affect their post-war behavior? Was their ethnicity such a painful marker that they did everything they could to erase it after they were released from confinement? And did white Americans, out of some retrospective sense of guilt, lower the barriers against Japanese Americans so that the latter could finally assimilate--at least during the 1960s and 1970s when Levine carried out his surveys? As for Jewish Americans, is their concern with their "survival" as a "solidary ethno-religious group" a result of the holocaust? And is their relative social insulation the result of the anti-Semitism that still exists?

Another interesting finding of Levine's that he does not delve deeply into, and which has a direct bearing on the relationship between race/ethnicity and class, is that for both the *Nisei* and *Sansei* (second- and third- generation Japanese Americans, respectively), behavioral (though not attitudinal) acculturation is positively correlated with socioeconomic status. Not only that, but there is also a positive correlation between these two generations' degree of acculturation and the socioeconomic status of their fathers, the *Issei*, as well as with that of their grandfathers in Japan who did not even emigrate to the United States! As Levine puts it, "the degree to which a *Sansei* in the 1980s becomes economically and socially integrated into American society is associated with the educational and economic accomplishments of his great-grandparents a century earlier." Levine concludes that "socioeconomic mobility can best be understood within families and over generations." I believe it is possible to go beyond this conclusion to say something more, and that is, the acceptance of nonwhite minorities into white American society may largely (though not entirely) be a class-specific phenomenon. Members of immigrant/ethnic/minority groups who already possess the behavioral characteristics associated with middle-class membership will be accepted much more readily, while those who do not, will find innumerable obstacles in their way. Worse, any efforts by the latter to act "above their station" may bring reprimands, as I suggested earlier. Individuals from middle- or upper-class backgrounds in their countries of origin who get integrated economically, socially, and culturally into the host society, therefore, are simply moving horizontally from one country to another, while remaining in the same class.

There being few intergenerational mobility studies of nonwhite groups, the theoretical implications of Levine's findings on Japanese Americans may most readily be compared with recent studies of European immigrant groups. Contrary to the image of the melting pot, in many localities in the United States European immigrants did not move up the socioeconomic ladder at a rapid rate. Only in large cities during periods of industrial expansion did certain groups of immigrants with particular skills find the kind of opportunities that had served as a lodestone to lure them to America's shores. For example, in the case of Jewish immigrants in New York City, education did not initially serve as a channel of upward mobility, as earlier writers had believed. Rather, revisionist studies have shown that second-generation Jewish Americans began going to college only after their immigrant parents had established a secure economic foundation through (urban) skilled crafts and retail trade.[16] In other words, intergenerational mobility was from one kind of middle-class status (skilled crafts and retail trade, which provided middle-class incomes but not concommitant social status) to another (the professions, which provided both middle-class earnings and social status). New York's Jewish Americans were able to obtain higher education and to enter the professions at the beginning of the twentieth century in increasing numbers only because of a fortuitious conjuncture of circumstances: tuition-free City College of New York opened its doors to them, changes in the American economy increased the need for professionals, and most importantly, several decades of Jewish immigration had cumulatively created a sufficiently large coethnic clientele in the city to allow many newly-minted professionals to earn a viable living. But the middle-class is where most Jewish Americans have remained; relatively few have joined the ranks of the true upper crust, despite their spectacular artistic, literary, and intellectual achievements in the United States. This same pattern of movement from one segment of the middle class to another is being repeated today by Cuban and Asian immigrants.[17]

Ethnicity, gender, and class status are more than group phenomena, however. They also affect the psyches of individuals. To get at the psychological component of ethnic identity, Karen Leonard analyzes one man's changing concept of himself and of society over his life cycle in "Immigrant Punjabis in Early Twentieth-Century California." She documents how Moola Singh, her informant, an adherent of the Sikh faith from the Punjab region of India, slowly learned different behavior and gave new cultural meaning to his experiences within the scope of his personal life. In addition, she briefly discusses how political changes in India, U.S. legislation, and changes in American immigration policies, all affected Singh's life profoundly. Leonard thus provides an individualized illustration of the point that Gutiérrez makes in his paper about the impact of history and politics on concepts of ethnicity.

Singh's life is particularly fascinating because he bridges four cultures: the Indian culture of his youth, the immigrant culture that evolved among his Indian compatriots in California, the lower-class white American culture represented by several of the women he was involved with, and the Mexican immigrant culture of other women in his life. Leonard shows how his ideas of love, sex, and marriage--at least by the time she interviewed him late in his life--had departed significantly from Indian norms and had become quite congruent with American ideals. In her view, the changes in his attitude towards women, sex, and marriage are the clearest indications of how he had redefined his ethnically-dictated values. Once again, we see how intergenderal norms (proper behavior towards the opposite sex) provide a crucial vehicle through which the contents of ethnicity are transformed.

An individual's view of his/her religion provides another angle of vision from which changes in the content of ethnicity may be viewed. Because their numbers were relatively small and American society was extremely hostile towards their presence, immigrants from India, who belonged to three different faiths--Sikhism, Hinduism, and Islam--muted their religious differences in the early years of this century and sometimes shared the same "temple" (built by the Sikh immigrants) for social occasions. A practice that may have grown out of necessity became a desirable phenomenon in the eyes of Moola Singh. He also liked the fact that those who frequented the temple adopted certain "American" practices, such as using chairs and eating on plates. After Indian immigration resumed in the late 1960s, the old pioneers became outnumbered by more recent immigrants, who succeeded in reimposing certain orthodox practices in the Sikh temple. Moola Singh's disapproval of the return to orthodoxy, like his censure of the way women were traditionally treated in India, provides another yardstick of the extent to which he has refashioned his ethnic identity. He is still a Punjabi Sikh, but his values and behavior differ greatly from those of other individuals who carry the same ethnic label.

Finally, though state policies and international politics strongly influenced the ethnic identity of Asian Indian immigrants by setting the parameters within which they could act, as Leonard shows, the final outcome nevertheless depended on conscious choices that the immigrants made. When exclusion laws barred further immigration after 1917, the main source of ethnic renewal was cut off, and those men who remained in the United States adapted to conditions here as best they could. However, after immigration resumed after 1968, social intercourse with India became possible again, and the old immigrants reacted in two diametrically opposite ways. Some left their Mexican, white, or black wives and mixed-blood children, returned to India, married (usually much younger) Indian women, and brought them and other relatives over; others, like Moola Singh, remained loyal to their American/Mexican families. What needs to be explained in this case, too, is why some individuals make the choices that they do.

Women play an especially crucial role as mediators between external forces and the culture of a people. The relationship between ethnicity and gender is analyzed in detail by Stephanie Reynolds in "The Role of Women in the Conservation of Culture: Gender Constraints in Tongan and Northern Ute Dance Forms." Reynolds looks at constraints in women's dance behavior--using the term "constraint" in a much broader sense than "limitation"--in order to test prevailing theories of women's art. She argues that an examination of changing constraints on women's dance behavior will reveal how the forms of a particular culture, as well as its internal cohesion, are being modified.

Reynolds focuses on three types of constraints: progenerative constraints related to women's biology, their role in reproduction, and the cultural meaning given those biological/physical aspects of women's existence; constraints on the extent to which women, compared to men, are allowed to be demonstrative in their art forms, particularly in dance; and hieratic constraints on women's participation in religious rituals, of which dance is a component part. Reynolds' evidence indicates that progenerative and hieratic constraints are dialectically related: in many societies, menstruation and childbirth are regarded as polluting phenomena, so that women in certain phases of their biological cycle are kept away from men while the latter are performing sacerdotal functions. Progenerative and hieratic constraints on women restrict the range of their activities, whereas constraints on demonstrativeness are manifested as greater abstraction in women's art forms.

Reynolds discusses how each of these types of constraints functioned in the past in Tongan and Northern Ute societies and how they have been eroded by the incursion of Western culture. Though women are now allowed to participate in hieratic dance forms, they are still prevented from engaging in certain kinds of action. To explain such continual restrictions on women, Reynolds cites Jorgensen's observation that in circumstances where men are losing power in real life (as the Northern Ute men have been in the past century under white American domination), they tend to seek it in a different--in this instance, spiritual--form. Hence their efforts to protect male prerogatives in rituals. This statement can be generalized to apply to male-female relations in other settings: when a group as a whole has been subjugated--whether politically, economically, socially, or culturally--by another, then its male members are likely to act defensively to preserve whatever traditional rights and privileges they may have enjoyed as men, while the female members are likely to challenge such prerogatives by making inroads into hitherto male domains.

The opposite phenomenon, however, can also occur. As Reynolds shows, instead of acting as the cutting edge in transforming gender relations, women in subjugated societies often play a stronger role in conserving traditional culture, because their cultural forms, being more abstract, are less easy to decipher and hence less threatening to the colonizing powers. In Reynold's words, "the fact that abstract forms do not appear to be subversive may facilitate their retention in a culture which is dominated by external forces. This may explain why women's art forms may persist longer under situations of domination." Seen in this light, more abstract art forms are in fact one expression of the private sphere of women, the nature of which theorists of patriarchy have tried to elucidate. That is to say, even though dance involves public performance, women dancers can convey meaning in a more private way through the use of symbols which, being nonliteral, can be understood only by those initiated or socialized into the culture. The significance of women's symbolic, abstract movements are opaque to outsiders. Thus, "feminizing" their art forms may be one way that members of a subordinated group can preserve their culture.

To expect women to play an active role in conserving traditional culture (and its corollary, ethnic identity), however, places an enormous burden on them. It means that women belonging to subordinated groups must choose between defending their culture's "integrity"--an integrity partly built upon the subordination of women--or liberating themselves from sexist oppression. Just as Matute-Bianchi's findings alert us to the importance of investigating the circumstances under which some members of a group are likely to assimilate while other members are likely to resist cultural domination, so Reynolds' data should lead us to inquire when women are likely to preserve traditional values and when they are likely to lead efforts to change ethnically-sanctioned sexist behavior.

Unlike Reynolds, whose analysis is based on an outsider's observations, Aida Hurtado and Alvina Quintana offer insiders' views of the consciousness of *Chicanas*. Like the writers whom Quintana explicates, they are "acting as their own ethnographers, using the word for self-representation . . . [which] provides an indispensable mechanism for deconstructing the Chicana cultural experience, because it effectively eliminates the possibility of outsiders misinterpreting cultural symbolic systems and allows the Chicana to express her own ambivalence towards her ethnicity and gender." A number of points should be made about these two essays. First, their authors use the terms *Chicano* and *Chicana* in the 1960s political sense and not in the way that Matute-Bianchi's students use these words. To distinguish between the two usages, in editing Hurtado's and Quintana's essays, I have not italized *Chicano* and *Chicana*. Second, Hurtado employs the analytical construct of the "ideal type," so that when she states that white middle-class women think this way, or women of color behave that way, she is not claiming that all white women or all women of color fit neatly into these binary types. Rather, she is counterposing two categories of women in order to extract the quintessential characteristics of each. Third, I have not italicized the Spanish words in the passages Quintana quotes--as I have done with non-English words elsewhere in this volume--because these citations illustrate how English and Spanish are being melded together to create a new and compelling medium of discourse among *Chicanos* and *Chicanas*.

In "Reflections on White Feminism: A Perspective from a Woman of Color," Hurtado argues that white women/feminists approach women's liberation differently from women/feminists of color for two reasons: sexist oppression is not imposed on the two groups of women in like manner, and white women/feminists and women/feminists of color have a different attitude towards white men in power because they relate to the latter in dissimilar ways. White women, according to Hurtado, are subordinated through seduction, whereas women of color are demeaned and controlled through rejection. Though women of color have been doubly oppressed because they have neither been protected as women--having had to do menial and undesirable work that no one else would do--nor been able to enjoy the same rights as men, they have also gained by being "freed . . . from the distraction of being offered the rewards of seduction in exchange for conforming to established gender expectations." Since "women of color have been degenderized by the dominant society," they do not have to try as hard as white women do to cast off the psychological and social sexist straight jacket that men have imposed on them.

Hurtado's ideal-typical white feminist and feminist of color have different social and political skills, and consequently, they often adopt different strategies for achieving women's liberation. Since a large majority of women of color have had to deal with outside authority figures from a tender age and have worked outside the home, they have never encountered the separation between the public and the private spheres that white middle-class women have experienced--at least during the age of industrial capitalism. (The qualifying phrase is necessary because in precapitalist societies, when the household was the main unit of production, women participated far more actively in producing goods needed for sustenance than they did in the two centuries after the industrial revolution and before women began joining the work force in large numbers.) In Hurtado's view, because women of color have had more experience fending off and fighting against the (public) power structure, they are more sophisticated than white women in their analysis of what needs to be done to remove gender inequality. White women, who have a more intimate relationship with white men, whom they have been socialized to please, are not as prepared psychologically--unless they are lesbians--as women of color to take the action necessary to overthrow white male domination.

Recognizing that women of color have political and social skills and specifying what these are, as Hurtado has done, allow us to move beyond the "victimization" framework for conceptualizing the existential dilemma faced by minority women. For years, women of color have repeated the litany that they suffer from "triple oppression" on account of their race, sex, and class. While such an observation is true, it is not particularly useful because it emphasizes oppression more than liberation. By pointing out that certain kinds of negative experiences--painful as they may be--also engender strength and useful skills, Hurtado has turned the oppression syndrome on its head to enable women of color to understand how they may use their history of suffering to advantage in their present and future struggles for equality. Hurtado observes that many white feminists think the issues that feminists of color consider important are too "male-identified." Perhaps this is so from a middle-class vantage point. However, once white feminists begin to understand more fully the total condition under which women of color live, they may begin to fathom why the latter have little choice except to be involved in struggles against racism, sexism, and class oppression all at once.

Concerned primarily with explicating the relationship between white women/feminists and women/feminists of color, on the one hand, and between women of color and white men, on the other hand, Hurtado makes no attempt to address the equally thorny issues of the relationship between women of color and men of color, and between white women and men of color. However, I think the relationship between women and men of color must be dealt with as a central fact in the lives of women of color if we are to develop a feminist theory that can truly take into account the overall conditions under which women of color live. As for the question of the relationship between white women and men of color, though it may not involve women of color directly, it nevertheless impinges on their existence, for there are surely spillover effects between the way men of color relate to white women and the way they interact with women of color.

That women of color themselves hold a panoply of positions on feminist issues is revealed in "Challenge and Counter-Challenge: Chicana Literary Motifs" by Alvina Quintana, who identifies four modes of Chicana literature: apology, rage and opposition, struggle and identification, and "new vision." She claims that their development is not necessarily sequential, that all four modes can exist simultaneously (even in a single work), and that the same authors may produce writings representing more than one mode.

The first two modes delineated by Quintana are really "internal" dialogues between *Chicanas* and *Chicanos*. The apologetic mode, by exposing how traditional *Chicano* culture has subordinated women, represents the efforts of feminist writers to "reappropriate" their history and their language. The oppositional mode, though different in tone, is also addressed to *Chicano* men and accuses them of using both history and religion to oppress *Chicanas*. By depicting la Malinche, the archtypal *Chicana*, as a traitor to her people, male writers have in effect banished *Chicanas* to the outer fringes of Mexican/Mexican American history. And, by associating the female body with sin, *Chicanos* have used religious precepts to further denigrate all that which is feminine. Analyzing the conflictual relationship between women and men of Mexican heritage this way, Quintana addresses a critical issue that Hurtado does not discuss in her essay.

As I understand Quintana's explication of them, the third and fourth modes--struggle and identificaiton and "new vision"--transcend the concerns of the first two modes by allowing women to break out of ethnically-defined boundaries and to place themselves at the center of a larger world. Quintana shows how such writings are often overcast with a tragic tone; the example that she cites to demonstrate what the literature of struggle and identification is all about is particularly poignant. By depicting the multiple burdens under which immigrant women of color labor, Gina Valdes' novel, *There Are No Madmen Here,* is both a happy and sad story. When Maria, the protagonist, leaves her husband and emigrates with her children to the United States, she is breaking away from sexist domination, and her courageous action warms the hearts of all feminist readers. However, Maria soon discovers that working in a sewing factory simply means exchanging Mexican patriarchal oppression for American capitalist exploitation. Furthermore, in the United States as in Mexico, her mind is controlled by male-defined Catholicism. Her story is ultimately a sad one because it reminds us that the tentacles that bind women of color are multi-layered and virtually ironclad.

In contrast to the literature of struggle and identification, the literature of "new vision" is affirmative in tone, because those who write in this mode are no longer concerned with overcoming negation, expressing rebellion, or coming to terms with the problems faced by women taking charge of their own lives, but are, instead, reaching for a "universal vision of womanhood." Such writers are conciliatory towards both white feminists and men of all ethnicities, with whom they can now interact as equals, having found their own, strong voices. According to Quintana, writers in both the third and fourth modes are able to "subvert and challenge" masculine as well as feminist "mainstream" texts; using words as weapons, they can now represent themselves in images of their own making. Quintana credits them with being involved deeply in the "politics of language and colonization," but I believe it is more accurate to characterize their action as the politics of language and *decolonization*.

A different example of how a subordinated group struggles to improve its lot is given in "The Union League and Agricultural Change in the Deep South during Reconstruction" by Michael Fitzgerald. In contrast to scholars who focus on the economic imperatives underlying the transition from plantation agriculture using slave labor to sharecropping, Fitzgerald argues that the "politics" of the Reconstruction era also helped to bring about the change. By definition, politics means a contention for power. Since planters held the preponderance of power, it is possible to think of a "struggle" between them and their former slaves only if one recognizes that the freedmen had some power of their own. And they did, by virtue of their possession of a key "factor of production"--labor. Without their sinews, no planting, cultivating, and harvesting could be done, and unless marketable crops could be grown on the land that planters owned, it was of little value. Hence, the freedmen's ability to *withhold* their labor from their former masters gave them some leverage. On the other hand, they could not withhold it indefinitely, as they, too, had to eat. Owning neither land nor implements, they could not support themselves through subsistence farming, so they had to work either for wages or a share of the crops. Since freedmen and planters both needed something that only the other could provide, neither could have things entirely their way. It was this fact that made politics possible.

From Fitzgerald's description, it seems that the freedmen were as concerned about their working conditions as they were about their subsistence. Though they were originally organized by the Union League, their goal differed from that of the League's agents. The latter were mainly interested in using the freedmen to gain electoral victory, while the freedmen themselves wanted to change the conditions under which they worked. What they wanted above all was to be free of the supervision and control of whites. Hence, even though sharecropping did not necessarily provide a better living than wages earned from gang labor, freedmen preferred it because the system allowed them to "set up for themselves." Fitzgerald recognizes that these upheavals were not simply "labor conflicts," as they were characterized by contemporary observers, but were, in fact, political efforts made by the ex-slaves to attain a new social status. The planters, for their part, came to accept sharecropping when they saw that it brought them the same economic returns with less trouble.

Valiant as the freedmen's attempts were, in the end they failed because the planters discovered a new weapon: terrorism. The use of extralegal terrorist tactics by the Ku Klux Klan moved the struggle between blacks and whites out of the realm of "normal" politics. Former slaves, who were unarmed and did not enjoy the protection of the law, were simply no match for the hooded nightriders. However, though the Klan crushed the Union League, it did not turn the clock back on sharecropping, because by the late 1860s planters had become sufficiently satisfied with the new arrangement to allow it to persist.

Though Michael Omi and Isidro Ortiz and Maguerite Marin discuss very different events that take place more than a century later, they echo two themes in Fitzgerald's paper: the balance of power between/among different racial groups is usually the outcome of political struggles, and such struggles can occur because even the objectively weaker side possesses a measure of power by virtue of society's need for something they have to offer.

In a sense, Omi and Ortiz and Marin are looking at opposite sides of the same coin--two outgrowths of the politics of the 1960s. In "Authoritarian Populism and Code Words: Race and the New Right," Omi analyzes the concerns and tactics of the New Right, whose adherents resent the gains allegedly made by people of color, by women, and by homosexuals in the last twenty years. In "Reaganomics and Latino Organizational Strategies," Ortiz and Marin examine one kind of response that a number of minority organizations have made to the conservative white backlash which, in turn, is a reaction to the radicalism of the 1960s. The two types of backlash mentioned by Omi and Ortiz and Marin, however, are not similar. One is populist in nature, while the other emanates from the very pinnacle of power in the United States--the administration of President Ronald Reagan. In addition to the "silent majority" and the Reagan administration, a third set of players has entered the arena of "racial politics." These are corporation executives who work to contain, rather than push back, the demands of the minority groups by mediating between them and those whites who are going on the offensive against them, not out of a sense of *noblesse oblige,* but because doing so serves the interests of the corporations they represent.

According to Omi, the New Right has been extraordinarily effective in its political efforts because its leaders have used innovative techniques, such as direct mail solicitations, to tap the emotional energy unleashed by the resentment that whites feel over the privileges they have lost. Though those against whom they direct their anger are ethnic or sexual minorities, New Right ideologues scrupulously avoid using racial vocabulary. Instead, in the terminology coined by Omi, they "rearticulate" racial issues in non-racial terms, by appealing to old fashioned "American" values, such as the right of individuals to choose their neighbors, the sanctity of the family, and traditional sexual and religious morality.

As I see it, one interesting side effect of the New Right's "rearticulation" of issues is that its spokespersons have managed to transform blacks, hitherto considered a racial minority, into an ethnic one. That is to say, they claim that if whites do not wish to send their children to the same schools that black children attend, it isn't because they object to the latter's color; rather, the two groups should not mix because they have different cultural values and lifestyles. Apparently, conservative whites have learned a crucial lesson from the turmoil of the 1960s: overt racism doesn't "wash" in the post-Civil Rights era, and using racist words detracts from the New Right's ability to build a political base. New Right strategists have even coopted some of the language that the New Left introduced into American politics, as they call for grassroots organizing, community power, networking, and direct action.

Another insight that the New Right capitalizes on is that people yearn for assurances that things will turn out all right after all. America's defeat in Vietnam, Nixon and Watergate, and other revelations of impotence and corruption in high places shook the self-confidence of ordinary Americans to the core. To find scapegoats to blame for this sad state of affairs, the New Right has lumped "feminists, the liberals, the university communities, minorities, residents of urban centers, and the media" together as the culprits that brought American society to the brink of disaster. The biggest culprit, in their eyes, is the federal government itself, which has acquiesced to the demands of the groups that surfaced in the 1960s as forces to be contended with. Pitted against this odd coalition is another alliance: pro-family advocates, New Right theorists, and fundamentalist evangelists, who will "save" America from its own folly.

This attempt at dichotomization is nothing new. Roger Daniels and Harry Kitano have characterized American racism as a "two-category system,"[18] while Benjamin Ringer has traced the origins of America's "duality" to the contact between Native Americans and Europeans, on the one hand, and the importation of enslaved Africans, on the other hand. Europeans, who were both colonists and colonizers, and their American descendants could go about building a democratic nation *while* subjugating people of color because they early distinguished between what Ringer calls a "People's Domain" and a "Plural Terrain."[19] New Right spokespersons have simply rearranged the groups that should be placed into these opposing categories. What is new is that they have designated the demarcation as a "class" division, based on economic, and not racial or ethnic criteria. As quoted by Omi, in the view of New Right thinkers, "a new economic division pits the producers--businessmen, manufacturers, hard-hats, blue-collar workers, and farmers--against a new and powerful class of non-producers comprised of a liberal verbalist elite (the dominant media, the major foundations and research institutions, the educational establishment, the federal and state bureaucracies) and a semipermanent welfare constituency . . ." And it isn't just New Right thinkers who divide American society that way. As Ortiz and Marin remind us, two liberal writers, Frances Fox Piven and Richard Cloward, also lumped organized labor, environmentalists, the elderly, the poor, women, social service workers and government agencies into a single "class," whose members, they hoped, would resist Ronald Reagan's budget cuts. Such analysis either reflects a hopeless confusion over "class" as an analytical category, or it may signal that a significant new class realignment is taking place. Future studies will have to assess whether the latter is a reality.

Faced with the double assault from the New Right and the Reagan administration, ethnic minority organizations have had to find new ways to survive. Ortiz and Marin chronicle one such effort by two influential Latino organizations, the Mexican-American Legal Defense and Education Fund and the National Council of La Raza. With federal funds for social programs run by community organizations drying up, MALDEF and NCLR have formed a symbiotic relationship with corporations that provide them with resources--financial and technical--in exchange for promoting the corporations' products and services among the Latino population. In several jointly sponsored conferences, corporation executives and the leaders of MALDEF and NCLR have collaborated to delineate the problems faced by Latinos, to identify their needs, and to propose ways to solve those problems and meet those needs. As reported by Ortiz and Marin, the partnerships thus developed seem very cosy indeed--so much so that even a corporation like Adolph Coors Company, which had been picketed by people of color for its discriminatory hiring policies, has signed a contract with NCLR and five other Latino organizations to improve its affirmative action track record and to donate at least two and a half million dollars over a five-year period to the Latino community. (At the same time, as Omi reveals, a member of the Coors family is a major donor to the Heritage Foundation, the New Right think tank.)

The behavior of the protagonists described by Ortiz and Marin warrents deeper scrutiny. First, while the strategy adopted by the leaders of MALDEF and NCLR can be understood in light of their desire to insure the survival of their organizations--so that they can continue to provide important services to the Latino community--such a choice is also explicable in terms of the class position of these officers, who are primarily professionals. In an advanced, industrial capitalist society such as the United States, professionals perform middlemen functions, whether they are providing technical services to those in power or to their clients. Minority professionals often play an additional role: they are called upon, or they take it upon themselves, to adjudicate potential conflict between the ruling elite and disenfranchised members of their own ethnic groups. In exchange for keeping "the masses" under control, minority professionals--especially those who have mastered the social interaction styles appropriate to their calling--are rewarded with recognition by the dominant society. They then become spokespersons for their communities. They do not see their acceptance by the dominant society as cooptation, because they believe that if it weren't for them, certain resources would not be funneled from the larger society to their own communities at all. Thus, radicals may accuse them of "selling out to the establishment," but they themselves feel good about keeping their organizations alive and serving their people.

Second, it is precisely because minority professionals have helped to establish a *modus vivendi* in an ethnically plural society that is inherently unstable that corporation executives, who are interested in maintaining a state of affairs that is "good for business," are willing to cooperate with them, even though doing so may mean they have to work against prevailing government policies or counteract the wishes of other groups within the white population. That two segments of the ruling class (the government and capitalists) should work at cross purposes is not surprising if we understand the basic tenets of the structuralist Marxist theory of the state, as it is expounded by Nicos Poulantzas.[20] According to Poulantzas, although the state and the owners of capital usually support each other, there are also times when they move in opposite directions, because insuring what Marxists call the reproduction of class relations in the long run is not necessarily the same as maximizing capital accumulation in the short run. Moreover, unlike classical Marxist theory that depicts class conflict as inevitable, structuralist Marxist theory asserts that class conflict can be regulated by bureaucratic procedures, so that even when "insurgent" groups are allowed to survive, they can be stripped of real power to such an extent that they are unable to disrupt the society or economy as a whole. In my interpretation of Ortiz' and Marin's findings, the corporation executives who come to the financial rescue of minority organizations fear that the retrenchments imposed by the Reagan administration may lead to racial uprisings that get out of hand. One mechanism for keeping minority populations under control is to make sure that community organizations which provide them services can continue to do so. Even though the officers of such organizations are not part of the state bureaucracy *per se,* they can nevertheless help to dampen potential unrest. Hence, corporation executives who are smart understand that supporting minority professionals/bureaucrats and their organizations will help to maintain an environment that is conducive to both the reproduction of existing class relations and the accumulation of capital. At the same time, they do not worry that such philanthropy will alienate them from the constituencies of the New Right, for they make it clear to everyone that their ultimate objective is to uphold free enterprise, that most cherished of all American institutions.

Conclusion

Though the authors of the essays in this volume did not design their studies collaboratively--many of them met each other for the first time at the conference during which the original versions of these papers were presented--the fact that I have been able to link their findings together conceptually means that there is an underlying common reality that their research is unearthing. By publishing the papers in one collection, I hope that some of the conclusions in these empirical studies will form the building blocks for the next round of theory construction in studies of race, ethnicity, gender, and class.

By way of conclusion, I would like to suggest that we researchers take several considerations into account when we design studies in the future. Because real life is far more complex than conceptual frameworks that scholars conjure up, we need to be less manichean in the way we categorize people and explain their behavior. For example, to resolve the ongoing debate of "race vs. class," it would save us a lot of wasted energy if we will recognize that people are not motivated to act simply on the basis of their interests as "workers" or as "racial/ethnic minorities." Both race/ethnicity and class (as well as other matters) affect their lives. Moreover, individuals' perceptions of themselves and of reality often change repeatedly over their lifetimes. Thus, it would be helpful to combine the methods used by historians and literary critics with those employed by social scientists, so that we can comprehend changes over time and see how human beings, all of whom are capable of acting as subjects of history and as agents of social change, not only react to their environment but also shape it. If we take seriously the injunction to place immigrants, minority group members, or women at the center of our studies, then one of the most urgent tasks facing us is the construction of a theory of choice--one that is more complex, though probably less elegant, than the ones now used by economists, political scientists, sociologists, anthropologists, and psychologists--that can explain (better yet, predict) why some individuals or groups make certain choices while others pick opposite outcomes under various circumstances. Since theory cannot be created out of thin air, many empirical studies, such as the ones in this volume, are needed to serve as the basis for theorizing. Finally, if we wish to decipher how race, ethnicity, gender, and class intersect, it seems to me the most expeditious way to do so is to understand, at many different levels, the lives of those who bear the mark of all four kinds of inequality--working women of color. Only by becoming more sensitive to the internal differentiation within a group can we understand the perceptions and aspirations of its members and analyze more compellingly the contradictory ways in which people of color and women have been treated by the dominant society in the United States.

Notes

1. Since the literature on race, ethnicity, gender, and class is voluminous, no attempt will be made to review or assess it here. For recent review essays, see John Higham, "Current Trends in the Study of Ethnicity in the United States," *Journal of American Ethnic History* 2 (1982): 5-15; Thomas J. Archdeacon, "Problems and Possibilities in the Study of American Immigration and Ethnic History," *International Migration Review* 19 (1985): 112-34; John Rex and David Mason, eds., *Theories of Race and Ethnic Relations* (Cambridge: Cambridge University Press, 1986); Joan W. Scott, "Gender: A Useful Category of Historical Analysis," *American Historical Review* 91 (1986): 1053-75; and Anthony Giddens, *The Class Structure of the Advanced Societies* (London: Hutchinson & Co. [Pub.] Ltd., 1973; New York: Harper & Row, Pub., 1973). G. Carter Bentley, *Ethnicity and Nationality: A Bibliographic Guide* (Seattle: University of Washington Press, 1981) and Francesco Cordasco, *The New American Immigration: Evolving Patterns of Legal and Illegal Emigration: A Bibliography of Selected References* (New York: Garland Publishing, Inc., 1987) provide guides to part of the literature.

2. Alejandro Portes and Robert L. Bach, *Latin Journey: Cuban and Mexican Immigrants in the United States* (Berkeley and Los Angeles: University of California Press, 1985), 26-27.

3. Although the intellectual roots of structural-functional theory go back to the work of anthropologists such as A. R. Radcliffe-Brown and Bronislaw Malinowski and sociologists such as Emile Durkheim, the modern foundation of equilibrium or consensus theory was laid by Talcott Parsons in *The Social System* (Glencoe, Ill: The Free Press, 1951) and in Talcott Parsons and Edward A. Shils, eds., *Toward a General Theory of Action: Theoretical Foundations for the Social Sciences* (Cambridge: Harvard University Press, 1951). For one of the most sophisticated studies of immigration using an equlibrium framework, see Brinley Thomas, *Migration and Economic Growth: A Study of Great Britain and the Atlantic Economy* (Cambridge: At the University Press, 1954; 2nd ed. 1973).

4. Oscar Handlin, *The Uprooted: The Epic Story of the Great Migrations that Made the American People* (Boston: Little, Brown and Co., 1951); and Robert E. Park, *Race and Culture* (Glencoe, Ill: The Free Press, 1950).

5. Most conflict theories are based on a Marxist view of history and social change, but works following other traditions also exist. See, for example, Lewis Coser, *The Functions of Social Conflict* (Glencoe, Ill: The Free Press, 1956), which derives its propositions from the theories of Georg Simmel. Ralf Dahrendorf, *Class and Class Conflict in Industrial Society* (Stanford: Stanford University Press, 1959) introduced conflict theory to American social scientists at a time when Marxist theory was still taboo in some academic circles, although Dahrendorf himself offers a critique of Marx. Anthony Giddens and David Held, eds., *Classes, Power, and Conflict: Classical and Contemporary Debates* (Berkeley and Los Angeles: University of California Press, 1982), is a useful collection of essays that provides an overview of the key issues. John Higham has called "conflict" theorists "hard pluralists," in contrast to "soft pluralists," who depict cultural diversity positively. Higham, "Current Trends," 8-9.

6. Milton M. Gordon, *Assimilation in American Life: The Role of Race, Religion, and National Origins* (New York: Oxford University Press, 1964).

7. For the best works on European immigration published in the last two decades--studies that take both the emigration and immigration contexts into account--see Mack Walker, *Germany and the Emigration 1816-1885* (Cambridge: Harvard University Press, 1964); Josef J. Barton, *Peasants and Strangers: Italians, Rumanians, and Slovaks in an American City, 1890-1950* (Cambridge: Harvard University Press, 1975); Kristian Hvidt, *Flight to America: The Social Background of 300,000 Danish Emigrants* (New York: Academic Press, 1975); Harald Runblom and Hans Norman, eds., *From Sweden to America: A History of the Migration* (Minneapolis: University of Minnesota Press, 1976); Caroline Golab, *Immigrant Destinations* (Philadelphia: Temple University Press, 1977); Virginia Yans-McLaughlin, *Family and Community: Italian Immigrants in Buffalo, 1880-1930* (Ithaca: Cornell University Press, 1977); Dino Cinel, *From Italy to San Francisco: The Immigrant Experience* (Stanford: Stanford University Press, 1982); Hasia R. Diner, *Erin's Daughters in America: Irish Immigrant Women in the Nineteenth Century* (Baltimore: The Johns Hopkins University Press, 1983); Kerby A. Miller, *Emigrants and Exiles: Ireland and the Irish Exodus to North America* (New York: Oxford University Press, 1985); and Jon Gjerde, *From Peasants to Farmers: The*

Migration from Balestrand, Norway, to the Upper Middle West (Cambridge: At the University Press, 1985).

8. Alison M. Jaggar, *Feminist Politics and Human Nature* (Totowa, N.J.: Rowman and Allanheld Pub., 1983).

9. Scott, "Gender."

10. Ibid., 1069.

11. Representative of the "race as ideology" approach are Thomas F. Gossett, *Race: The History of an Idea in America* (Dallas: Southern Methodist University Press, 1963); Winthrop D. Jordan, *The White Man's Burden: Historical Origins of Racism in the United States* (New York: Oxford University Press, 1974), much of which originally appeared as *White Over Black: American Attitudes Toward the Negro, 1550-1812* (Chapel Hill: University of North Carolina Press, 1968); and Reginald Horseman, *Race and Manifest Destiny: The Origins of American Racial Anglo-Saxonism* (Cambridge: Harvard University Press, 1981). See also Ronald T. Takaki, *Iron Cages: Race and Culture in 19th-Century America* (New York: Alfred A. Knopf, 1979); Richard Polenberg, *One Nation Divisible: Race, Class, and Ethnicity in the United States Since 1938* (New York: The Viking Press, 1980); and Michael Omi and Howard Winant, *Racial Formation in the United States from the 1960s to the 1980s* (New York and London: Routledge & Kegan Paul, 1986) for discussions that relate racial ideology to significant developments in American history.

12. Works that focus on racism as a form of economic exploitation include William K. Tabb, *The Political Economy of the Black Ghetto* (New York: W.W. Norton & Co., Inc., 1970); Raymond S. Franklin and Solomon Resnik, *The Political Economy of Racism* (New York: Holt, Rinehart and Winston, Inc., 1973); Victor Perlo, *Economics of Racism U.S.A.: Roots of Black Inequality* (New York: International Publishers, 1975) and Manning Marable, *How Capitalism Underdeveloped Black America* (Boston: South End Press, 1983).

13. Although not about racism and racists *per se*, T. W. Adorno *et al.*, *The Authoritarian Personality, Parts I and II* (New York: Harper & Row, Pub., Inc., 1950) was extremely influential in starting a trend in the study of racism as psychological pathology. Another classic in the psychological approach to

racism is Gordon W. Allport, *The Nature of Prejudice* (Cambridge, Mass.: Addison-Wesley Publishing Co., Inc., 1954). For two studies of how whites have become conscious of their own racism, see Larry L. King, *Confessions of a White Racist* (New York: The Viking Press, 1969); and David T. Wellman, *Portraits of White Racism* (Cambridge: Cambridge University Press, 1977).

14. So many internal debates and different strands of Marxism have developed that it is impossible to discuss them in a footnote. One of the earliest and clearest explications of Marx by an American is Paul M. Sweezy, *The Theory of Capitalist Development* (New York: Monthly Review Press, 1942). See also Paul A. Baran and Paul M. Sweezy, *Monopoly Capital: An Essay on the American Economic and Social Order* (New York: Monthly Review Press, 1966); and Michael Reich, *Racial Inequality* (Princeton: Princeton University Press, 1981). Labor market segmentation theory is most clearly developed in David M. Gordon, Richard Edward, and Michael Reich, *Segmented Work, Divided Workers: The Historical Transformation of Labor in the United States* (New York: Cambridge University Press, 1982), while split labor market theory is expounded by Edna Bonacich in "A Theory of Ethnic Antagonism: The Split Labor Market," *American Sociological Review* 37 (1973): 547-59 and "Advanced Capitalism and Black/White Relations in the United States: a Split Labor Market Interpretation," *American Sociological Review* 41 (1976): 34-51.

15. H. H. Gerth and C. Wright Mills, *From Max Weber: Essays in Sociology* (New York: Oxford University Press, 1946; 1958, ed.), 180-95. For expositions of Weber's thought, see Reinhard Bendix, *Max Weber: An Intellectual Portrait* (Garden City: Doubleday & Co., Inc., 1960); J. Freund, *The Sociology of Max Weber* (London: The Penguin Press, 1968); Giddens, *The Class Structure*, 41-52; and John Rex, "The Role of Class Analysis in the Study of Race Relations--a Weberian Perspective," in *Theories of Race and Ethnic Relations*, 64-83, ed. Rex and Mason.

16. Thomas Kessner, *The Golden Door: Italian and Jewish Immigrant Mobility in New York City, 1880-1915* (New York: Oxford University Press, 1977). See also Moses Rischin, *The Promised City: New York's Jews, 1870-1914* (Cambridge: Harvard University Press, 1962).

17. On Cuban immigrants, see Portes and Bach, *Latin Journey;* Sylvia Pedreza-Bailey, "Cuba's Exiles: Portrait of a Refugee Migration," *International Migration Review* 16 (1985): 4-34; and Lisandro Perez, "Immigrant Economic

Adjustment and Family Organization: The Cuban Success Story Reexamined," *International Migration Review* 20 (1986): 4-20. The tendency of Asian immigrants to go into small business has been best studied among Korean immigrants. See Hyung-chan Kim, "Ethnic Enterprise Among Korean Immigrants in America," in *The Korean Diaspora: Historical and Sociological Studies of Korean Immigration and Assimilation in North America,* ed. Hyung-chan Kim (Santa Barbara: ABC-Clio, Inc., 1977), 109-28; David S. Kim and Charles Choy Wong, "Business Development in Koreatown, Los Angeles," in *Korean Diaspora,* 229-48, ed. Kim; Illsoo Kim, *New Urban Immigrants: The Korean Community in New York* (Princeton: Princeton University Press, 1981); and Kwang Chung Kim and Won Moo Hurh, "Ethnic Resources Utilization of Korean Immigrant Entrepreneurs in the Chicago Minority Area," *International Migration Review* 19 (1985): 82-111.

18. Roger Daniels and Harry H. L. Kitano, *American Racism: Exploration of the Nature of Prejudice* (Englewood Cliffs, N.J.: Prentice-Hall, Inc., 1970).

19. Benjamin B. Ringer, *'We the People' and Others: Duality and America's Treatment of Its Racial Minorities* (New York: Tavistock Publications, 1983).

20. Nicos Poulantzas, *Political Power and Social Classes* (London: New Left Books, 1973) and *Classes in Contemporary Capitalism* (London: New Left Books, 1975).

Changing Ethnic and Class Boundaries in America's Hispanic Past

Ramón A. Gutiérrez

There is a tendency in historical and sociological literature to describe the Spanish/Mexican-origin population of the United States as a homogeneous group. The prevalent assumption about this population is that it is an immigrant group experiencing structural assimilation at the macro-level via market integration and personal acculturation at the micro-level through exogamous marriage, English-language mastery, and participation in the dominant society's political institutions.[1]

Assimilation theorists of the immigrant experience in the United States have generally assumed that Mexicans, like other ethnic groups before them, would eventually forsake their initial cultural conservatism and gradually blend into that big caldron of stew--"the melting pot"--called America, first as hyphenated Americans (e.g., Mexican-Americans, Italian-Americans, Polish-Americans, Afro-Americans, etc.) and someday as full participants in American middle-class culture. I shall challenge this traditional wisdom by examining the internal stratification of the Spanish/Mexican-origin population in the United States. Far from being a homogeneous group, the Hispanic population of the Southwest is complexly stratified and has a variety of historically constituted social boundaries which define it. I intend to show that the process by which people define themselves and are defined by others is dynamic. Cultural identity is not a fixed and static entity; rather, it ebbs and flows as history unfolds. I hope that the findings presented here will serve as a corrective to the prevailing notion that there are core features in the Mexican

A slightly different version of this essay has appeared as "Unraveling America's Hispanic Past: Internal Stratification and Class Boundaries," *Aztlan: International Journal of Chicano Research* 17 (1987).

immigrant culture, and that those features, regardless of regional, class, and generational differences, can be miraculously transformed into American middle-class culture.

The history of the Spanish-speaking people in the United States is a long one. Several decades before Jamestown was founded and before the Pilgrims landed at Plymouth, Spain's citizens had already established permanent settlements on soil that would become part of the United States. The colonization of the Kingdom of New Mexico (then encompassing roughly the current states of New Mexico and Arizona) was launched in 1598.[2] Texas' first Spanish settlements date from 1691, and the settlement of Alta California began with the founding of San Diego in 1769. The Kingdom of New Mexico, Texas, and Alta California were all situated at the northern edge of Spain's empire. They were isolated from each other, surrounded on all sides by Indians who resisted Spanish presence, and too distant from the major centers of Spanish culture in central Mexico for frequent communication. In each of these provinces distinct regional subcultures developed that were Iberian in form but thoroughly syncretic in content, due to prolonged contact with local indigenous cultures.

National consciousness, that is, identity as citizens of a nation-state, was not strong among the colonists Spain initially dispatched to settle the Southwest. What common identity they did share was religious: they were Christians first and foremost. The fervor of their religious sentiment had been forged during Spain's Reconquest, those years of warfare between 711 and 1492, when the Moors occupied the Iberian peninsula. Then the Christian monarchs rallied their populations behind the standard of the cross to push the forces of Islam back into Africa and the Middle East. What victories they won were won in the name of Christianity.[3]

Next in importance in the formation of the identity of these colonists was the *patria chica*, the "small fatherland," or region of origin. Each of Spain's kingdoms had a well-developed *conciencia de sí* or self-consciousness. After men and women proclaimed themselves Christians, they boasted of being Aragonese, Catalans, Leonese, Galicians, Castilians, etc. It should come as no surprise that the Indians of the southwestern United States first used the word *Castilla*, meaning Castile, to describe their European overlords. Though the Indians understood little of what Spain's soldiers told them, they did nonetheless repeatedly hear the soldiers call themselves *castellanos*, announce that the Indians were subjects of *Castilla*, and that the king of *Castilla* was their new lord. Gaspar Pérez de Villagrá, who participated in the 1598 conquest of New Mexico and in 1610 made those feats memorable in his *Historia de la Nueva México*, wrote that the Indians at Acoma Pueblo "called to me, crying,

Castilian! Castilian! . . . Zutacapan [their chief] asked me if more Castilian followed me and how long before they would arrive."[4]

The colonists in the Southwest gradually lost their identity with Spain's various regions, but not their habit of identifying with the region in which they lived. The literary evidence indicates that by the beginning of the nineteenth century, residents of the Kingdom of New Mexico were calling themselves *Nuevo Mexicanos,* those in California were referring to themselves as *Californios,* while those in Texas were proclaiming themselves *Tejanos.*

The Spanish conquest of America brought men together from different regions and, by so doing, helped to shape a common experience and cultural identity. Men who had never before really identified themselves as Spaniards now came to think of themselves as such in cultural terms, particularly when confronting indigenous peoples as the latter's new overlords. By calling themselves Spaniards or *españoles,* the colonists in the Southwest acknowledged that their culture and social institutions were of Iberian origin and thus quite different from those of the Indians or *indios.* Three hundred years of contact between these two groups, through intermarriage and cohabitation in a common ecological zone, would radically transform what it meant to be *español* and *indio,* but that is another story.[5]

The *españoles* who colonized the Southwest were extremely status-conscious and viewed society as hierarchically ordered by a number of ascriptive status categories based on race, legitimacy of birth, occupation, citizenship, and religion. Whenever anyone came before a legal tribunal, be it civil or ecclesiastical, the judge was always eager to determine the person's *calidad,* or social status, for punishment was meted out differentially according to one's status. Thus, legal dockets always began with a formulaic statement that *Fulano de tal es de calidad mestizo, obrero, hijo legitimo de tal y tal y cristiano nuevo* (John Doe's social status is *mestizo,* worker, the legitimate son of so and so, and a New Christian). A person's racial status was defined according to the biological criteria outlined in the *Régimen de Castas* or Society of Castes, that artifact of Spanish Purity of Blood statutes which attempted to measure one's genealogical proximity to socially tainted peoples by scrutinizing qualities of blood. In Spain, even faintly impure blood, contacted from Jews, Moors, and heretics, disqualified a person from high honorific posts. In America, contact with Indians or black slaves was deemed equally polluting. To describe the various racial groups created through miscegenation in America, an elaborate legal racial vocabulary was devised. A mix between a Spaniard and an Indian produced a *mestizo*; a Spaniard and *mestizo* produced a *castizo;* a Spaniard and a black beget a *mulato,* and so on.[6]

Of equal importance in every local status hierarchy was whether one worked with one's hands or not. The assumption was that blacks toiled because of the infamy of their enslavement and Indians worked because of their vanquishment by a superior power. Racial status was similarly adduced from one's legitimacy or illegitimacy of birth. The legal scholar Juan de Solórzano y Pereira in his *Política Indiana* maintained that illegitimates were

> those born of adulterous or other illicit and punishable unions, because there are few Spaniards of honor who marry Indian or negro women; this defect of birth makes them infamous, at least *infama facti*, according to the weighty and common opinion of serious scholars; they carry the stain of different colors and other vices.[7]

Throughout the colonial period, illegitimacy was seen as an indecent and shameful mark because of its association with mixed racial unions. Finally, to differentiate Christians of peninsular origin from those recently converted to the faith, the categories "Old Christian" and "New Christian" were widely used. To call someone a "New Christian" was to recognize his or her indigenous ancestry and consequent infamy or low position in the status hierarchy.

All of these categories, which defined a person's *calidad*, were intricately related. In fact, a person's social standing in a community was a public summation of these various measures. We see this very clearly in social action. The fiercest fighting words one could utter were slurs that impugned a person's total social personality--race, ancestry, and position in the division of labor. On June 3, 1765, for example, there was a fight in Albuquerque between Eusebio Chavez and his father-in-law, Andres Martin. Chavez beat Martin with a large stick and dragged him by his hair, leaving Martin's arm badly bruised, his chest covered with black and blue welts, his scalp swollen out of shape, and his hair completely tangled and caked in blood. The reason: Martin had called Chavez a *"perro mulato hijo de puta"* (mixed-blood dog son-of-a-bitch). One insult, perhaps, would have been enough, but Martin not only inferred that Chavez was less than human and a mixed-blood, but that--if he were truly a son-of-a-bitch--he was illegitimate. Martin had thus combined three statuses to insult.[8]

Another social distinction that deserves mention here is a legal category which was widely used in the Southwest during the colonial period, particularly in California, that is, *gente de razón*, literally "people of reason," or rational beings. There is a great deal of confusion among contemporary scholars as to who this category encompassed and what precisely it meant. The category is best understood by looking at its opposite, that is, *gente sin razón*, "people lacking reason," or irrational persons. The Holy Office of the Inquisition concocted this legal distinction to protect the Indians from prosecution for heretical ideas. The Indians were *gente sin razón*, mere children lacking the rational faculties to understand dogmas of the faith. Everyone else was deemed *gente de razón* and could be punished by the Inquisition for acts judged heretical. With the demise of the Inquisition, the term *gente de razón* remained as a way to classify the non-Indian population of an area.

The word *genízaro*, which appeared in New Mexico at the beginning of the eighteenth century, also referred to a specific class of Indians in Spanish society. The *genízaros* were primarily Apache and Navajo Indians enslaved during Spanish raids, and secondarily Pueblo Indians who had abandoned their indigenous towns or were exiled from them for some transgression. Approximately 4,000 *genízaros* entered New Mexican society during the eighteenth century. For most of that and the following century, they were considered marginal persons because of their slave, ex-slave or outcast status.[9] They spoke a distinctive (broken) form of Spanish, were residentially segregated, married endogamously, and shared a corporate identity, living together, said Fray Carlos Delgado in 1744 "in great unity *como si fueran una nación*" (as if they were a nation).[10] In 1776, Fray Atanacio Dominguez described the *genízaros* as "weak, gamblers, liars, cheats, and petty thieves."[11] This caricature stuck, for today when New Mexicans say, "*No seas genízaro*," they mean, "Don't be a liar."

Other folk classification systems also existed among Spain's colonists in the Southwest. *Españoles* referred to half-breeds as *lobos* and *coyotes*, denoting a mixture between a Spaniard and an Indian. With both of these labels, the mixed-blood individual was portrayed as a low species close to an animal. *Lobo* and *coyote* were maintained in the common parlance over the centuries and today are used to refer to persons who are a mix between Anglo and Mexican.

There can be no doubt that the Indians the Spanish conquered and dominated had a linguistic arsenal of their own to describe the Europeans. Though I have searched hard for this lexicon I have had only slight success. The evidence I unearthed comes from the Pueblo, the Yaqui, and the Mayo Indians. All three groups were impressed by the sacrament of baptism and devised words to describe the Spaniards which made reference to it. Among the Pueblo Indians, the Spaniards were called "wet-heads" because of the water poured on a person's head at baptism. For similar reasons, the Yaqui and Mayo Indians called the Spaniards "water-fathers" and "water-mothers."[12]

As Mexican independence approached in 1821, other status categories came into use. Residents of the Southwest at times employed the *peninsular* and *criollo* categories to differentiate *españoles* (i.e., people born in Spain) from *españoles mexicanos* (i.e., people of Spanish origin born in Mexico). At the beginning of the nineteenth century, however, the only persons in the Southwest who could genuinely claim peninsular Spanish origin were the priests, and it is among them that one sees the *peninsular/criollo* categories used most frequently. For the rest of the population in New Mexico, Texas, and California, little seems to have changed as a result of Mexico's independence from Spain. One does not find a rapid increase of people calling themselves *Mexicanos*. The category did appear in the 1830s but was used by a very small number of people. In New Mexico, for example, only about 5 percent of all individuals who married legally during 1830-1839 claimed they were *Mexicanos*; the rest still preferred to call themselves *españoles*.[13]

There were, nonetheless, forces of change operating in Hispanic society in the Southwest that would radically transform it after 1821. Internally, the increased level of economic activity in the Southwest, fostered by the Bourbon monarchs in the 1770s to safeguard the area and to integrate it into larger marketing centers in northern Mexico, shattered the traditional bonds of society. With the rise of wage labor and the growth of a large landless peasant class, the status system based on ascription slowly gave way to one based on achievement. International rivalries, large-scale migration, and other political events also helped to change the nature of society. In 1836, Texas won its independence from Mexico through revolution. A decade later the rest of the Southwest was ceded to the United States as a result of the U.S.-Mexican War of 1846-48. As a new political order was established and people moved back and forth across the Rio Grande and west across the Great Plains, a new conception of society emerged. Just as when colonists from various parts of Spain first arrived in the Southwest and defined themselves culturally as Spaniards vis-à-vis the Indians, so too, after 1848 did settlers from various parts of the United States define themselves as Anglos and Americans when confronted by the Mexicans and Indians.

From the moment *Americanos* entered the Southwest, the Mexican population residing there concocted a variety of ethnic terms for the invaders. There were names for the *Americanos* that focused on the peculiarities of their skin, eye, and hair color, and the size of their feet. Thus we find in the folklore *canoso* (grey-hairs), *colorado* (red face), *cara de pan crudo* (bread dough face), *ojos de gato* (cat eyes), and *patón* (big foot). Other Spanish ethnic labels for the Americans resulted from difficulties with and misunderstandings of the English language. *Gringo* comes from the corruption of the words in a song the Mexican soldiers heard the Texas rebels singing at the Alamo. The first two words of the prairie song, "Green grows the grass," were heard by Mexicans as "grin gros," and finally *gringos*. Because the *Americanos* loved cabbage in their diet they were called *repolleros*. And because of their penchant for chewing tobacco they were called *masca tabacos*.[14]

Of course, Anglos were themselves quite adept at calling the Mexican-origin populace names. From the Mexican diet came such derogatory terms as "greaser," "grease ball," "goo-goo," "pepper-belly," "taco-choker," "frijole guzzler," "chili picker," and for a woman, "hot tamale." From the word Mexican several slurs were corrupted: "Mex," "Meskin," "Skin," and "Skindiver."

When the Anglo-Americans entered the Southwest, much like when the Spaniards entered in 1598, they saw few distinctions among the residents of their newly conquered territory, although long-standing cleavages of the sort I described above existed. In addition, the long-established Spanish residents of the area clearly saw themselves as different from Mexican immigrants who started to cross the border in large numbers after 1848, and particularly after 1880. But to the conquerors of the land, people were either Americans, Mexicans, or Indians. The United States had won the territory from Mexico through war, thus the most appropriate term for the population in the Southwest seemed to be Mexican. In American eyes, the residents of the area all looked alike, dressed alike, spoke Spanish, and were fanatic Catholics, therefore they were all Mexicans. The *Americanos'* deep-seated racial prejudice against blacks was easily transferred to persons of Spanish origin, due to their swarthy skin color.[15]

To counter the tendency among Americans who referred to all residents of the Southwest as Mexicans, the long-resident population of the area employed old ethnic categories in new ways. In so doing, the Hispanic population that had resided in the Southwest since before 1848 wanted to differentiate itself from the constant flow of lower-class Mexican immigrants coming in. In addition, they wanted to clearly establish that they were Spaniards of white European ancestry, and not of a mixed Indian, and therefore inferior, background.

Since the massive influx of population into California after 1848, due to the gold rush, radically transformed the ethnic mix of this state first, let us begin with a discussion of its ethnic dynamics. The *Californios*, the original colonists who settled the area--first under Spain's control, then after 1821 under Mexico's control, and finally after 1848 under the control of the United States--were faced with the arrival of numerous Mexican nationals who came to make it rich in the mines. The *Californios* referred to these immigrants as *Mexicanos* because they were indeed Mexicans. Anglos, however, saw no apparent physical or cultural differences between the *Californios* and the *Mexicanos* and so referred to both of them as Mexicans. To counter this perception and to clearly differentiate themselves from the recent lower-class immigrants, the *Californios* increasingly referred to themselves as "Spaniards," and insisted that English-speakers do the same. This tendency was particularly strong at the old Spanish pueblos at Santa Barbara, San Fernando, Los Angeles, and San Francisco.[16]

But the sheer number of Mexican immigrants entering California after 1848 drastically dissipated the numerical strength of the *Californios*. The first good statistics on Mexican immigration to the United States start with the decade 1911-1920. Mexican immigrants in the United States then totaled 219,000, representing approximately 20 percent of all immigrants to the United States. From 1921-1930, the official number more than doubled to 459,287. In that decade, Mexicans were the largest immigrant group, representing close to 10 percent of the national total. Most of these immigrants went to California and, increasingly after the 1920s, the terms "Mexican" and "Mexican American" became prominent and "Spanish" and "Spanish American" virtually disappeared.

Ethnic identity in New Mexico was similarly shaped by population dynamics and a new political order. But here the process of redefining the ethnic boundaries did not begin until after World War I. Unlike California, where the *Californios* were quickly outnumbered by Mexican immigrants and hence lost their cultural dominance, in New Mexico the native Spanish-speaking people retained their cultural identity as *Españoles* or Spaniards for a long time. When faced with the arrival of Mexican immigrants in the 1920s and 1930s, they referred to themselves as "Spaniards" or "Spanish Americans." Some went so far as to claim that they were the direct descendants of Spanish conquistadores who colonized the region in 1598, and that over the centuries they had maintained their blood lines free from any taint by inferior races. Of course, this was more fiction than fact. Most of the people who settled New Mexico were racially *mestizos* and few, if any, after three hundred years of miscegenation could claim "pure" Spanish ancestry. But whatever the ideology, it was put to service primarily to resist being called Mexicans.

If we examine the linguistic context in which ethnicity was defined, we see the logic of their defensive ideology. When Arthur L. Campa in the 1950s asked long-time New Mexican residents in Spanish what their ethnicity was, most responded: *"soy Mexicano"* (I am Mexican). When he asked these same individuals what they liked to be called in English, they responded: "Spanish-American." Campa then asked in Spanish, "What do you call a person from Mexico?" *"Mexicano de México* (Mexican from Mexico)," they responded. In English such a person was simply a "Mexican." One New Mexican said that she did not like being called "Mexican" because "Mexican . . . is most used when someone is being rude . . . Example--'dirty Mexican'." Another woman echoed her sentiments: "I'd rather not be called Mexican because of the stereotype remarks that are associated with it. Such as lazy, dirty greaser, etc."[17] Thus, part of the New Mexican's hostility to the term "Mexican" stems from its association with Mexico and Mexican nationals. New Mexico was always marginal to Spanish imperial politics and isolated from Mexico City. This fact prompted one man to state:

> My identity has always been closer to Spanish as an ethnic
> group and for that reason I consider myself Spanish . . . but
> the civil laws under which I live and which make me proud
> are American . . . being from northern New Mexico the only
> connection I have with anything Mexican is as a tourist and
> not as my national origin.[18]

Erna Fergusson has argued that "Spanish American" came into popular use in New Mexico after World War I to counter the Anglo perception that soldiers who called themselves *Mexicanos* were aliens from another country. Nancie González agrees that the term "Spanish American" emerged in response to an upsurge of prejudice and discrimination against Spanish-speakers during the 1920s.[19]

The ethnic categories employed by *Tejanos* or Texans of Spanish/Mexican origin require more explanation. One would assume that as with the *Californios* and *Nuevo Mexicanos*, they too would opt for being called Spanish or Spanish-Americans when differentiating themselves from recent Mexican immigrants in the 1920s and 1930s. They did not. Instead they called themselves *Latinos* and "Latin Americans." History provides some, but not all, of the reasons why this was so. When the *Tejanos* joined forces with the American settlers of Texas to form their own independent republic in 1836, they clearly rejected their Mexican identity. Faced with the same prejudice that the Mexican immigrants suffered in the 1920s, the *Tejanos* insisted on being called "Latin American" in polite English-speaking company. Obviously, they did not want to be called "Mexicans" or "Mexican Americans." Why they rejected "Spanish" and "Spanish American" I still do not know. Whatever the reason, in 1929 the first major civil rights group in Texas named itself the League of United Latin American Citizens.[20]

Survey data collected by Leo Grebler between 1965 and 1970 found that in San Antonio, the self-use of the label *Latino* was positively associated with income. The higher one's income, the greater the preference for being called a *Latino;* the lower one's income, the greater the incidence of calling oneself *Mexicano.* [21] However, when Michael Miller replicated Grebler's study in 1976 among South Texas high school students, he found that virtually no one called himself or herself "Latin American," *Latino/Latina*, "Mexican American," or *Mexicano/Mexicana*. The preference among these students was *Chicano/Chicana*, thus exposing the strong generational undercurrents in ethnic identity.[22]

As with other areas that had a native core of settlers who considered themselves culturally "Spaniards," Arizona also experienced the same Spanish/Mexican tension when confronted with massive immigration. One of the first civic organizations in Arizona during the early twentieth century was the Spanish American Alliance of Tucson. But again, given the rapid influx of Mexicans into the area with the development of irrigated agriculture, "Mexican" and "Mexican American" rapidly gained ascendency.[23]

The tension between Spaniards and Mexicans created in the Southwest by the arrival of Mexican immigrants was couched in broad cultural terms; it also expressed a basic class tension, and showed a generational rift. I turn now to explicit in-group terms which differentiated the Hispanic population by class.

Pocho is perhaps the most popular of these terms. It refers to a lower-class individual who has assimilated middle-class habits. There is a folksong that captures the meaning of *pocho* well:

> *Los Pochos de California*
> *no saben comer tortilla*
> *porque solo en la mesa*
> *usan pan con mantequilla.*

> The Pochos of California
> Don't know how to eat tortillas
> For at mealtime on the table
> All they serve is bread and butter.[24]

Another class-based term is *Chicano*. There are several possible origins for the word. Researchers at the Center of Hispanic Linguistics at the Universidad Nacional Autónoma de México in Mexico City believe that the word is a *pochismo* (a corruption) created through the linguistic process of metathesis, whereby the order of letters in a word is reversed. They maintain that *Chicano* possibly comes from *chinaco* which means "tramp" or "guttersnipe."[25]

Tino Villanueva, taking a slightly different linguistic approach, has sought the origins of *Chicano* in the speech play between adults and small children. Many adults employ "baby-talk" with their infants, shortening words and exaggerating those which a child has difficulty pronouncing. Thus, when a child cannot pronounce the name Eugenio it is shortened to Cheno; Mauricio becomes Wicho and Socorro becomes Choco. In each of these examples a shortening of the name and the addition of "ch" produced the nickname. This, Villanueva argues, was how *Chicano* emerged. According to him, it comes from the word *Meshicas*, which was the ancient Aztec tribe that settled the Valley of Mexico. *Meshicas* slowly corrupted to *Meshicanos, Shicanos,* and finally *Chicanos.* Curiously enough, numerous informants associated the word *Chicano* with children. One woman said that she wanted to be called "Mexican" and not "Chicana" because "the true meaning of Chicano is small boy--coming from the word chico--meaning small." Professor Carlos A. Rojas, emeritus professor of Spanish at Fresno State University, also believes that *Chicano* stemmed from *chico,* which means "young one" or "small one."[26] In each of these explanations of the origin of the word *Chicano*, the implication is that the power dynamics in the parent/child relationship are the model for upper/lower class relations in the Hispanic community.

Leaving the origins of *Chicano* aside, we find that it has always been a derogatory term for lower-class Mexicans. One informant said he disliked being called *Chicano* because "people . . . mean a lower class of people." Another interviewee stated his objection to the term: "This word to me is equal to 'chicanery' or *'Surumato'* and is insulting." (A *Surumato* is a rough lower-class Mexican immigrant.) Michael Miller found in his survey of South Texas youth that a negative relationship existed between socioeconomic status and the use of the word *Chicano* as an ethnic self-referent. Only teenagers of recent-immigrant origin preferred it.[27]

José Limón maintains that *Chicano* as a derogatory in-group term has two meanings: 1) a person of dubious character, and 2) a recent immigrant of lower-class standing. However, the word is used folklorically as in-group banter and a form of social self-affirmation in the face of wide-spread discrimination, just as a black may call another black a "nigger," or an Italian may call another Italian a "wop." Thus is the case when a Chicano tells another, *"No seas chicano."* If an out-group member used any of these terms he would be considered racist, and his use of the word an explicit attempt to humiliate. Survey data bears this out. One New Mexican said that among his friends he wished to be called a *Chicano,* but at school he always insisted on being called a "Spanish American."[28]

Militant and politically conscious Mexican-origin residents of the Southwest in the early 1960s embraced this term of out-group insult and in-group banter as a sign of self-determination and ethnic militancy. There is no doubt that *Chicano* was popularized to establish a genealogical tie to a militant, warrior Aztec past. The meaning that *Chicano* acquired in the 1960s is well stated in the following poem.

> *La palabra Chicano es un reproche,*
> *Una angustia con algo de esperanza.*
> *Es un rato, quizas una bandera,*
> *El estandarte terco de una raza.*
> *La palabra Chicano es una flecha*
> *Y el arco es el aliento de una raza.*

> The word Chicano is a reproach,
> An anguish with something of a hope.
> It is a challenge, perhaps a banner,
> The stubborn standard of a race.
> The word Chicano is an arrow
> And the bow is the inspiration of a race.[29]

But some Hispanics objected to the use of the word *Chicano* because, as one woman stated, "All my life I claim [sic] myself Spanish-American . . . Chicano to me is like someone who is radical." Studies by Metzgar and by Gutiérrez and Hirsh found that the use of *Chicano* was inversely related to age. Older individuals preferred such terms as "Mexican," "Mexican-American," "Latin-American," and "Spanish-American," while younger persons chose *Chicano*.[30]

I have tried to show in these few pages that the peculiarities of Spain's colonization of the Southwest led to the development of three regional subcultures, located in the Kingdom of New Mexico, in Texas, and in California. In each of these provinces, the Hispanic residents interacted with indigenous populations and, as a result, devised various ways of defining themselves and others. During Spain's and Mexico's control of the Southwest, society was complexly stratified by ascriptive status hierarchies based on race, religion, occupation, and legitimacy of birth. With the development of a market economy and the proliferation of capitalist relationships of production, status was increasingly achieved and decreasingly ascribed. The ethnic confrontations created by the Texas Revolution, the U.S.-Mexican War, the California gold rush, and finally the large-scale immigration of Mexican nationals into the United States starting in the 1880s, profoundly transformed how the long-established Hispanic residents of the Southwest defined themselves and those with whom they shared numerous cultural affinities. When faced with an assault on their social standing by Anglo-Americans in the wake of the influx of large numbers of Mexican immigrants, the Hispanic residents of the Southwest repeatedly returned to their oldest identity as Spaniards or Spanish-Americans. In addition to this, new terms were brought into the ethnic vocabulary to clearly delineate those boundaries within the Hispanic community that had developed along class, age, generation, nationality, and political lines. My goal in describing all of these ethnic and class categories has been to debunk the persistent assumptions about the monolithic characteristics of the Spanish/Mexican-origin population in the United States. Once this is recognized, perhaps we will be able to move beyond the facile application of European immigrant models to that history. I do not deny that assimilation and acculturation have taken place, and that these are indeed powerful explanatory tools. Rather, I herald a cautionary note. If we do not begin our studies of the past with a thorough understanding of the basic cleavages that have divided society, and particularly if we propose that the driving aspiration of the Hispanic population has been to achieve Anglo-American middle-class goals, we are doomed to wrong conclusions.

Notes

1. The classic statements of this perspective are Milton M. Gordon, *Assimilation in American Life: The Role of Race, Religion, and National Origin* (New York: Oxford University Press, 1964) and Leo Grebler, Joan Moore and Ralph C. Guzman, *The Mexican American People: The Nation's Second Largest Minority* (New York: Free Press, 1970).

2. Saint Augustin in Florida was founded in 1565. I did not mention this town in the text as the first Spanish settlement in the United States because the focus of this essay is the Southwest.

3. Américo Castro, *The Spaniards: An Introduction to Their History* (Berkeley and Los Angeles: University of California Press, 1971), 1-94.

4. Gaspar Pérez de Villagrá, *History of New Mexico* (Los Angeles: Quivira Society, 1933), 173. See also Aurelio M. Espinosa, "El desarrollo de la palabra *Castilla* en la lengua de los Indios Queres de Nuevo Mejico," *Revista de Filologia Española* 19 (1932): 261-77 and "La palabra *Castilla* en la lengua de los indios Hopis de Arizona," *Revista de Filologia Española* 22 (1935): 298-300.

5. The details of contact between Spaniards and Indians can be found in Ramón A. Gutiérrez, "Marriage, Sex and the Family: Social Change in Colonial New Mexico, 1690-1846" (Ph.D. diss., University of Wisconsin, 1980).

6. Magnus Morner, *Race Mixture in the History of Latin America* (Boston: Little, Brown and Co., 1967).

7. Solórzano y Pereira, quoted in Verena Martinez-Alier, *Marriage, Class and Colour in Nineteenth-Century Cuba* (Cambridge: Cambridge University Press, 1974), 83-84.

8. *Spanish Archives of New Mexico*, Reel 9, frames 789-820.

9.   Fray Angelico Chavez, "Genízaros," *Handbook of North American Indians* (Washington, D.C.: Smithsonian Institution, 1979), Vol. 9, 198-201; Steven M. Horvath, "The Social and Political Organization of the Genízaros of Plaza de Nuestra Señora de los Dolores de Belen, New Mexico, 1740-1812" (Ph.D. diss., Brown University, 1979); David M. Brugge, *Navajos in the Catholic Church Records of New Mexico 1694-1875* (Window Rock, Ariz.: The Navajo Tribe, 1968), 30.

10.   Archivo General de la Nación (México): *Historia* 25-25: 229.

11.   Fray Atanasio Dominguez, *The Missions of New Mexico, 1776* (Albuquerque: University of New Mexico Press, 1956), 259.

12.   Elsie C. Parsons, "Tewa Mothers and Children," *Man* 24 (1924): 149; Edward H. Spicer, *The Yaquis: A Cultural History* (Tucson: University of Arizona Press, 1980), 22-23; Ross N. Crumrine, *The Mayo Indians of Sonora: A People Who Refuse to Die* (Tucson: University of Arizona Press, 1977), 69.

13.   Gutiérrez, "Marriage, Sex and the Family," 145-46.

14.   Américo Paredes, "The Problem of Identity in a Changing Culture: Popular Expressions of Culture Conflict Along the Lower Rio Grande Border," *Views Across the Border: The United States and Mexico,* ed. Stanley R. Ross (Albuquerque: University of New Mexico Press, 1978), 68-94.

15.   Raymond A. Paredes, "The Mexican Image in American Travel Literature, 1831-1869," *New Mexico Historical Quarterly* 1 (1977): 5-29; Deena Gonzales, "The Spanish-Mexican Women of Santa Fe: Patterns of Their Resistance and Accomodation, 1820-1880" (Ph.D. diss., University of California, Berkeley, 1986); John R. Chavez, *The Lost Land: The Chicano Image of the Southwest* (Albuquerque: University of New Mexico Press, 1984); Philip A. Hernandez, "The Other Americans: The American Image of Mexico and Mexicans, 1550-1850" (Ph.D. diss., University of California, Berkeley, 1974); Susan R. Kenneson, "Through the Looking Glass: A History of Anglo-American Attitudes Toward the Spanish-American and Indians of New Mexico" (Ph.D. diss., Yale University, 1978); Jack D. Forbes, "Race and Color in Mexican-American Problems," *Journal of Human Relations* 16 (1968): 55-68; Manuel Gamio, *Mexican Immigration to the United States* (Chicago: Arno Press, 1930), 129 and 209.

16. Leonard Pitt, *The Decline of the Californios: A Social History of the Spanish-Speaking Californians, 1846-1890* (Berkeley and Los Angeles: University of California Press, 1966), 53, 157, 174, 188, 204, 259, 267, and 309; Arthur L. Campa, *Hispanic Culture in the Southwest* (Norman: University of Oklahoma Press, 1979), 5.

17. Joseph V. Metzgar, "The Ethnic Sensitivity of Spanish New Mexicans: A Survey and Analysis," *New Mexico Historical Review* 49 (1974): 52.

18. Ibid., 60.

19. Erna Fergusson, *New Mexico: A Pageant of Three Peoples* (New York: Alfred A. Knopf, 1964), 218; Nancie Gonzalez, *The Spanish-Americans of New Mexico* (Albuquerque: University of New Mexico Press, 1969), 80-81.

20. Richard Nostrand, "Mexican American and Chicano: Emerging Terms for a People Coming of Age," *Pacific Historical Review* 42 (1973): 396.

21. Grebler, et. al., *The Mexican American People*, 386-87.

22. Michael V. Miller, "Mexican Americans, Chicanos, and Others: Ethnic Self-Identification and Selected Social Attributes of Rural Texas Youth," *Rural Sociology* 41(1976): 234-47.

23. Gamio, *Mexican Immigration*, 133.

24. Campa, *Hispanic Culture*, 5.

25. Ibid., 7.

26. Tino Villanueva, "Sobre el termino 'chicano'," *Cuadernos Hispano-Americanos* (1978): 387-410; Metzgar, "Ethnic Sensitivity," 59; Nostrand, "Mexican American and Chicano," 398.

27. Metzgar, "Ethnic Sensitivity," 55, 72; Miller, "Mexican Americans," 241.

28. José Limon, "The Folk Performance of 'Chicano' and the Cultural Limits of Political Ideology," *And Other Neighborly Names,* ed. Richard Bauman and

Roger Abrahams (Austin: University of Texas Press, 1980), 197-225; Metzgar, "Ethnic Sensitivity," 66.

29. Campa, *Hispanic Culture*, 7.

30. Metzgar, "Ethnic Sensitivity," 51; Armando Gutiérrez and Herbert Hirsch, "The Militant Challenge to the American Ethos: 'Chicanos' and 'Mexican Americans'," *Social Science Quarterly* 53 (1973): 830-45.

The Americanization of Mexican Women and Their Families during the Era of De Jure School Segregation, 1900-1950

Gilbert G. Gonzalez

No history of the Mexican community in the Southwest would be complete without recognizing the attempt by the state's educational apparatus to change the culture, influence the political consciousness of individuals, and restructure the family within the Mexican American community from the early 1900s to the mid-1950s. The Americanization of the family was as significant a chapter as segregation was in the educational history of Chicanos.[1] In fact, the Americanization of women and the family was perhaps even more important than the secondary education of Mexican youth during the segregation period.

Americanization programs encompassed the entire Mexican community, although they differentiated between programs for men and women, and youths and adults. Separate classes in Americanization were created for boys and girls. Within the adult category, special programs were offered to women, particularly mothers and wives. The adult programs were developed to complement the school programs, as well as to extend them into the community. The essential purpose of Americanization--the social, political, and economic integration of 'foreigners' into U.S. society--remained constant, whether the focus was upon children in schools or on adults in their communities. The curriculum, teaching methods, and objectives differed, of course, for children and adults. However, the similarities were striking: the stereotype of cultural inferiority, the emphasis upon cultural reformation, the stress on English instruction, and the segregated facilities. All these characteristics were found in Americanization programs developed for, and applied to, the Mexican community throughout the Southwest.

Historical analyses of Mexican women and the family have not included discussions of the Americanization efforts of the segregated schooling system. Richard Griswold del Castillo, for example, has written an insightful and important study of *la familia* but he did not delve into the role of the public educational system as a factor in the evolution of the Mexican family.[2] Ricardo Romo's excellent account of the history of East Los Angeles briefly discusses Americanization in the segregated schools but does not recognize that Americanization had a particular purpose in relation to girls, women, and the family.[3] Maxine Seller's essay on the education of immigrant women, covering the years 1900-1935, does recognize the Americanization emphasis of schooling and does include discussion of Mexican women,[4] but her analysis, like Romo's, does not acknowledge the particularity of Americanization, especially in the Southwest, upon women and the family.

Despite this lack of attention both to Americanization in general and to the programmatic focus on women and the family in particular, the topic warrants notice as one of the key processes occurring in the segregated schools. The goal of Americanization was nothing less than the elimination of the Mexican as a distinct cultural entity in the United States. The attempt proved to be a failure--it could not change the reality that the Southwest has been, and probably always will be, a bicultural and bilingual region.

The Home

The Americanization of the Mexican child was not limited to the teaching of educational skills such as reading, writing, and arithmetic. Nor did it merely teach allegiance to the country and its institutions. Americanization involved separating the child from the home and family in such a way that the child would desire a different model of home and family. Educators perceived the Mexican home as a source of Mexican culture and consequently, a reinforcer of the "Mexican educational problem." A critical objective of Americanization was the transformation of the Mexican home into an American home. In their "Course of Study for Mexican Children," the Arizona Department of Education urged that the home should be a "continuous topic through the school days" since "home life is the basis of custom and culture."[5] Arizona teachers were told that the measure of an effective educational program was whether or not it had "a lasting effect on home life."

The superintendent of the Chaffey School District in Southern California concluded that the learning "disability" of Mexican children (his research "discovered" that Mexican children learned at 58 percent the rate of "normal" American children) could be resolved only through an

Americanization program. However, if Mexican children learned English in school but had no English-language books, magazines, or newspapers at home, then "an educational background is lacking for them." Americanization programs, he wrote, "supply in some way what the home conditions lack."[6]

The focus upon the home had several aspects: the first dealt with the relations of boys and girls within the home and was a regular part of the Americanization curriculum; the second focused upon the young girl as a future wife, mother, and homemaker, while the third discussed the women of the community, most often the wives, mothers, and homemakers. The first two were part of the Americanization program imparted within the regular schedule of the school; the third took place within the community, assuming several different forms, e.g., classes held in community centers, settlement houses, and evening schools, or day cottage classes in the neighborhood.

The Americanization and Homemaking instructor in the Covina City elementary schools, and author of a teacher's manual, *Americanization Through Homemaking*, wrote that the "surest solution of the Americanization problem lies in the proper training of the parents of a future citizenry."[7] The home was clearly very much a part of the total Americanization effort. However, the focus of homemaking was on the future effect that the Mexican girl would have, as mother, in creating an American-like home. Therefore, homemaking courses for Mexican girls were intended to "instill in the minds of girls . . . an appreciative understanding . . . and a sincere respect for the ideals of Democracy."[8] Courses combined Americanization and homemaking to teach Mexican girls to "adopt our customs, our ideals, and our country" and meanwhile were expected to raise the standards of health, cleanliness, diet, and child-rearing in the Mexican community.[9]

Moreover, cautioned the instructor, teachers must be cognizant of the relationship between the home and political behavior. She wrote that "the man with a home and family is more dependable and less revolutionary in his tendencies . . . the influence of the home extends to labor problems and to many other problems in the social regime." "The homemaker," she continued, "creates the atmosphere, whether it be one of harmony and cooperation or of dissatisfaction and revolt."[10] Thus, home economics for the Mexican girl had a wide range of objectives, including the political socialization of the Mexican community via the future mother.

The Young Mexican Girl

In an era when it was assumed that the future of all girls was motherhood and homemaking, the practice of a near-universal training for Mexican girls to become mothers and wives was unquestioned. Americanization, therefore, was deliberately directed at changing the relationship of the child to the home.

However, home economics was not to be taught uniformly to both American and Mexican girls; several factors differentiated the coursework for the two groups. First, home economics for the Mexican girl was an essential component of an overall Americanization program. Secondly, it was common practice to impart such training to Mexican girls at an earlier age than to American girls because of the former's early drop-out problem. Thirdly, the young Mexican girl was defined as a potential "carrier" of American culture, the social gene, who, upon her marriage and subsequent motherhood, could raise the next generation in an American cultural atmosphere. Consequently, the problem of the Americanization of the Mexican community could theoretically be resolved in a generation through a program of home economics integrated with Americanization.

The training of Mexican girls in a combination of Americanization and home economics, geared to their alleged personality, intelligence, aptitude, and culture was widely practiced throughout the Southwest, in the segregated elementary schools and in the integrated junior and senior highs. A two-tiered curriculum for Mexican children was implemented, one for boys emphasizing vocational courses but having little to do with Americanization, the second for girls emphasizing home economics intrinsic to their Americanization and the Americanization of future generations.

If Mexican culture was the general target for reform, Mexican girls and women were considered the key agents in achieving that transformation. If America is to assimilate the Mexican, wrote a home economics teacher, "we must begin at the basic structure of their social order--the home." However, the "main hope lies with the rising generation," she continued, and "since the girls are potential mothers and homemakers, they will control, in a large measure, the destinies of their future families."[11] There was a widespread belief that the Mexican girl should be educated not only for her personal development, but also to alter her habits, customs, and language, so that she might accomplish what the school would perhaps not be able to: the Americanization of the Mexican-descent *community*.

However, before the transformation of the girl could become fact, teachers needed to know what it was that made her different. Since the "needs of the Mexican home and community," argued a home economics teacher, were "vastly different from those of our own people," the course of instruction in home economics should be shaped to "fit the needs of these people when they come to us."[12] Another home economics teacher wrote that the effective education of Mexican girls required a knowledge of "the racial characteristics" because "many Mexican traits are exactly opposite of those of the Anglo-Saxon . . . "[13] The Mexican girl, the same teacher continued, must be clearly "understood and appreciated" before the curriculum for her could be provided. Various images of the Mexican girl were depicted in the literature which shaped teachers' knowledge and expectations of the Mexican girl. The following is a sampling:

> The Mexican girl develops emotionally at an early age. She becomes conscious of the opposite sex while she is still in the lower grades. This fact creates problems in the school which are difficult to cope with.[14]

> Mexican girls have inherited this remarkable aptness with the needle. We should strive to foster it in them . . . [15]

> Mexican girls need a great deal of training in serving and table etiquette, as being a waitress may be their method of obtaining a livelihood.[16]

> Mexican girls frequently create very bad impressions with gaudy, inappropriate clothes, brilliant nails, cheeks, and lips, a mass of very oily curls, cheap dangling earrings, and heavily scented perfume.[17]

> Many of the [Mexican] girls will very likely find employment as house servants. They should be taught something about cleaning, table-setting, and serving.[18]

> . . . the background of the American and that of the Mexican girl differ[s]. The former has learned the little courtesies of table etiquette in the home, but the latter, who may not have had a table in the home, must obtain her knowledge in the school room.[19]

> It is important that there is saving. . . . If we can get the [Mexican] girls to see the wisdom of doing this there will be . . . fewer county charges.[20]

The specific educational goal in relation to the Mexican girl was to train her for a future as an Americanized wife, mother, and homemaker, as well as to qualify her for occupations such as laundry worker, servant, waitress, seamstress, and others of a similar nature. In addition, the young girl was to be re-trained according to more appropriate standards of sexual behavior, appearance, diet, personal hygiene, and child-rearing. The schools then selected the Mexican girl for a 'personalized' home economics curriculum, which channelled her into at least three quite related directions: she would become an efficient wife, mother, and homemaker; she would be an Americanizing influence on her children and husband; she would become a potential wage earner in that unskilled labor market limited to women and utilizing her domestic skills. These three qualities were the central focus in the curriculum generally offered (or should one say forced upon?) the Mexican girl. Thus, across the Southwest, from Brownsville to Los Angeles, the Mexican girl was taught the "practical arts," a "curriculum more suited to her needs."[21] "For [Mexican] girls," wrote the superintendent of the Needles (California) School District, "we have sewing, cooking, and general household management, and we try to lay much stress upon ideas of sanitation."[22] In one Rio Grande Valley Mexican school, girls were routinely separated from the boys for special coursework in home economics, emphasizing sewing and cooking. At Belvedere Junior High School in Los Angeles, which was 50 percent Mexican, a demonstration home was devoted to home economics instruction, and only those girls in the 'slow-learner' track were required to enroll. According to the instructors, "The . . . courses aim to teach the girls to do all work better which is required of them at home . . . "[23]

It was quite common for Mexican children to be placed in slow-learner and educationally mentally retarded tracks. Often the two curricula did not have a clear demarcation; consequently, the "average" Mexican girl, as well as the "slow learner" and the "educationally mentally retarded" Mexican girl, had quite similar coursework. In Los Angeles it was an accepted policy that Mexican girls in elementary and junior high schools took home economics as their main coursework. This policy was well fixed for those girls whose grades and scores on I.Q. and achievement tests were low in comparison to the norm and were judged intellectually sub-normal. In addition, it was commonly assumed that the "typical" Mexican girl was an early drop-out and that her home economics training should begin in the elementary grades.

The principal at the Delhi Mexican Elementary School in Santa Ana (California) altered the curriculum to accommodate this pattern of early leaving. She found that a "need for a simple, practical course in household economics is even more essential to the girl from the Mexican home than to the average

American girl and it is also essential that it be given at an earlier date."[24] Her views were generally echoed across the Southwest, as this Southern California teacher stated:

> The fact that the Mexican girl marries young and becomes the mother in the home at the age the American girl is in high school means that the junior high school is trusted with her education for homemaker. For this reason, it seems to me that all or most of her junior high school training should be directed toward making her a better wife, mother and homemaker.[25]

In most school districts, the drop-out problem for Mexican girls began in the junior high years; however, those who did move from the segregated elementary school to the integrated junior high commonly found themselves in the slow-learner track or in the classes for the mentally retarded. Another practice placed overage elementary pupils into junior highs regardless of whether they had finished the preceding coursework. Los Angeles followed this policy, which affected Mexican children "more than it [did] any other group."[26] The special policy of transferring overage children to junior highs considerably enlarged the "low mentality" track. In one San Fernando Valley (Los Angeles) school, "out of a group of thirty-six special girls, twenty-six of them [were] Mexican."[27] One observer commented that the "problems of the Mexican girl are learned and taken care of" through these classes.[28] In other words, since most of the Mexican girls were enrolled in the low mentality classes, it would follow that the information regarding Mexican girls provided to teachers and administrators would emanate from these classes. Not all Mexican girls were in the special classes, but an overwhelmingly large percentage were: in one Valley school "twenty-five percent of all Mexican girls enrolled" were in the "special group"; in another school, "fifty-five percent or over one-half of the Mexican girls enrolled in this school" were in the "special group." In the remaining junior high school of the Valley, one-third of the Mexican girls were in special classes.[29] Not only were the Mexican girls enrolled in home economics, they also received "hands on" experiential learning by cooking and serving food in the cafeteria. In one case, Mexican girls were given maintenance chores as part of their training. The school with the highest Mexican enrollment routinely placed Mexican girls into "cafeteria work or janitor service."[30]

One of the more interesting aspects of this policy of placing Mexican girls into home economics classes was that "sub-normal," or "intellectually deficient," girls were also placed, as a matter of course, in the traditional Mexican girls' curriculum. Warburton, Wood, and Crane reported that the schools in the Rio Grande Valley had "special ungraded rooms in which home economics was emphasized for the girls . . . " and that these "were sometimes provided for retarded children."[31] The California State Department of Education recommended that those students categorized as "mentally retarded minors" begin a special course tailored to their abilities and future occupational potential. The Department therefore recommended special classes "equipped with tools and materials for appropriate forms of handiwork, such as weaving, woodwork, sewing, cooking, and other manual activities of educational value."[32] The type of equipment recommended was selected according to its suitability "for handicraft and homemaking classes."

Despite some difference in the class material, presentation, and intensity of teaching, all in all, Mexican girls were channelled into home economics, regardless of their abilities. The justification used for this practice was the Mexican family structure--that is, a family culture which defined the role of women as child-bearers, nurturing mothers, and faithful wives. Thus, oddly enough, home economics instruction in schools for Mexican children probably contributed to *maintaining* the traditional Mexican family organization, rather than promoting changes that would have brought it more in line with the American family structure. Paradoxically, the schools capitalized on an existing cultural pattern even though their objective was to reconstruct the Mexican family to conform with American standards.

Women and the Family

The creation of the Commission of Immigration and Housing in 1913 placed California in the forefront of the Americanization effort in the Southwest. The Commission's mandate was to "protect and deal with problems of foreign labor and of the communities in which they live." The Act establishing the Commission empowered the state to investigate "all things affecting immigrants, and for the care, protection, and welfare of immigrants."[33] The Commission was also authorized to cooperate with all other agencies in order "to bring to the immigrant the best opportunities for acquiring education and citizenship."

However, the Commission could not enforce policy; it could only make recommendations on the basis of its investigations. The outlines of future Americanization programs were already emerging when the Commission was founded. The law stated that the Commission was authorized to design educational programs for the proper instruction of adult and minor aliens in the English language and other subjects . . . It shall be the aim to communicate this instruction as soon after his arrival as practicable. The Commission shall cooperate with authorities to extend this education for both children and adults to labor camps and other localities from which the regular schools are not easily accessible.[34]

In 1915, the Commission successfully convinced the legislature to pass the Home Teacher Act, enabling the State, through local school systems, to enter into immigrant communities and to Americanize them through the use of community-based teachers or "home teachers." "It shall be the duty," read the Act,

of the home teacher to work in the homes of the pupils, instructing children and adults in matters relating to school attendance and preparation therefore; also in sanitation, in the English language, in household duties such as purchase, preparation and use of food and of clothing, and in the fundamental principles of the American system of government.[35]

The Act then "recognized the family not only as the social, but as the educational unit"[36] and gave local school systems the right to incorporate home teachers into their programs, should they so choose. Thus the law did not require school districts to hire home teachers, but merely enabled them to do so. The Act was supported by a number of patriotic organizations, such as the Daughters of the American Revolution, the United Daughters of the Confederacy, The Women's Christian Temperance Union, the Colonial Dames, and others of a similar political outlook.[37] Given the nature of the Act, the state tried to persuade school districts to employ home teachers by using Los Angeles schools to demonstrate the efficacy of home teachers. Several years after the Los Angeles experiment and after home teachers became a fixture in urban areas with large immigrant populations, Will C. Wood, State Superintendent of Public Instruction, stated in a report that

California was the first state to recognize the mother as the important factor in the home education, and to give her public school service, whether her child had shown any maladjustment or not. It is not because the child is undernourished or tardy or absent or dull or sleepy that the home teacher visits the foreign mother. It is because she is a foreign mother. If her child is doing well in school so much the better. It is still important that she learn English, have contact with American life and create for the child a home which will not be in conflict with his American education.[38]

If California did indeed lead the nation, then Los Angeles led California, so that by 1916 the city had established a Department of Immigrant Education, a title often given to the office responsible for the Americanization program in California school districts. Thus, at the close of the second decade, the home teacher was a prominent aspect of the schooling of the Los Angeles population. The purpose was to "devise means of placing within reach of all [immigrant] groups adequate facilities for becoming familiar with American social, economic and civic institutions and ideals."[39] One of the principal methods used was to establish Americanization centers in "cottages" in the community. By 1928 there were nineteen such centers with 280 classes meeting regularly, teaching English and "new world methods of housekeeping," whereby "a home may be made colorful and dainty and also may be kept clean and orderly."[40] More than seventy home teachers worked in these Americanization centers, which were often refurbished and decorated so that they would represent "any attractive, modest American home."[41] Cottages usually had "a pleasant porch with flower boxes . . . " and "fresh wallpaper, dainty window curtains, and . . . brightly painted furniture."[42] The district's assistant supervisor of Americanization stated that the home instruction emphasized English but that "cooking, sewing, millinery, budget making, thrift, home nursing, diet and nutrition" were also taught on an ongoing basis.[43] The location for Americanizing the children was the neighborhood school, that for Americanizing the adult was the neighborhood itself--through the use of a home-like structure, which was in reality a parallel state educational institution.

Los Angeles, like several other large districts, utilized a variety of means to Americanize the immigrant. Teachers were sent to the General Hospital, Olive View Sanitarium, the Central Jail, the Lincoln Heights Jail, railroad camps, and a number of industries, such as laundries, which employed large numbers of Mexican women.[44] Again, the curriculum emphasized the traditional subjects: English, American ideals and customs, homemaking, nutrition, sanitation, child-rearing, and the like.

Los Angeles had reason to commit itself early to Americanization: 22 percent of its population was foreign-born as the third decade of the twentieth century began, and 13 percent of the school population were Mexican as the decade closed. In that same period, one-half of all foreign-born children in Los Angeles were Mexican. Throughout its history, Los Angeles has had a large Spanish-speaking population, so, when Americanization was launched, there was a significant effect upon the Mexican community. The allegedly "backward" culture was challenged by the "progressive" culture, leading one home teacher to comment that the Mexican's "tendency to wander and live in a shiftless way," which was "not checked by the economic conditions in which this type of family finds itself here," should be eliminated through the Americanization efforts of the schools and the home teachers.[45]

By the mid-1920s, there were twenty-eight cities in California offering special courses to immigrant adults, with well over 30,000 persons enrolled. In each of these centers, the foreign mother was defined as "the important factor" in the responsibilities of the home teacher. Outside of city systems, the home teacher was not generally employed; instead, other methods were utilized which will be discussed below.

California established a statewide adminstrative bureaucracy, the Department of Immigrant Education, with centralized responsibility for Americanization work, which reported to the Superintendent's Office, whereas other states chose decentralized systems. Arizona and Texas, for example, did not create specific state-run adult immigrant programs, but they did recognize the importance of adult Americanization and sought to extend the influence of the classroom into the home. The *Course of Study for Elementary Schools of Arizona Instruction of Bilingual Children,1939* emphasized the importance of "actual contact with the homes of the children" by their teacher. Through the extension of the school program to the home, the role of the Mexican mother would be changed to fit American standards. The *Course of Study* underscored the importance of home contact for the "marked improvement in standards of living" of the immigrant communities.[46] As a consequence of such programs,

> many young immigrant mothers are now caring for their babies in a much better way than they themselves were cared for. . . . The use of English at home slowly gains ground. Receptivity to American culture slowly increases.[47]

Examples of such practices were also evident in Texas, where the effort to Americanize the child was extended to the family. However, some authorities urged that "Americanized" Mexicans rather than Anglo teachers be used as the main agents of cultural reformation. Texas urged its school districts to devise specific methods for the Americanization of the Mexican community: "new and original methods will have to be worked out," stated the State-sponsored *Report on Illiteracy in Texas, 1923*. One of these methods was the employment of "capable English speaking Mexicans themselves." "For this reason," the *Report* continued,

> the women's clubs, the Church societies, and all educational leaders interested in Mexican education should be ever on the alert for the enlistment of capable Mexican talent . . . The work of Mexican education can best be done by the intelligent Americanized Mexicans themselves. No persons can understand the Mexican mind better than they.[48]

Thus, while California was constructing state administrative apparatus to assimilate Mexican adults, Texas and Arizona left that function to the local districts. About all that Texas and Arizona did, in regard to adults, during the Americanization period was to encourage evening school programs in Mexican schools and teacher-training programs sponsored by the normal schools and the school districts.[49] Texas school districts often tried to extend their Americanization practices to the parents, so that in the Grandfalls Mexican school, for example, Halloween was especially devoted to breaking down superstitions "of the Mexican families."[50] It appears in retrospect that Arizona, Texas, New Mexico, and Colorado emphasized Americanization among children and allowed adult Americanization to proceed without a great deal of administrative leadership. It is therefore on California, and especially the work in Southern California, that attention will be focused in the rest of this essay.

Long Beach, Fullerton, Santa Ana, Riverside, La Habra, San Bernardino, Pasadena, and the Pomona Valley each had adult programs which emphasized reforming the role of the Mexican mother in the home. Generally, Americanization was the result of a cooperative effort among various agencies, with the school district performing the key role. Often social work agencies, churches, and women's clubs joined together to offer classes. Some localities offered evening classes on the school grounds; one in particular had a school bus refurbished as a traveling classroom that moved from one labor camp to another; Fullerton and La Habra had a labor camp cottage system whereby an Americanization "teacher lived in one camp in a 'model' house which also functioned as a school and would travel by car to offer classes in model cottages in other camps"; Riverside utilized a "settlement house" approach; Santa Ana offered classes in the county jail. Thus, Americanization programs took on many shapes, although the essential qualities remained constant.

Settlement houses within Mexican communities were used for Americanization programs in Pasadena and Riverside. The Edna P. Alter Mexican Settlement House in Pasadena promoted a program aimed at the

Chihuahuita *colonia*. The articles of incorporation stated that its work was

> to maintain, conduct and operate one or more Settlement
> Houses for the use of said Mexican population; to conduct
> nurseries and kindergartens for the Mexican children and
> schools for the Americanization of said people, and for the
> teaching and inculcating of the essentials of good citizenship
> . . . 51

The house sponsored "sewing classes for women and girls, English classes for men, women, boys and girls, . . . part time classes for working girls, . . . [a] girls' club, [a] maternity hospital, rug weaving, [an] employment bureau" and similar activities.52

The Riverside Community Settlement Association sponsored Americanization in the Mexican community but also offered separate classes for "colored women" with the support of the school district. Classes in "sewing, weaving, cooking" as well as a "Boys' Club and Girls' Club, Scout troop and various social activities"53 were given. In addition, a maternity hospital where for "thirteen dollars, a Mexican or colored mother can . . . stay for ten days," and "a bath house charging ten cents a shower," were major features of Americanization.54 Sewing was taught on a segregated basis to Mexican and black women, and a store in the building sold used clothes as well as the clothes and weavings made by the women.

Santa Ana offered classes to adults in the Mexican community and in the county jail. Two home teachers, a nurse, and five evening school teachers were directed by the supervisor of the school district's Department of Americanization. There were classes in "English, sewing, cooking, naturalization, orchestra, typing, and athletics at the various centers" located in the three Mexican communities.55 The courses in the jail were devoted to English and to instructing "some of the men why they are there."56 According to the warden, the courses had done much to raise the morale of the inmates. Each of the localities' programs "is organized with the ideal of making the [Mexican] immigrant a valuable factor in the life of his community."57

In the Labor Camps

The Americanization work carried out in the agricultural areas of the state was generally of a different nature from that of the urban areas. In the Imperial and San Joaquin valleys, some attempts were made at assimilating the

Mexican laborer. In El Centro, the school board and the local women's club cooperated to hire a "director of immigrant education" who spent "most of her time in the homes and in the teaching of the Mexicans."[58] In the neighboring town of Calipatria, the school board employed a "spirited young Mexican women with an American education" to carry out the Americanization program. Santa Paula, in Ventura County, had a director of Americanization who organized "schools for the workers in the various little foreign communities" located near the large ranching corporations using the Mexican laborers.[59]

The biggest effort at Americanization in the rural areas took place in the citrus-growing districts, rather than in the vegetable or cotton farming areas, because the Mexican communities in the citrus belts, primarily in Southern California, were composed of more or less permanent residents, whereas the vegetable and cotton farming areas utilized migrant labor to a far greater extent. Citrus growers often had "company towns" or labor camps where Mexican workers either leased or purchased lots at minimal prices.

Self-interest on the part of citrus growers spurred them to sponsor traditional assimilationist courses on their ranches and in their labor camps. The citrus industry found that improving their workers' language ability and work habits led to better labor-management relations. The Industrial Relations Bureau of the California Fruit Growers Supply Company realized that they had an interest in Americanization and thus actively promoted it among their affiliates. The local and state departments of immigrant education, for their part, found it convenient to work through the agribusiness firms. George B. Hodgkin, an official of the California Fruit Growers Supply Company, reflecting on this mutual interest, noted that the "sole object of building a labor camp is to provide a satisfactory supply of labor to do good work at the lowest possible cost."[60] However, he continued, very often, after the camp is built "it is not an uncommon occurrence to find that the cost of upkeep is unexpectedly high" due to the "ungentlemanly manners of some of the tenants."[61] The official charged that those camps which were left unsupervised had a high incidence of gambling, unemployment, brawls, and disease, and were marked by an "undependable and disappointing" supply of labor.[62] "In order to make the labor camp pay, to make it produce the desired workers," the official stated,

> it is necessary to create an atmosphere that will attract and hold such workers. The Mexican is reached most easily through his home and friends. If his family is well and happy, if his house is good and clean, and his meals good--and above all if his yard is full of vegetables and flowers which he has planted--he will be pretty certain to

think twice before uprooting himself. Moreover, if he
becomes a member of a local society, or baseball team or
band, or if he joins an English class and finds pleasant
companionship in the Camp he will probably think even
three times before leaving.[63]

Furthermore, there was a relationship, argued Hodgkin, "between
picking costs and teaching the Mexican women to sing 'Open the Window' in
English."[64] However, the Growers Exchange did not merely propose and
support Americanization, it also published its own "textbook of lessons in
industrial English" which functioned as a "compact description of the several
processes using foreign laborers."[65] The book was used in English classes for
men, teaching them "not only the English vernacular" of their jobs, but also
the skills of the "related processes of growing, cultivating, pruning, picking,
and irrigating."[66] An Americanization teacher in this setting devoted herself
mainly "to the labor camp, paying special attention to the housemother and her
problems," but the hired laborer was also a center of attention. In some cases,
as in La Habra, the Americanization teacher lived in one labor camp but also
provided classes for neighboring camps.
Every adult program had its graduation exercises, and at La Habra, as
in most other locales, they were well orchestrated rites of cultural passage. At
the 1921 graduation ceremonies, the small number of women who completed
their English classes were assembled before a "large group of growers, directors
of the La Habra Citrus Association, merchants, educators and camp dwellers to
receive their diplomas."[67] The cottage was "decorated with streamers and gay
paper flowers." The graduates were "attired in white graduation dresses . . .
bedecked with multi-colored paper flowers."[68] Before the women stood a table,
and upon it "were miniature beds, wash pans, brooms, dolls and other
household paraphenalia."[69] As proof of their expertise as English-speakers,
each graduate came before the table, picked up an object, and in English
described what she was doing: "making a bed, dressing the doll or sweeping the
floor."[70] Then, in unison, "they sang songs in English about opening the
windows, washing the baby and learning English."[71] Graduation was but a
certification that desirable cultural traditions had been learned, and in so doing,
an effective method of camp supervision and of worker dependability was
allegedly making its appearance. It was the efforts of the Americanization
teacher, remarked Hodgkin, that created "a desire for higher, healthier standards
of living," which in turn "will be more likely to achieve lasting results than
the supervisor who attempts to force the tenant to walk the chalk line."[72]
Thus, through the process of such education, the laborer was expected to

become self-directed, rather than externally directed, manifesting such qualities as thrift, good health, homeownership, clean-living, and sobriety--in short, all those characteristics that he or she had not previously possessed because of Mexican culture.

By the end of the 1920s, "industrial" Americanization had grown to encompass more than citrus belts, as laundries, sugar mills, and "industries of all sort having special vocabularies such as vineyards, canneries, railroads, and factories" began to hire or sponsor Americanization teachers and programs for their workers.[73] Given the demand, the state's normal schools early began to develop special Americanization curricula, teaching methods, and teacher training. Indeed, by 1920 the state offered a special Americanization Teaching Certificate which certified that the credentialed teacher had completed the required training coursework to qualify him or her for Americanization classwork. At mid-decade, nearly 3,000 teachers had "taken the required training courses" and over half of them were employed in Americanization education.[74]

When the Americanization program emanated from a cooperative arrangement between the school board and a business, an industry, or a grower, generally that teacher organized the coursework along the lines desired by the employer. Thus, for example, Arletta Kelly, who taught at the La Habra camp, was expected not only to teach courses, but also to keep "closer track of them [Mexicans]" than would normally be the case without the program.[75] At the Riverside school, a 'home visitor' was to report "all unsanitary conditions to the city health department," to "keep a careful check on domestic affairs, and cooperate with the district attorney if need arises," and to work with the county welfare organizations.[76] In the latter example, the 'home visitor' performed the function of an overseer for the public authorities, whereas in the La Habra case, the teacher was the overseer for the employer. In both instances, the Americanization programs introduced a system of surveillance into the Mexican community that was largely unnoticed by the community. One may only surmise the extent of this practice in the Southwest, but whether the programs were community- or home-oriented, the opportunity for activities exceeding the scope of Americanization were certainly available. Nevertheless, many employers, especially the citrus growers, saw value (meaning profit) in Americanization and did not hesitate to offer their support. Their motives were encapsulated in a statement in the biennial report of the Department of Education: "The Mexicans who are regular attendants at school are taught to *think*, the employers say, and are consequently better workmen."[77]

Generally, before Americanization courses were offered, the school district consulted with local employers to get their input into the program design. "The employers of alien labor," stated the Superintendent of the Chaffey

Union High School District, "should be consulted about the matter [Americanization]."[78] This was indeed done before the "class for Mexicans was opened in the Mexican camp." The officials of the Lucas Co., Inc., a ranch of some 4,000 acres in the Pomona area, gave their approval and a "bunk house" was remodeled at high school expense for Americanization instruction.

In neighboring Upland, the growers' associations built labor camps for their workers, "three roomed houses . . . rented . . . at ten dollars per month."[79] The Upland camp, called "Sonora Town," was populated by several hundred families and was similar to the towns found "in practically every citrus section."[80] After consultations between the grower's association and the Chaffey Union High School, "it was arranged that a . . . house in Sonora Town . . . should be fitted up as a school and a community center" for the exclusive use of the workers and their families. The superintendent of the school district felt that cooperation "between school authorities and employers of labor is absolutely necessary in the development of a successful plan of Americanization."[81]

Americanization teachers were impressed not only with the power of their employer, the school district, and their students' employers, the industry or grower, but were also imbued with a deep sense of professional commitment that greatly influenced their performance on the job. The Americanization teacher at La Habra, Jessie Hayden, stated that her colleagues "have been the sources of the greatest improvement in human living" when instructing Mexicans in the camps. Their responsibilities as Americanization teachers, she added, not only

> set forth to the Mexicans the rules of health, but also [brought] them in direct contact with a deep, overflowing, sympathetic source of human action where American ideals, ambitions, attitudes and aspirations for clean, pure, healthful thinking and living are born.[82]

In spite of the success of Americanization in the cities and towns, the Depression had a big effect upon the adult programs. Whereas Americanization work would continue in the segregated elementary schools until the termination of segregation, adult Americanization began to wane in the late 1930s. By the end of the decade, the high tide of community and adult Americanization among Mexicans had been reached and a slow decline followed, as World War II became the major point of interest. This was due, in part, to the massive repatriation drives which reduced both the number of Mexicans in the United States and the flow of new immigrants into the country. In addition, the financial costs of employing special Americanization teachers and a separate curriculum must have had a decided effect in curbing any extension of, as well as in cutting back, the adult Americanization work. Thus, the chief of the State Division of Adult and Continuation Education (within which Immigrant Education was administered) reported in 1933 that Americanization would increasingly "concern itself with the children of foreign-born parents . . . "[83]

In spite of the chauvinistic character of Americanization, Mexican adults undoubtedly gained some benefits from it. Courses in English, sanitation, hygiene, or sewing, were not entirely unnecessary. The high rate of illiteracy among Mexicans and the traditional methods of health care were often problems in the Mexican community which would have benefited from the instruction offered in these programs had they been free of Americanization objectives. And it is highly probable that many people did gain from learning English, or new methods of child care, or cooking. But this was not the essence of Americanization--and it is precisely because learning was not separated from political and economic interests that Americanization programs did not serve the Mexican community, but functioned, instead, to maintain the community as an oppressed group of workers. English was not taught as "English," but was shaped to fit the needs of employers and was aimed at making Mexicans more efficient and reliable workers. Americanization for mothers and housewives proposed to make them more effective reproducers and training agents of future laborers. Americanization, consequently, was a particular form of assimilation, but not of social change, and therefore provided a state institutional structure for strengthening the unequal social relations between Mexican laborers and their employers, and between Mexican and Anglo communities. Further, the theoretical basis for Americanization, the alleged cultural inferiority of the Mexican community, which was nothing more than academic sociological racism, would never have provided a foundation for a democratic educational experience.

Consequently, the theoretical argument that Mexican culture was antithetical to the continued economic development of the United States, was not consistently upheld in practice. For example, the Mexican patriarchal family was easily absorbed into the structure of capitalist agriculture and proved to be an instrument in maintaining its profitability and productivity. Furthermore, the attributes of being cheap and flexible labor, which grew out of the Mexicans' origins as immigrants from peasant villages, were highly prized by employers.

Thus, a kind of schizophrenic policy emerged in the Southwest: on the one hand, an opportunistic incorporation of Mexican laborers, valued because of their peasant background, into modern capitalist agricultural production, and on the other hand, an aggressive policy of de-culturalization aimed at eliminating the ethnicity of the Mexican community. The former practice preserved key elements of Mexican culture, especially the traditional family and language; the latter policy weakened Mexican culture. Often both practices were applied by public educators to the very same community--what one hand gave, the other took away. Further, Americanization was expected to occur in a segregated setting, an environment that contributed to separation rather than assimilation.

Mexican immigrants were involved in the culture of their communities of origin even while in the United States. However, the argument that ethnicity was antithetical to economic progress has never been fully proven, and it is more likely that the justification for Americanization stemmed from the chauvinism inherent in the popular sociological concepts of the period. American culture was nationalistic, racist, chauvinistic, and prone to that arrogance characteristic of a rising world power. Consequently, social theory, too, inevitably contained those same ideas that promoted the anti-democratic subordination of ethnic minorities.[84]

Notes

1. Maxine Seller, "The Education of the Immigrant Woman, 1900-1935," *Journal of Urban History* 4 (1978).

2. Richard Griswold del Castillo, *La Familia: Chicano Families in the Urban Southwest, 1848 to the Present* (Notre Dame: University of Notre Dame Press, 1984).

3. Ricardo Romo, *History of a Barrio, East Los Angeles* (Austin: University of Texas Press, 1983).

4. Seller, "Education."

5. "The Course of Study for Elementary Schools of Arizona," *Instruction of Bilingual Children Bulletin* 13 (Phoenix, Ariz.: State Department of Education, 1939), 59.

6. Merton E. Hill, *The Development of an Americanization Program* (Ontario, Calif.: Chaffey Union High School District, 1928), 75.

7. Pearl Idelia Ellis, *Americanization Through Homemaking* (Los Angeles: Wetzel Publishing Co., 1929), 3.

8. Ibid., 65.

9. Ibid.

10. Ibid., 31.

11. Ibid., 6.

12. Ibid., 13.

13. Laura Lucille Lyon, "Investigation of the Program For the Adjustment of Mexican Girls to the High Schools of the San Fernando Valley" (Master's thesis, University of Southern California, 1933), 8.

14. Ibid., 49.

15. Ellis, *Americanization*, 15.

16. Ibid., 35.

17. Katherine Hollier Meguire, "Educating the Mexican Child in the Elementary School" (Master's thesis, University of Southern California, 1938), 122.

18. Ibid., 117-18.

19. Ibid., 33.

20. Ibid., 41.

21. John E. Branigan, "Education of Overage Mexican Children," *Sierra Educational News* 12 (1929): 39.

22. Ibid.

23. Gladine Bowers, "Mexican Education in East Donna," *Los Angeles School Journal* 10 (1927): 58.

24. Hazel Peck Bishop, "A Case Study of the Improvement of Mexican Homes Through Instruction in Homemaking" (Master's Thesis, University of Southern California), 87.

25. Ibid., 91.

26. Lyon, "Investigation," 30.

27. Ibid., 31.

28. Ibid.

29. Ibid., 35.

30. Ibid., 54.

31. Amber Warburton, Helen Wood, and Marian Crane, "The Work and Welfare of Children of Agricultural Laborers in Hidalgo County, Texas," U.S. Department of Labor, Children's Bureau Publication 298 (Washington, D.C.: Government Printing Office, 1943), 33.

32. Frances W. Doyle, "Questions on the Education of Mentally Retarded Minors in California," *California Department of Education Bulletin* 19 (January 1950): 21.

33. Grace Elizabeth Reeves, "Adult Mexican Education in the United States" (Master's thesis, Claremont Colleges, Claremont, California, 1929), 21-22.

34. Ibid.

35. Ibid., 23.

36. Mary Cunliffe Trautwein "A History of the Development of Schools for Foreign Born Adults in Los Angeles" (Master's thesis, University of Southern California, 1928), 58.

37. Ibid., 60.

38. Ibid., 67.

39. Ruby Baughman, "Elementary Education for Adults," *The Annals of the American Academy*, 1920, 103.

40. Beulah Amidon, "Home Teachers in the City," *Survey Graphic*, June 1926, 306.

41. Ibid.

42. Ibid.

43. Harry M. Shafer, "Americanization in the Los Angeles Schools," *The Los Angeles School Journal* 7 (1924): 31-333.

44. Alice Osborne McKenna, "Americanizing the Foreign Home," *The Los Angeles School Journal* 9 (1925): 13.

45. Vera Sturges, "Home Standards Among Our Mexican Residents," *The Los Angeles School Journal* 9 (1925): 15.

46. "Course of Study for Elementary Schools," 62.

47. Ibid.

48. Everett E. Davis, *A Report on Illiteracy in Texas*, University of Texas Bulletin no. 2328, 22 July 1923, 35.

49. Ibid., 50.

50. Laura Frances Murphy, "An Experiment in Americanization," *The Texas Outlook* 23 (1939): 24.

51. Anna Christine Lofstedt, "A Study of the Mexican Population in Pasadena, California" (Master's thesis, University of Southern California, 1922), Appendix A.

52. Ibid.

53. Reeves, "Adult Mexican Education," 43.

54. Ibid., 44.

55. Ibid., 48.

56. Ibid., 47.

57. Ibid., 49.

58. Ethel Richardson,"Doing the Things that Couldn't be Done," *Survey Graphic*, June 1926, 298.

59. Ibid., 299.

60. George B. Hodgkin, "Making the Labor Camp Pay," *California Citrograph*, August 1921, 354.

61. Ibid.

62. Ibid.

63. Ibid.

64. Ibid.

65. Baughman, "Elementary Education," 165.

66. Ibid.

67. Hodgkin, "Labor Camp," 354.

68. Ibid.

69. Ibid.

70. Ibid.

71. Ibid.

72. Ibid.

73. Mary S. Gibson, "Schools for the Whole Family," *Survey Graphic,* June 1926, 303.

74. Ibid.

75. Interview with Arletta Kelly by B. E. Schmidt, California State University, Fullerton, Oral History Literary Tape no. 48.

76. Reeves, "Adult Mexican Education," 45.

77. *The Thirty-Fourth Biennial Report of the California State Department of Education, Sacramento, California* (California State Printing Office, 1933), 68.

78. Hill, *Americanization Program,* 10.

79. Ibid., 11.

80. Ibid.

81. Ibid., 12.

82. Jessie Hayden, "The La Habra Experiment in Mexican Social Education" (Master's thesis, Claremont Colleges, Claremont, California, 1934).

83. California State Department of Education, Biennial Report, 1931/1932.

84. See, for example, Stephan Jay Gould, *The Mismeasure of Man* (New York: W. W. Norton and Co., Inc., 1981).

An Ethnographic Study of Mexican-Descent Students in a California High School

Maria Eugenia Matute-Bianchi

To understand the responses that different minority students have made to the demands of schooling, it is important to distinguish between those minorities who do well in school and others who do not, because minority status *per se* does not account for differences in school success and failure.[1] Even within the same ethnic group, there are considerable variations in school performance. In a California high school that I studied, which I shall call Field High, subgroups of Mexican-descent students showed vastly different rates of graduation and diverse modes of behavior. This essay analyzes how the way members of each subgroup perceived themselves and how the value they placed on education affected their school performance.

Categories of Mexican-descent Students

In general, Mexican-descent students at Field High can be divided into five categories: recent Mexican immigrants, Mexican-oriented, Mexican Americans, *Chicanos*, and *Cholos*.

Recent Mexican immigrant students, the Mexican *recién llegado*, are Spanish-speaking, Mexican-born, and frequently identified through diagnostic English placement tests as Limited English Proficient (LEP) students. These students dress differently from the rest of the students, who consider their

---

This essay is a greatly abbreviated version of "Ethnic Identities and Patterns of School Success and Failure among Mexican-Descent and Japanese-American Students in a California HIgh School: An Ethnographic Analysis," *American Journal of Education* 95 (1986): 233-55.

clothing to be unfashionable. When interviewed, these students identify themselves as *"Mexicanos"* and they consider Mexico their permanent home. They most frequently cite economic opportunity as the reason for their families' immigration to the United States. Some came here legally, others illegally. Some have established a relatively permanent base in the community and do not migrate seasonally back to Mexico, others return to Mexico or travel to other areas with their families. Students within this group make distinctions among themselves, using the reference framework of Mexico: rural versus urban, upper class versus working class, and *mestizo* versus *indio*.

Students within the Mexican-immigrant category differ significantly in their level of proficiency in Spanish. Those who function below grade level in Spanish, perhaps at the 4th or 5th grade level, are likely to enroll in a special curriculum, as well as in the beginning ESL (English as a Second Language) class. Others who are at approximately grade level in Spanish are enrolled in one or two ESL classes, beginning English reading, bilingual math, bilingual social studies, bilingual science, and physical education.

Among these immigrant students, those who are relatively proficient in Spanish in both oral and written expression tend to succeed academically more often than those who function below grade level in Spanish. Hence, proficiency in their primary language is related to their academic performance. Proficiency is often due to the length of schooling in Mexico: before coming to the United States, many of the more proficient students had successfully completed *primaria* (grammar school) and, in some cases, had entered the pre-collegiate *secundaria* or the *preparatoria* in Mexico.

The length of schooling in Mexico also reflects the extent of a student's socialization into Mexican culture. Teachers and staff frequently describe these immigrant students as more courteous, more serious about their school work, more eager to please, more polite, more industrious, more well-behaved, more naive, and less worldly than other students. Such behavior, apparently, is conducive to relatively successful school performance in the United States.

Students in the second category, The Mexican-oriented, are most often bilingual, with varying degrees of proficiency in English, and they usually do well in academic work in classes conducted exclusively in English. They use English and Spanish interchangeably with their peers and speak Spanish at home but speak English exclusively with the school personnel. These students are usually identified as Fluent English Proficient (FEP) students. Many of them enroll in the general or remedial English classes but not in the ESL or beginning English reading courses. Spanish-surname students enrolled in the college prep courses are frequently from this

Mexican-oriented group.

Mexican-oriented students have strong ties with both Mexico and the United States, but they identify themselves as *"Mexicanos"* and see differences between themselves and the Mexican *recién llegado*, the Mexican American, the *Chicano*, and the *Cholo*. They show pride in their Mexican heritage, which they feel distinguishes them from other more "Americanized" students of Mexican-descent in the school. To these students, the terms *Chicano* and *Cholo* seem derogatory and they would rarely, if ever, use them as self-descriptors. Neither do they identify themselves as Mexican Americans. They attended elementary and junior high schools in the United States, although some may have attended the first year or two of *primaria* in Mexico. Other students consider their style of dress more "American" than that of the recent immigrant group, but not "quaddie," a local term for "preppie."

Mexican-oriented students are among the more successful Mexican-descent students in the school. Although not all members of this group succeed in school, virtually all of the Mexican-descent students in the top 10 percent of the 1985 graduating class were identified by teachers and other students as members of the Mexican-oriented group. The vast majority of them were effectively bilingual, had lived in this country for more than five years, and had plans to attend college and to establish themselves in a career in this country.

Mexican-oriented students see themselves as "more *Mexicano*" than the Mexican American, *Chicano*, or *Cholo* groups. They view Mexican Americans as "people of Mexican parents who were born in the United States." They often describe some Mexican American students as arrogant, people who make fun of the more Mexican-oriented students and who feel "superior" to them. Mexican-oriented students tend to view *Chicanos* and *Cholos* as "people who have lost their Mexican culture," and the terms *Chicano* and *Cholo* as negative labels associated with gang membership and a host of offensive qualities.

The Mexican immigrant and the Mexican-oriented students, who are either Spanish-speaking or bilingual, are more likely than other groups to participate in school clubs such as the *Sociedad Bilingüe* or in soccer. The *Sociedad Bilingüe* club serves as the most visible organizational symbol of Mexican student involvement in the school. The club raises funds for scholarships which are awarded to students going on to college, organizes dances, sponsors cultural events like the *Semana de la Raza* during *Cinco de Mayo* week, and plans field trips to university campuses. *Sociedad Bilingüe* was founded in the late 1970s by a group of Mexican immigrant and Mexican-oriented students who wanted an organization to help them bridge the social distance between themselves and the "Anglos" in the school. They hoped to have both "Anglos" and "Mexicans" in the club. However, the club's membership has been virtually exclusively "Mexican," and the club's activities attract mostly the Mexican-descent students, particularly the Mexican-oriented.

The third category of Mexican-descent students, the Mexican Americans, comprises those born in the United States of Mexican parentage who identify themselves as Mexican Americans or Americans of Mexican descent. They are much more "American"-oriented than the first two groups, and school personnel frequently describe them as "totally assimilated." They often do not speak Spanish well, and even if they do, they prefer to speak English in school. There is a range of oral Spanish-language proficiency among this group, depending on the extent to which the student must use Spanish at home and in the community. Students in this category see differences between themselves and the Mexican immigrant and Mexican-oriented students, on the one hand, and between themselves and the *Chicanos* and *Cholos*, on the other hand. They find the term *Chicano* offensive and consider it to be synonymous with *Cholo* and "Low Rider."

Some of the most active and successful Mexican-descent students in the school belong to this group. They participate more in the mainstream school clubs and in student government than either the Mexican immigrant or Mexican-oriented students. They are members of clubs and organizations which also have white and Japanese-American members. For the most part, they do not participate in the more "Mexican" clubs, such as the *Sociedad Bilingüe* or more *"Chicano"* clubs like M.A.T.A. (Mexican Americans Taking Action).

The fourth group, the *Chicanos,* encompasses a large segment of the Mexican-descent population in the school, perhaps 40 to 50 percent of the Spanish-surname students. When queried, these students identify themselves as "Mexican" or *"Mexicano,"* but they do not find the term *"Chicano"* offensive or derogatory. They frequently call themselves "homeboys" or "homegirls" and derisively describe academically successful Mexican-descent students as "schoolboys" or "schoolgirls"--students who attend classes regularly, carry books around the campus, and abide by the school rules. To distinguish themselves from more "Americanized" students of Mexican descent, *Chicano* students call the latter "Wannabee" which means "wants to be white" or "wants to be Anglo."

These students' high level of alienation from the school distinguishes them from the three groups described above. They are less actively involved in school programs and activities, they typically do not enroll in college prep courses, and they are much more likely to be in the general or remedial courses. Many teachers think members of this group are primarily concerned with being

Chicano and behave as though "school isn't important." They listen to music that is different from the music that mainstream students in the school are fond of; they frequently cite this as a reason for not attending school dances. Students in this group may try to do well in school and often express a desire to do so, but they behave in ways that promote failure--frequent absences, disruptive behavior, not bringing books and materials to class, and not doing their homework.

The *Cholos* are the fifth, and by far, the smallest of the five subgroups of Mexican-descent students in the school--almost to the point of disappearing from the school community--but its members are the most distinguishable because of the obvious stylistic and cultural symbols they display. Students who affect the *Cholo* style are frequently identified by others as "gang-oriented" or gang sympathizers. Not all of these students belong to gangs, but because they affect the *Cholo* style, they are usually considered to be sympathetic to the *Cholo* as a cultural subgroup.

Other Mexican-descent students in the school, as well as mainstream students, hold *Chicanos* and *Cholos* in low esteem and express fear of, or contempt for, them. Both *Chicanos* and *Cholos* have low status in the school and are disaffected, marginalized members of the school community. They do not actively participate in school functions, nor are they usually considered successful students.

A teacher who had taught at the school for more than eight years indicated that so many Mexican-descent students now attend the school, with varying degrees of success and failure, that the staff has been "forced" to make distinctions among this growing student population. The general image of these students, according to this teacher, has changed from a " . . . distinctly negative one to one that is more positive or at least ambivalent."

The stereotypical view of the "more Mexican" students held by teachers is that they are more polite and respectful, more serious about school, more eager to please, more motivated, and much less sophisticated in ways to undermine school rules and practices than are the more "Americanized" Mexican-descent students, especially *Chicanos* and *Cholos*. When asked to compare *Chicano* students and students more oriented to Mexico and Mexican culture, many adults said the former are "less interested in school," "more irresponsible," "more smart-mouthed," "more street-tough," and "less motivated" than the latter.

The staff members do not consider all Mexican-oriented and Mexican-immigrant students to be successful; however, the difficulties they have are perceived to be different from those attributed to unsuccessful *Chicano* students. Staff members feel that unsuccessful Mexican-immigrant students have difficulty in school because they do not have satisfactory English language skills, lack competency in academic skills in general, and/or come from a rural, peasant Mexican background which has not prepared them to meet the demands of schooling in the United States. Despite such difficulties in school, staff freqently describe these students as "shy but unfailingly courteous," "cheerful," "grateful for what you can do for them," and "well-behaved."

Unsuccessful *Chicano* and *Cholo* students, on the other hand, are perceived to lack motivation, interest, and respect for schooling. Staff members believe they fail in school because they reject what the school has to offer. They are said to be more "apathetic," "sullen," "withdrawn," "mistrusting," and "discourteous" in general than are Mexican-immigrant and Mexican-oriented students.

Perceptions of Adult Opportunities and the Value of Schooling

Thirty-five Mexican-descent students were interviewed over a two-year period to understand their aspirations, their knowledge of adult occupations and strategies to achieve adult success, their definitions of adult success and failure, and their perceptions of the value of schooling in achieving their expressed goal.

The more successful Mexican-descent students are achievement- and goal-oriented, even when they lack a specific career goal. In general, they come from the Mexican-oriented and Mexican American subgroups. They see a definite connection between their experiences in high school and their potential success as adults. Virtually all of them express an interest in going to college, although some indicate that family circumstances (e.g., return to Mexico or financial difficulties) may make this difficult or impossible. Many of these students look to adults in the school--Anglo as well as Mexican-descent--as role models of success. They recognize a practical value in meeting the demands of high school and manifest a marked sense of purpose in doing well in school. They know generally which are the "right" courses to take in preparation for college, they know that it is important for them to participate in school activities, and they have a generalized understanding that what they do today will serve them well later on in life. Many of them were born in Mexico and received their earliest schooling there. Others were born in the United States and received all of their schooling in the Pajaro Valley area. All were the sons and daughters of agricultural workers, cannery workers, or laborers in some kind of low-skilled occupation.

Many of the successful students express confidence in their ability to succeed in their adult lives and recognize the importance that school can play in their adult lives. They are willing to expend considerable effort to do well in school because they anticipate benefits from such an investment. They often define adult success in terms of "having a nice car, a nice house, a nice job," and having "enough money that you don't have to worry about it any more." A few of the students have a definite occupational choice, such as interior designer, engineer, or lawyer. But for the most part, they only express a desire to work "in a big company," "in a large corporation," "with something in computers," or "for a bank." One student, a senior going on to a University of California campus, said, "I guess I want to hold a job that pays at least $10 an hour, where I can make at least more than my brother [a computer assembly line worker]." Another, also a 12th grader, said, "I would like to have a very good job where I could get good money and meet new people, like working in a bank or as an accountant." A third senior said, "I don't know exactly what. Probably working for a big company, like the telephone company."

When asked about the purpose of education, the successful Mexican-descent students express a strong belief in the link between doing well in school and being a successful adult, in "being someone" and "earning good money." As an 11th grader expressed it, "*Es una preparación que te está llevando a pasos más grandes.* [It is a preparation which is carrying you to greater things]." Another 11th grader said:

> My mother keeps telling me, *"Ai mi hija, tienes que sacar buenas calificaciones en la* high school *para que no te estes chingando igual que yo.* And you know, she has a point. I don't want to be doing that. I've been in the cannery before. Like taking things to my uncle who works there with my mother. Just being there I can tell I wouldn't want to work there. I don't like it. I've got to do well in school so that I don't have to face this in my future.

Despite the fact that these students are remarkably achievement-oriented in school, they often do not know people holding the kind of jobs they would like to have as adults. Nonetheless, they believe in the link between doing well in school and attaining rewarding, high-status adult occupations. And "doing well in school," according to these students, means attending classes regularly, doing the homework, asking teachers for help when they don't understand something, trying "as hard as you can," and getting along well with the teachers.

Most, but not all of the students, indicate that one reason for their success in school is their parents' interest and support. Some of the girls, however, reveal that their parents have not supported them, and that their encouragement to do well in school has come from teachers and counselors. These same girls say that their parents fear that should they go to a university or college, they would live away from home.

Unsuccessful Mexican-descent students are among the most visible students on campus. Their manner of dress, walk, and speech frequently identify them as *Chicanos* or *Cholos*. Moreover, they congregate in specific places on campus which they consider their "turf." Just as the mainstream "quaddie" students "hang out" in the area between the main administration building and the swimming pool, the *Chicano* and *Cholo* students most often meet further away from the center of the campus. The more gang-oriented "hang out" in certain areas which are considered the exclusive province of one of the two major gangs in the community.

Chicano and *Cholo* students frequently roam the campus after the class bell has rung. They walk across the street to a fast-food stand, meet friends in the faculty parking lot, or just "hang out" in the corridors of remote hallways. They are also quite visible in the 'study center'--located in the cafeteria--during each class period. This 'study center' is reserved for students who are prevented from entering class because of tardiness, or who have been permanently expelled from a class and have no other class in which to enroll.

Chicano and *Cholo* students are much more likely than other students to enroll in the school's alternative 'school within a school' program, which was established for students unable to function effectively in the regular classrooms. Classes do not last as long (40 minutes versus 50 minutes), and students take four core courses in the morning and after lunch. Afterwards, they can take additional courses, such as physical education or social studies, in the regular curriculum or they can go home. Students enrolled in the program earn graduation credits, but their transcripts indicate they earned the credit in 'alternative education'. The curriculum is less structured and rigorous than in many of the courses in the regular program, although students must participate in reading, writing, and discussion exercises in class. In a class containing all boys, the students assemble model cars, many of them in the "Low Rider" style. The content and structure of the program reinforce the students' marginality and alienation from the school community, although the staff believes the program provides an educational opportunity for students who would otherwise have dropped out of school.

The relationship between most of the unsuccessful students and the school is characterized by conflict and resistance. The students are disillusioned and lack confidence regarding the rewards of schooling because they perceive that their chances of getting desirable jobs when they finish school are very limited. They perceive an incongruence between the requirements of schooling and those of the alternative survival or resistance strategies they have developed to cope with their manifestly restricted economic and social opportunities.

However, some unsuccessful *Chicano* students express high-status career aspirations--they want to be lawyers, engineers, or architects--while others have no definite plans. These students espouse the conventional notions about going to school in order to get "good jobs," but most of them anticipate having continuing difficulties in school, express uncertainty about their future, and doubt they will graduate. One of the students, for example, expressed a commonly shared sentiment: "I would like to graduate but I don't know if I will."

Unsuccessful *Chicano* students frequently would like to work in an office or in some occupation which is less physically demanding or "more interesting" than the work their parents, siblings, and relatives do, yet frequently they do not know how one goes about getting such jobs. Often, they get intrigued with the idea of working "with computers" after a school-sponsored field trip to a local computer firm, but they usually lack the specific information or are misinformed about how to secure a job with such a company. Many of these students do not know what kind of career their parents or family would like them to pursue and have not discussed this with their elders. Moreover, they often say "it would be okay" with their parents if they drop out of school before graduation. They often cite economic necessity as a reason for leaving school before graduation.

All students interviewed were asked to describe successful and unsuccessful adults and to elaborate on the reasons for such success or lack thereof. Many of the *Chicano* students could not name a single successsful Mexican-descent adult whom they know well. They could only point to an Anglo teacher or youth counselor as a successful person. Or, if they could describe a Mexican-descent adult whom they considered to be successful, the adult pursued activities which society at large would not consider valuable. For example, one *Chicano* 10th grader carefully described his uncle as a "successful adult": he is a leader in Northside [a local gang] and he is "smart with money." He became successful because of "being on the streets" and "knowing what's happening." Another 10th grade student described his grandmother as a successful adult: "she used to own several restaurants and bars in town but she isn't here no more because they kept closing her places down because of the gangs and stuff."

When asked to explain how young people become unsuccessful adults, these students responded in various ways: "they were lazy and dropped out of school"; "they got too much into partying and doing drugs"; "they had teachers who didn't care if they were learning"; "they got a rotten education"; "Mexicans don't have a chance to go to college and make something of themselves"; "people like us face a lot of prejudice because there are a lot of people who don't like Mexicans"; "there aren't enough good jobs to go around"; "some people, no matter how hard they try, just have bad luck"; "some people are just lazy and before they realize it, they have messed-up too much to start going right."

These students often don't know what the future holds for them. They have a difficult time articulating what they expect to be doing in ten years: "Gee, I don't know. I hope I have a job, but I don't know." "I haven't really thought that far ahead but I hope I finish school." "It's hard to think that far ahead." They find it easier to discuss at length their concerns and hopes for today, tomorrow or, possibly, the coming weekend.

Despite the fact that these students frequently wish to do well in school and to graduate, they often behave in ways that are counterproductive to these achievements. Many of them expend a great deal of energy during the school day subverting some aspect of the school program. One group explained how they "worked the system": many of the textbooks have answers in the back of the chapters, so when the teachers assign homework, there is no need to read the chapters because you can "get by" just copying the answers. Some of them meet during lunch in certain remote areas of the campus to "smoke dope and get high and just hang out." After school they ride around town or "hang out" by the 7-11 store near campus. When asked why they come to school, many replied that they come to see their friends. To them, the most onerous aspect of being suspended from school is that it means they "won't be able to see their buddies."

Conclusion

Mexican-descent students have multiple identities in which symbols, stereotypes, and styles assume great significance. Among these students, maintaining separate identities as "Mexican," "Mexican American," *"Chicano,"* or *"Cholo"* appears to be important in their lives at school. These labels are emblems that carry meaning both to those who so name themselves and to outside observers.

At Field High, ethnic identity is used by Mexican-descent students to cope with their subordinate status in the school community. The various identities consist of powerful symbols around which social negotiation takes place. It means a great deal to students who call themselves *"Mexicanos"* that they *not* be identified as *"Chicanos"* or *"Cholos."* Maintaining an identity as *"Mexicano"* or as a "Mexican American" means that one is not held in low esteem by others in the school. Being a *"Mexicano"* or "Mexican American" allows one to be identified as a successful student because in the eyes of teachers, being a good student is not inconsistent with being a *"Mexicano "* or a "Mexican American."

To be a *"Chicano,"* on the other hand, means to hang out by the science wing; it means not eating lunch in the quad where all the *"gringos,"* "white folks," and "schoolboys" hang out; it means cutting classes by faking a call slip so you can be with your friends at the 7-11 store; it means sitting in the back in a class of *"gabachos"* and *not* participating; it means *not* carrying books to class or doing one's homework; it means not taking the "hard" classes; it means doing the "minimum to get by." In short, it means not participating in school in ways which will promote academic success and achievement.

This study suggests that students use different strategies to cope with the demands of schooling and that these strategies are both anticipatory and reactive. That is, students anticipate their future adult roles and develop a set of skills, behaviors, and orientations in response to those expectations. In particular, they respond to education in terms of its perceived role in determining their future lives.

Ethnicity seems to be problematic for Mexican-descent students. The differences among them are manifested as *primary cultural differences* which are associated with the "more Mexican" students and in *secondary cultural differences* which are associated with the "more *Chicano"* or "more *Cholo"* students. The primary cultural differences are due to the students' non-English speaking ability, unfamiliarity with school rules and expectations, lack of an informed knowledge of the school curriculum, and so forth. These existed *prior* to the immigrants' arrival in the United States. To overcome such problems does not threaten the students' identity as *Mexicanos*. Nor do such students suffer from affective dissonance or emotional distress and ambivalence when they make an effort to learn the behavior and other cultural features of the dominant culture. They can maintain an identity as Mexicanos even when they cross cultural boundaries.

Secondary cultural differences are the collective result of a group's responses to subordination and exploitation by the dominant group. They develop *after* the subordinate group becomes involuntarily incorporated and evolve as part of a boundary-maintenance mechanism or *oppositional process* between the minority group and the dominant society. Secondary cultural differences signal a group's reluctance to accept or learn certain features of the dominant group's culture and some of its behavioral codes of conduct.*Chicanos* and *Cholos* appear to resist certain features of the school culture, especially the behavioral and normative expectations required for scholastic achievement, because these norms, assumptions, and codes of conduct are associated with being "white" or *"gringo"* or "quaddie" or "rich honkie." To them, adopting these cultural features--participating in class discussions, carrying books from class to class, asking the teacher for help in front of others, trying to do well in school--will subject them to the derision, condescension, and mockery of other *Chicanos*.

These students are faced with a forced-choice dilemma: they must choose between doing well in school or being a *Chicano*. From this perspective, it is not possible or legitimate to participate in both the culture of the dominant group, i.e., the school culture, *and* in the *Chicano* culture. To cross these cultural boundaries means denying one's identity as a *Chicano* and is considered to be incompatible with maintaining the integrity of one's *Chicano* identity. The school policies and practices are viewed as forces to be resisted, subverted, undermined, challenged, and opposed. Often the opposition takes the form of mental withdrawal in which the students find themselves alienated from the academic content of the school curriculum and the effort required to master it. The observed pattern of school failure among many Mexican-descent students at Field High School suggests a reactive process, an intensive intragroup reliance in developing a collective identity as a disadvantaged, disparaged minority group. The construction of this identity is thus at once a product of both historical exclusion and structural subordination imposed by the dominant group, *and* a vehicle used by the oppressed group to resist structured inequality.

Notes

1.   John Ogbu and Maria Eugenia Matute-Bianchi, "Minority Status and Schooling in Plural Societies," *Comparative Education Review* 27, no. 2 (1983):168-90; John Ogbu and Maria Eugenia Matute-Bianchi, "Understanding Sociocultural Factors: Knowledge, Identity, and School Adjustment," *Beyond Language: Social and Cultural Factors in Schooling Language Minority Students* (Los Angeles: California State University, Los Angeles, Evaluation, Dissemination and Assessment Center, 1986).

References

Castile, George R., and Kushner, Gilbert, eds. *Persistent Peoples*. Tucson, Arizona: University of Arizona Press, 1981.

Ogbu, John, and Matute-Bianchi, Maria Eugenia. "Minority Status and Schooling in Plural Societies." *Comparative Education Review* 27 (1983).

Ogbu, John, and Matute-Bianchi, Maria Eugenia. "Understanding Sociocultural Factors: Knowledge, Identity, and School Adjustment." *Beyond Language: Social and Cultural Factors in Schooling Language Minority Students.* Los Angeles: California State University, Los Angeles, Evaluation, Dissemination and Assessment Center, 1986.

Royce, Anya. *Ethnic Identity*. Bloomington, Ind.: Indiana University Press, 1982.

Social Science Research Council. *Comparative Research on Ethnicity: A Conference Report*. New York: Social Science Research Council, 1974.

Spicer, Edward. "Persistent Identity Systems." *Science* 4011 (1971).

Assimilation in Comparative Perspective: Jewish and Japanese Americans

Gene N. Levine

Given the problems of conceptualization, getting funding, drawing samples, and unforeseen exigencies in field work--to say nothing of arriving at an appropriate analytic model--it is no surprise that comparative surveys of ethnic groups and communities are rarely attempted. It is hard enough to do justice to the study of one ethnic group and to look for differentiation within it. The monocultural study, however, cannot answer a multitude of questions.

We know that within any ethnic group, there are differential rates of acculturation by its members. Some may learn English more quickly than others, men may be more privileged than women, and the younger (or second) generation may have an advantage over their immigrant parents. Even within families, though this has been little documented, one brother may ascend the socioeconomic ladder, while another experiences no mobility.

But what of intergroup comparisons? In what ways, if any, does one group achieve rapid integration into the larger milieu, while another lags behind? And what accounts for the difference? Obviously, common measures must be employed to arrive at answers to these questions.

I have chosen to study differences in the acculturation and assimilation of Japanese Americans and Jewish Americans in Los Angeles. That I did not at the outset of my work plan any such comparison will be apparent. Nonetheless, it is possible to compare data from two separate studies. The data on Japanese Americans were collected at UCLA between 1965 and 1968 as part of the Japanese American Research Project, which had been established to collect both historical and sociological data about the *Issei*, the immigrant generation. The project was soon expanded to include the second *(Nisei)* and third *(Sansei)* generations. The Japanese sample consisted of 1,047

Issei slated for interviews--out of a total of some 18,000 then still alive on the United States mainland. Then we also found some 2,300 of the *Issei's* 3,700 children who consented to be respondents. We went on to solicit mail questionnaires from all *Sansei* at least 18 years of age. Almost nine in ten responded, which gave us a total of over 800 respondents. Our instruments covered a variety of subjects (some early *Issei* interviews lasted over 10 hours), but we focused upon questions about jobs and job histories (including those of the *Issei's* parents in Japan) and upon acculturation. We used both attitudinal and behavioral measures of the phenomenon. Our Japanese American data set includes information from over 4,000 respondents. And, increasingly over the years since the project ended, secondary analysts have been plumbing the data along a number of avenues.

My data on Jews come from a sample survey sponsored by the University of Judaism's Institute for Contemporary Jewish Life in 1976-1978. The study was limited to metropolitan Los Angeles. The Jewish sample came from 424 respondents who were contacted by knocking on over 6,000 doors in putatively densely-Jewish, mixed, and sparsely-Jewish census tracts. The Jewish Identity Study, as it was called, had two aims: to search for correlates of identity and to assay the state of Jewish acculturation. To the latter end I decided to use some of the same questions in the Jewish interview schedule that were in the surveys of Japanese Americans. I wanted to use these studies in acculturation to standardize key items so that intergroup comparisons could be made, just as there have been like efforts in the systematization of questions about demographic characteristics. The original intention was not actually to make comparisons between Japanese and Jewish Americans, but I reasoned that what worked for one group might work for the other as well. Only later did the idea emerge to compare the two groups.

The Japanese American data lent themselves to the identification of five behavioral variables that were correlated with significant independent variables. These were: (1) friendships with Caucasians; (2) whether or not the main earner worked with Caucasians and informally associated with them off-the-job; (3) neighborly associations with Caucasians, including reciprocal home visits; (4) membership in formal organizations that had a mostly Caucasian membership; and (5) intermarriage, particularly between *Sansei* and Caucasians. (Only 10 percent of the *Nisei* had outmarried.)

There was one other variable of interest, but we failed to ask the critical question to correlate it to social relationships. We queried the respondents about their religious affiliations and asked Protestants about their denominations but neglected to ask about the ethnic composition of their churches. This nullified the use of the variable as a social-relational measure of acculturation.

Because the Japanese American study was nation-wide and the Jewish study was limited to Los Angeles, for the comparative study we chose from the Japanese generational samples *Nisei* and *Sansei* residing in 1967-1968 in Los Angeles--almost half of each group. On the Jewish side, we excluded immigrants, and looked only at the second, third, and an increasingly numerous fourth generation.

In analyzing the findings of the Japanese American Research Project, I discovered that many of the *attitudinal* variables relating to acculturation and assimilation failed to differentiate among the respondents by socioeconomic status. For example, persons of high socioeconomic status were no more likely than those of lesser accomplishments to adhere to either "American" values or to ancestral "Japanese" values. However, *behavioral* indicators of the same phenomenon, acculturation, yielded different results.

Taking the first four as an index, we found that higher socioeconomic status was correlated with high scores on behavioral acculturation both for the *Nisei* and the *Sansei*. Further, the *Issei's* accomplishments were very good predictors of the social position of their children and grandchildren. And socioeconomic status in the American-born generations was prefigured to an unanticipated degree by the attainments of the *Issei's* parents in Japan. In short, the degree to which a *Sansei* in the 1980s becomes economically and socially integrated into American society is associated with the educational and economic accomplishments of his great-grandparents a century earlier. This finding affirms the proposition that socioeconomic mobility can best be understood within families and over generations.

In terms of interethnic comparisons, what did the findings show? Each group had experienced considerable intergenerational mobility. The large number of proletarians and small farmers of the immigrant generations had all but disappeared in the second generation. Where the immigrants had a problem with English, the second generation used it as a matter of course. By the third generation the professionals and managers already evident in the second had become predominant over petty traders and shopkeepers.

Each group, by the second, and notably by the third, generation had made great strides in educational accomplishment. By the third generation it had become a common assumption that a *Sansei* or his or her Jewish equivalent would pursue higher education.

Despite these similarities, differences were also found between the two groups. Jews were more likely than *Nisei* or *Sansei* to undertake postgraduate studies, and proportionately more had finished college; Jews were engaged in a wider range of occupational pursuits, often at higher levels of responsibility; and the Jewish income level exceeded that of the Japanese. Jews, then, had attained a higher level of educational and economic achievement than the Japanese. Partly, this is due to the longer time Jews had been engaged in urban pursuits. The *Issei* had typically been small cultivators. (There are other factors contributing to the disparity in income which I shall not examine here.)

But if Los Angeles Jews had made more of a mark on the economy of the area, were they also more acculturated in terms of friendly relations with the dominant group? Put another way, was the one group more involved than the other in the informal networks that create social integration?

The answer is clear: Japanese are far more likely than Jews to be included in the social relations of society's dominant group. In terms of friendship patterns, two out of every three of our *Nisei* respondents count at least one Caucasian among their best friends. Only about four out of ten of the Jewish respondents number at least one non-Jew among their inner circle. Likewise, Japanese are more likely than Jews to work with white Gentiles and to associate with them after work. And Japanese are more likely than Jews to belong to outgroup formal associations with Caucasians. Finally, Japanese are much more likely to live in Caucasian neighborhoods than Jews are to live in Gentile neighborhoods. The *Nisei* are no longer ghettoized, as they moved to white suburbs in the 1950s and 1960s when they had recovered economically from the losses suffered during their internment in relocation camps in World War II. Prejudice against them has apparently dissipated; by 1968 two-thirds of non-Japanese Californians polled were not disturbed at the prospect of a child of theirs marrying a Japanese American.

In contrast, the Jews of Los Angeles, as their numbers grew after World War II, tended to congregate in certain quarters of the city; and this is still true, even though there has been some inevitable dispersion to the largely Gentile suburbs. Incidentally, Jews living in sparsely-Jewish neighborhoods are more likely than those in densely-Jewish neighborhoods to be affiliated with the formal Jewish community organizations--that is, to belong to a temple or a Jewish organization.

Intermarriage is common for both groups. Six in ten *Sansei* have married or are likely to marry Caucasians. This is a result of their residence during the school years in Caucasian neighborhoods, of the lack of a parental ban on such marriages, and of their attendance at colleges where they are typically a small minority. The rate of intermarriage for Los Angeles Jews is over 30 percent (higher in the fourth generation) despite the negative Jewish view on such unions. One would guess that Jews have to worry far less than Japanese on this score; in fact, they worry much more.

The Japanese American community has shrunk and will shrink in size as a consequence of interracial marriage. But this does not seem to have caused great alarm. Jews, in contrast, are greatly concerned about intermarriage and about the low fertility of Jewish couples. They view the issue in terms of survival versus assimilation and many solutions are advanced. There is no counterpart to such concerns among Japanese American survivalists. The continued life of a racially homogeneous Japanese American community does not appear to be a high priority for Japanese Americans. They are more oriented toward individual accomplishment. Jews certainly value that, too, but they also seem to place a high priority on their durability as a solidary ethno-religious group.

That Jews tend to be a solidary group, knitted together by networks of intensive social relationships, is displayed with other data which, unfortunately, do not allow for any comparison with Japanese Americans. Of the over 13,000 respondents interviewed in the General Social Surveys by the National Opinion Research Center, cumulatively from 1972-1982, there are 349 Jewish respondents. Jews are radically different from the majority of Americans in their opinions and attitudes on a variety of issues. For example, they are staunch supporters of certain sections of the Bill of Rights, much more so than white Gentiles, blacks, and Latinos. More than other groups, they favor the legalization of marijuana, the Equal Rights Amendment, a ban on handguns, abortion, and equal rights for homosexuals. It is not difficult to discern how Jews, purportedly assimilated, are able to maintain otherwise unpopular positions on issues of the age. They may not even be aware that they are different. The Jewish singularity is maintained and sustained within the confines of a still solidary community in which liberal norms are reinforced in their everyday associations. What relatively little data I have from the Japanese American Research Project show less consensus on social and political issues among Japanese Americans. Such a lack shows again the comparative weakness of communal bonds.

The history of each ethnic group is unique, its current preoccupations differ, politicization is varied, group membership is more or less valued. And importantly, group size and dispersion are structural variables of no small import. Perhaps to compare Jews and Japanese is like comparing apples with pears. There are fewer than 6,000,000 Jews in the U.S. and fewer than 700,000 Japanese Americans (excluding those in Hawaii). Nevertheless, the attempt to make exact intergroup comparisons is worthwhile and should be pursued. Acculturation differs between groups, and one group will advance along lines different from another. It is instructive to account for these different routes in a systematic way. Comparative survey research on ethnic groups, fraught with difficulty and open to criticism on many counts though it may be, presents important challenges to the scholarly community.

Immigrant Punjabis in
Early Twentieth-Century California

Karen Leonard

From the perspective of the anthropology of emotions, Indian immigrants from the Punjab region who came to the American West were men who experienced a redefinition of self in a new context. The anthropology of emotions is based on the notion that emotions are socially structured and that it is possible to find generally shared, stable interpretations of immediate experience among members of a group. For historians, the challenge is to trace the bearers of such a cultural consensus over time and under different conditions. The group I studied consists of some 2000 Punjabi men who left India early in the twentieth century to work and live in California. Several hundred of them married Hispanic women.[1] Not only did these men move from one society to another, adapting themselves to a new cultural context and changing their expectations of themselves and of others, but their political status in both India and California changed drastically in the 1940s, forcing them to confront for a second time emotion-laden personal and political choices. In this study, I shall show how one of these men changed his concept of himself and of society. I shall also show that the impact of state policies on individual and family experiences was substantial, suggesting that we need to investigate carefully the ways in which individual life cycles, family life cycles, and state policies interpenetrate.

The Punjabi immigrants defined themselves vis-à-vis the new context in which they found themselves in two central ways. First was their relationship to political authority: both in India and in the United States, they saw themselves as the disenfranchised subjects of non-Indian rulers who denied them political rights. Their experience as immigrants in the United States sharpened their sense of deprivation and produced the Ghadar party, an anti-British revolutionary movement which contributed strongly to the cohesiveness of the Punjabi immigrant community in California.[2]

Secondly, those who married Hispanic women consciously encountered new cultural meanings and learned different behaviors at a personal level within their marriages and homes. Such personal values and behaviors often focused on questions of ethnicity: for these men, the Punjabi component of their self-image played a major role in shaping the emotional life of the so-called Mexican-Hindu families they established.

The Punjabi men who came to California in the first two decades of this century undoubtedly shared a cultural consensus when they first arrived. Most of the men were between the ages of 16 and 35; most were from the three districts of Ludhiana, Jullunder, and Hoshiarpur; and most were Sikhs. (Some 10 percent were Muslims, and perhaps 1 percent were Hindus.) The primary economic relationships they established in the United States were, first, with each other in partnerships and work gangs, and second, with white American landowners and politicians who employed them and helped them stay in farming after laws were passed to prohibit them from owning land. At least half of these immigrants had been in the British Indian military or police service, often overseas; such prior experience prepared them well for economic relationships in the American West.

These early Punjabi immigrants encountered great cultural diversity in early twentieth-century California. White Americans dominated political life, but immigrants from many places worked in California agriculture. U.S. restrictions on Asian immigration prevented all but a handful of Punjabi women from joining their husbands, so Hispanic women, most of them also recent immigrants, very often became the wives of Punjabi men in the United States. The accompanying table shows where the men and their spouses setteled. Southern California, with over 200 couples of Punjabi men and Hispanic women, was the heartland of the so-called Mexican-Hindu community. I have been tracing family and individual life cycles for these men, women, and children, and one of the most fascinating aspects of the study is the variation in the meaning systems they created and experienced over time.

At least half of the Punjabi men had been married before leaving India, but many married again in the United States at least once. The first recorded marriage between a Punjabi man and a Hispanic woman occurred in 1916; most of the Mexican-Hindu children were born in the early 1920s and came of age in the early 1940s. Two immediately obvious problems in the majority of the bi-ethnic marriages were the different languages spoken by the men and women--Punjabi and Spanish--and the large difference in their ages at marriage. The Punjabi men were significantly older than the Hispanic women they married (the mean difference was 12 years, the median 14)[3] and this difference became increasingly important as the couples grew older. I have written elsewhere about some of the cultural accommodations and conflicts within these families; in this essay, I can only note that the children, through their names, language, and biological and ritual kinship (the *compadrazgo*) systems were strongly socialized into their mothers' Hispanic culture.[4]

The external pressures and constraints on the immigrants were many. The marriages to Hispanic women, in fact, owed much to these constraints: restrictions on Asian immigration into the United States, which made it impossible for the men who came and worked here to bring their families over or to travel easily to and from India; the anti-miscegenation laws which prevented them from marrying white or black women, or anyone whom the County Clerk perceived to be racially different from Punjabi men; and the 1913, 1920, and 1923 California Alien Land laws, which prevented "aliens ineligible to citizenship" from leasing or owning agricultural land and which may have encouraged these men to marry women eligible for citizenship.[5] After the Alien Land Law was applied to them in 1923, they devised various strategies to stay in farming.[6] To obtain political rights, they organized the Ghadar party in North America to fight for their freedom in India,[7] and they also lobbied for U.S. citizenship, contributing much time and money to these efforts. The outcome of such efforts had consequences for their self-concepts and feelings about their families.

To illustrate the men's responses to the environmental constraints and opportunities, I shall discuss one oldtimer's account of his life here, his feelings, and the meaning he gave to his experiences. (See the appendix.) A farmer in the Imperial Valley in his early years, Moola Singh now lives in Selma, just south of Fresno in California's Central Valley. He speaks Spanish like a native speaker,[8] but I took down his life story in English. (I have kept one segment of the text as I transcribed it to give an idea of his English).[9]

Moola Singh came to California in 1912 at the age of fifteen, after spending a year in Hong Kong and the Philippines *en route*. He was young when he emigrated; he knew the Punjabi context only briefly, but he was attentive to context (or "context and cases")[10] throughout the account he gave me. As he said at one point:

> Brothers-in-law in India might be different, I don't know,
> after marrying there I came here. I can remember India, but
> that I don't know. I never knew about brothers-in-law there. I
> left home, married here, and worked hard.[11]

I am focusing on Moola Singh's feelings of love and loneliness and feelings about institutions--religion, marriage, and divorce--which differ in Indian and American cultures. I hope to show that while emotions are indeed culturally defined to some extent--Moola Singh experienced tensions between what he understood by "love" and "religion" in the Punjab and in the United States--the stronger differences are found in the ways in which these emotions were related to societal institutions like marriage and divorce. And, to a surprising extent, emotions and their expression were conditioned by the constraints and opportunities set at the highest level of the political system, by the laws governing immigration, citizenship, and access to economic opportunities.

Let us start with love. Moola Singh is very clear that he learned its "meaning" here. Women had fallen in love with him before his arrival in California--his young Punjabi bride and a Filipino girl who wanted to follow him here. But he said he did not know what love really meant until his first affair with an older white woman in the Imperial Valley, which taught him that love could make one crazy. In 1919 he married Carmen, his first wife in the United States, for love. And it was shortly after this marriage that his wife in India died, with a love letter from him clutched to her breast, so, by this time he obviously loved her, too. He married Maria, his second wife in the United States, for 'mix 'em up,' or sex, rather than love, but it was a troubled relationship. When talking about his third wife, Susanna, he did not use the word love, but the feeling pervades his discussion and their relationship has been a lasting one.[12]

Moola Singh came to view love as a passion which renders marriage and divorce contracts irrelevant. He had married Maria (*La Tocharia*, he always called her) but when she began to love someone else, he felt powerless to prevent her from leaving. He simply kicked her out, without bothering to divorce her, although he had previously divorced Carmen, whose departure had caused him far more regret and anger. When he met Susanna, his third partner in the United States and mother of eight of his fourteen children, in 1937, he did not bother with marriage.[13] He firmly believed by this time that love was the necessary and sufficient condition for a relationship and both he and Susanna (twice widowed) were content to simply live and work together. When they finally married much later, it was for legal reasons. (They had a civil marriage in 1962 and a Catholic one in 1975.)

In his personal life, he became committed to the idea of love based on sexual attraction between men and women as the best basis for a relationship. He shows little or none of the negative or ambivalent Indian attitude towards female sexuality; he makes no attempt to control or punish it.[14] Rather, he seems to have accepted it as a positive catalyst to love, which he endorses in a typically American romantic fashion. And as he talks about Susanna, his words evoke that phrase "diffuse, enduring, solidarity" used by Schneider.[15]

Furthermore, marriage to Moola Singh seems to have become a legal contract, a government affair, something outside the sphere of his personal life and of interest only for record-keeping.[16] This attitude differs greatly from Indian ideas about marriage. I cannot make detailed contrasts between his attitudes and traditional Punjabi meanings and behaviors here, but as he observes, parentally-arranged marriages do not take individual feelings into account, and marriages in India are almost never civil ceremonies recorded by the government but are religious events recorded by genealogists for families and castes. (Moola Singh and several other Punjabi Sikhs went through Catholic ceremonies late in life to please their partners. These ceremonies were personally meaningful to the Hispanic women, but their Punjabi husbands did not request similar ceremonies performed according to their own religious traditions.)

Another feeling which runs through his account and connects the people important to him is that of loneliness. At first he defines this in terms of other Punjabis, his father and "cousin-brothers," who went back to India or died and left him feeling lonely. He talks about his brother and how he had brought him from Manila, and then of his mother and how he had brought her from India. Then he speaks of Susanna, his wife, who felt lonely when his brother threatened to take him away, and he fully recognizes her feeling and the claims she and their Mexican-Hindu family had on him. In his decision to stand by his Mexican-Hindu wife and family, Moola Singh represents one set of Punjabi immigrants; others found it easy to turn away from their American families in the 1950s when marriage to Indian women became possible again.

Religion provided another source of emotions. The Punjabis in California had built a *gurdwara*, which they called a temple, in Stockton when they first came; it was the only Sikh temple in California from 1911 to 1946. It served political and social as well as religious purposes, with Sikhs, Muslims, Hindus, and their Mexican-Hindu families attending it for various reasons until the 1950s. While the men encouraged their wives to keep their own religious beliefs and practices and they at times served as godfathers in the Catholic *compadrazgo* system, they nontheless continued to practice their own religions.

The Sikhs did modify some of their religious practices in the United States. Most of the men took off their turbans, shaved off their beards, and cut their hair. They also reformed certain religious practices at the Stockton temple.[17] Moola Singh alludes to most of these in his comments: seating on chairs, *prasad* on a plate eaten with a spoon, napkins, men and women seated together.

When Moola Singh encountered the new (post-1965) Sikh immigrants at the Stockton temple, the behavioral changes they instigated aroused strong emotions in him. To him, the return to traditional religious practices, including seating on the floor and maintaining the inferior status of women, signifies the inferiority of Indian culture which has failed to change with the times. He has separated religious beliefs from practices, a separation not typical of the Hindu or Sikh traditions in India, which are often said to emphasize orthopraxy far more than orthodoxy.[18] He believes that the Sikh practices being reinstated by these newcomers from India are meaningless, and he uses the concepts, "clean" and "dirty," to differentiate between those like himself who truly understand Sikhism and those who are ignorant of its real meaning.[19]

Moola Singh's confrontation with the new immigrants reminds us that the American environment in which the Punjabi men had lived had changed dramatically in the 1940s. The passage of the Luce-Cellar bill in 1946 made them eligible for U.S. citizenship through naturalization, and therefore they could finally lease and own agricultural land in their own names. The 1946 Act also allowed a small quota of immigrants from India to enter. The achievement of independence in India and Pakistan in 1947 made the early immigrants tremendously proud, and many resumed connections with relatives, went for visits, or planned to retire in South Asia. The trickle of new immigrants became a flood when U.S. immigration laws changed again in the mid-1960s, and the surviving pioneers were overwhelmed by the large number of new Punjabi immigrants entering rural California, particularly the Yuba City/Marysville area.[20]

These developments produced strong emotions in many of the Punjabi pioneers. Although the creation of Pakistan came as a surprise to many California Punjabis, great enthusiasm for the two new nations resulted in divisions between Sikhs and Muslims in the United States. In earlier decades these men all had accepted the American misnomer "Hindu," but to many it now became unacceptable. The Muslims devised a new name, "Spanish-Pakistanis," to distinguish themselves sharply from the "old Hindus" (mostly Sikhs) and the Mexican-Hindus, and they established a mosque in Sacramento.[21] The Sikh temple in Stockton began to bring over more specialized priests, while other Sikh temples were built around the state.

The emotions released by these momentous events were less predictable in the arena of family life. Some of the men enthusiastically took their Hispanic wives to visit their native villages in India or Pakistan, and a few Mexican-Hindu children went as well. Other men sponsored nephews (or sons and grandsons) to immigrate to the United States, sometimes at the expense of further investment in their Mexican-Hindu children. The long-awaited legal right to own land in their own names coincided with the sudden availability of relatives from India to serve as partners or heirs; all too often, these new options coincided with growing tensions within the Mexican-Hindu families.

The families were large (a subset of mothers for whom fertility records could be assembled had 6.4 children each)[22] and the children's socialization into their mothers' Hispanic culture and the dominant Anglo society was thorough. As the men aged, disagreements between husbands and wives increased; the age difference between them also became important. Some of the men divorced or left their Hispanic wives and brought over their Indian wives or journeyed to the Punjab to bring back Punjabi brides. Daughters and sons began dating, usually with the mother's but not the father's approval. Frustrated fathers tried to arrange marriages for their children or (belatedly) educate them about what the proper caste and regional origins of their spouses should be.

Not surprisingly, conflicts over property and inheritance proved most explosive within these families. It is hard to separate material interest from emotion when analyzing these families' experiences,[23] and hard to see whether "material flow systems" shaped "cultural meaning systems" or the other way around.[24] Father-son relationships became particularly difficult. To avoid the restrictions imposed by the Alien Land laws, most Punjabi farmers had put land in the names of their minor children, who were United States citizens, while they managed it as the latter's guardians. The Mexican-Hindu sons farmed alongside their fathers, and upon reaching adulthood, tried to take more active roles in running the farms. Typically, they were denied such roles by the Punjabi men who had just received title to their own land and would not give up any control. With stalwart young Punjabi nephews available as alternatives to sons named Armando Singh, Jose Akbar Khan, or Rudolfo Chand--sons who spoke Spanish, played in mariachi bands, and dated and married whomever they pleased--some men turned away from their American-born families. One fellow sold all his land and retired to Pakistan, leaving his son and grandchildren with nothing. Another tried to become executor of a former partner's estate in order to prevent its going to the latter's Hispanic widow and children. A third old man brought over not his son but his grandson; when he died, however, his son came and tried to take the estate away from the boy and the Hispanic widow. Someone else brought over a nephew to inherit his property; later that boy's brothers in India sued the widow for their shares. And active intervention by Punjabi men in the United States often helped U.S. Courts to contact men's first wives in India and award estates to them rather than to wives they married in California.[25]

Moola Singh stands in contrast to those who assuaged their loneliness in their old age by returning to their Punjabi culture and relatives. As his own account makes clear, he had learned to give different meanings to many feelings and their relationship to social and religious institutions. By the time I inerviewed him, he clearly no longer shared the Punjabi cultural consensus. Perhaps some of the changes occurred, as Levine might suggest, because Moola Singh came of age in a different house.[26] But he was not alone in diverging from the culture of his childhood. Such divergence expressed itself particularly in the men's attitudes towards, and relationship to, women. Many other men reportedly wrote home urging relatives to abandon the arranged marriage system. Donations for the construction of girls' schools back in Punjabi villages were probably second only to donations to the Ghadar party. Finally, there were many other Punjabi-Hispanic couples whose relationships were long-lasting--relationships that embody successful and creative adaptation to the conditions these pioneers encountered in California.

Moola Singh: Excerpts from His Life Story

Love: his first wife in India and first relationship in the United States

(Moola speaking) I was the oldest child, with a younger brother and two sisters. In 1908, my father left for Manila in the Philippines and he did business there in Manila. He had me married in 1910 or 1911. In India you don't get to stay together when you marry, because you're too young; but he married me off. We spent two or three months together, and she came to my family home. Then I went to Manila and left her with my relatives.

"You're leaving me here?" she asked.

"Yes," I said, "my mother is here."

"What do I need a mother for? You started love; I need you."

"I'll come back in six years," I said.

"I'll give you three years," she said.

I left in 1911 and she died in 1920. She lived with my mother and my sister and her husband.

My wife in India, she nearly had a baby. Women, they say, if they eat too much hot food, they throw the baby, you know. Anyway, I had some stuff over there in my store and they told me to bring it: coconut, meva, raisin, and a pan of hot water. I don't know much about this, the baby came out, only five months or something. Then next year I came here. I wish she'd had that baby. I didn't know then about love. I didn't know what that meant.

She said, "love"; I said, "mother"; she said, "I don't want mother, I want you." We married too young.

Then I came here, to this country, and a white girl made me crazy with love, see. She was on one side with her lawyer, my father was on the other side with our lawyer. We 'mix em up'. So they tried to make a case against me, they tried to shoot, to hurt me; anyway they didn't do anything.

In El Centro, they didn't like a Hindu man to have anything to do with a white woman. Even a Mexican woman, they didn't want us to like them, see, because of jealousy.

* * * * *

1917, live four miles east of El Centro, in house, with my father, another Singh, Bhan Singh, Lalu, always stay together. Nobody married, that time that woman, housekeeper, stay there, the one that get me shot, 1917. She had kids, three kids, two girls, one boy, I fathered the boy, that's why make me suffer, I father the boy. Then she divorce her husband, same year, white woman, want to live, start love. I don't want to marry, my father said no marry, I seventeen year old, she twenty-nine. She told me, mix em up you know, love no can stop, love's crazy, you know. So anyway I pay the divorce, I pay her living expense, when living nearby, one town like small town, I come over there to see her from El Centro. My father, he no want . . . he say "go ahead, good time but no plans marry." He said, "lots of women in India, you got a wife there."

My wife not dead yet, only three-four year after I come here, ten year after I come here, she die. She worry. Maybe she love, you know, she love, she don't like nobody, and she worry and worry and maybe then she die. She good, nice looking, healthy, but she love. You know love, person no eat, worry, then maybe die. Mother wrote one time letter, "she sick, you gotta come." Then I write her letter from Arizona, to her I say, "I'm coming, don't worry, I be here." Another letter she's sending me, she die. One letter, on chest, love letter, she die. Good one, very good one, nice letter, very good letter. She come from Matwandi Padhori, village Matwandi Padhori, my village Wada Johl Singh. She live close by Nakodar, Nakodar city.

I see two year ago a Padhori man here, worked here. I say, "come see, Padhori man, my wife's village"; another time he come back to me. He know my wife's family, but they don't know me.

I go once, twice; my mother-in-law told me, "you come here," and I wanted to come. "I have money to give to you, to put a store business." And she living with her sister, you know, had daughter, she got nobody, only mother, daughter. One time I send money to my mother-in-law, young then . . . . yeah, feel bad. That's the trouble, couldn't bring her, this country that time give the passport to go, no come back, no come back. After that pass law, she cannot bring my wife here, I no can do. When they no let come back, that's too bad, you know, tough.

I dream, but she no come close. At first wedding, I was fifteen, she same age, but she smarter than me. She smart woman, good woman. That way she suffer, no touch no man, feeling, think, worry. Lot of time some time I dream, she come close to me, she's with me, you know. No, she don't want come close, she go round, round, no come close in my dream . . . that's a life gone.

* * * * *

In this country, it's a different class of people. You can't force love here, women go where they want to, even if they're married, even with three or four kids. In India, you could only get a divorce after India got freedom. Here, women go away, here it's different. The woman is the boss in this country. A woman can have four husbands, a man can have two or three women. What you gonna do, that's the way with love.

I married Carmen in 1919 in Phoenix, Arizona. My father told me, "Why do you want to marry here, there are plenty of good people in India--let her go." Sometimes I feel like I'm suffering here, you know, trouble at home. Here, when you marry, you have woman trouble, kid trouble, not like in India. When I got here, I saw you have liberty, women have liberty, you know. The way it is here, I've been separated, divorced. In India, you stay together all your life. In this country, you have love. When you love a person, you stay with her, with her kids and everything.

In India, lots of time in India, I feel, the woman is a slave. I say no, that's no good. You should have a duty to them, women have rights, even more than men. When you want to make a marriage in India, you never see the boy; the boy and girl never meet each other. That's no good. Maybe the boy's all right, maybe the boy's no good. Maybe he's blind, maybe he has an arm broken, maybe a leg broken. You never know, you see, the mother and the father ask for him. Today I feel that it's more important to love. First you love, then you should marry. It happens too young over there. The relatives do it all, and they can make a mistake. No I don't like that way. I like it when a woman and a man get together, fall in love, and marry.

Divorce: his first and second marriages in the United States

1924 [the year after the Alien Land Law first affected Indians] was when I leased to Alfredo Barrentos [his wife's brother], in 1925 the crop came, and then he went to Mexico, Mexicali. Carmen, she didn't want to go away, you know, she wanted to live with me. But I couldn't keep her, her mother and father made trouble. They took her away. They had only one daughter, you know. I could speak Spanish, I talked to them, but no use. So they went to Mexico, they all went to Mexicali: Carmen, my father-in-law, my brother-in-law. Then Carmen came back, but she had a baby by another man. They all came back, but I wouldn't take her back. She left me in 1928.

I divorced Carmen, when she went away to Mexico. I couldn't do anything, so I filed for divorce. She had two more kids by then. My wife in India, she'd died already by that time. Yes, I knew about divorce. In this country, I no sleep. Everybody was divorced, I could see what they were doing. It's only normal, you see the customs of the country, and so you have to do that. Bhagat Singh divorced too. In 1925, Carmen went away.

* * * * *

I married Maria, La Tocharia, in 1932. She, Maria, lived a quarter mile from my ranch. She came and borrowed things from me all the time, so we began loving. She came and lived on my ranch, she worked there. I didn't like to marry her, but I did marry her finally. In 1930 a boy was born to us, but still I didn't marry her; I only married her in 1932 or so. Then I went to El Paso, Texas, and I brought my mother-in-law and my sister-in-law, and Mota Singh married her, Julia Consuelo. Then another girl came, another sister, Hortencia, with one girl already, and she married Natha Singh.

* * * * *

Then, in 1934 or 1936, this Maria went away. She went to a man who worked for me, Galindo. We were having a big party, with my cousin Lalu, the single one, my cousin-brother who farmed with me, and Buta Singh and his wife, and Mota Singh and Julia, and my father. It was a big party, we all drank. And that Mexican boy . . . I wanted someone to make food, so I called Maria to get him to come in the kitchen to make food. She said, "Yes, he'll come, if I call him." And he did come, he made *roti* and other things. We ate, and we Hindu men all watched the lovers. We saw how they looked at each other. We all knew.

Mota said, "You know what she's doing, I won't let mine do that."
I asked her, "Do you love him more?"
She said, "Yes, I love him more; you're worth the sole of a shoe."
So I hit her, and I kicked them both out. They went to Mexico.

* * * * *

She said, "Okay, this is my friend, I'm going with him."
I couldn't say, "No you can't go."
In this country, when she wants to go, my wife, she says, "All right, sonny honey, I'm going," and I say, "I can't stop you." It's because of love, therefore I couldn't stop her.

* * * * *

I talked to Judge Griffin in Brawley.
I told him my kids said, "Daddy, we're hungry, we haven't eaten." So I hit her, hit Tocharia.
"What are you going out for, the kids haven't eaten, why are you going?" One day I hit her. Then she cried, she cried. These Mexicans, they go play cards, don't feed the kids, don't clean the house, don't do anything. So I hit her.
She went to an attorney, and they sent a paper to Brawley. She went to see Judge Griffin. I went to the court.

I said, "Judge Griffin, did my wife come here today?"

"Yeah, Moola, she came. What did you do, you hit her hard." He told me, "Moola, it's okay to hit her a little, but don't make bruises."

"Okay, Judge. She doesn't take care of anything--what can I do?"

He said, "Moola, a woman needs to keep busy, do something, go pick eggs or pull the garden, something to keep her mind happy. Mrs. Griffin, she's a bookkeeper now, I go to the Court and so does she."

But Tocharia wouldn't do that. She wouldn't pick eggs, she wouldn't work outside around the house, nothing. All the time she went out. What could I do?

Judge Griffin said to come back with her again. And she struck me, so we went back to him.

She said, "Here we are, Daddy Griffin."

He said, "You want to go home or stay here?"

She said, "I'll go back home."

I said, "You want to stay, you stay. You want something to eat?"

She said, "Yes, I want something to eat, I'm hungry," so we went to eat.

Then we had the same trouble, in Calipatria. She didn't take care of the kids.

Judge Griffin told her, "You're a bad woman, you don't take care of the kids. Moola's a good man, he doesn't drink in bars."

Judge Griffin told her to go away and stop bothering me. She took the furniture, there was more trouble. That woman was the most trouble for me. The mother-in-law was there too, she tried to advise me, but I wouldn't fight for her, she was a no count woman. My father had gone to Manila, he was ashamed of her; he went to my brother there. He wrote me a letter advising me to quit that woman.

My second wife here, Tocharia, I divorced only in 1950. I bought a piece of land here in 1948-49, and Tocharia came. Women, you know how they are, she followed me, she wanted to come back to me. I divorced her late, divorced Carmen first, then divorced Tocharia in 1950, I think.

Susanna: his third U.S. marriage

When I met Susanna, she did sewing, she's a good farmer girl. She cut all the kids' hair, she made all their clothes. She was brought up in Holtville, her father worked in the Irrigation Company. We got married years later, in Reno, Nevada. She didn't want to marry me, at first; I went out to buy things for her, she wouldn't buy for herself. We got married later.

* * * * *

I found Susanna in 1937, and then everything got good. Susanna, she didn't want to buy anything, she only wanted to buy groceries. She chopped cotton, she worked, she didn't even want to buy a dress. I went to the store, I bought her a dress. She didn't want to go to the store, I had to buy it. She did go shopping for something, a sewing machine. She was no dummy, she was very smart, that woman. She sewed. For all of our girls, she never bought a dress. She sewed, she worked hard, she didn't want money. She never cared about money, she didn't spend it.

* * * * *

After a long time, I married Susanna. I didn't want to marry, I'd have to pay for the divorce, I didn't want to pay for the divorce again. Two women, I'd already had to pay for divorces. But the Social Security man told me to marry.

"You better marry, make :t legal," he said, so we married.

And for the citizenship paper too, I didn't want trouble. And our kids were not legal until we married, so I had to marry.

* * * * *

I've been with Susanna since 1937 but we never married. I wanted to keep free for other ladies, see, wanted to be able to throw away another woman, too (Susanna laughing in background) . . . Yeah, sure . . . no, you're a good woman. ("Working too hard," said Susanna.)

Loneliness

I brought my mother here in 1962, and she died here in 1973 at age 115. See the newspaper clipping over my fireplace. My brother had come here too, to be the priest at Stockton, in 1957. After my father died back there, who was to look after my mother? I brought her here, to look after her.

I was never lonesome here in the U.S., my father was here, my cousins were here, my cousin-brothers all were here. How could I be lonesome, everybody was here, we had plenty of good times here. Only when my father went away, my cousins went away, or they died here, three of them died here, then I got lonesome. Then I felt lonesome.

I said, "I have only one brother, in Manila, and I don't know if I can see him or not."

So mother [Susanna] said, "Don't worry, somebody gonna come."

Then I got Hindi records and she played them for me, she likes them too. Then I thought, my brother is in Manila, how can he come?

"Someone will come," she said.

He came. He said, "What do you do here?"

I said, "I farm, that's all."

"Don't do that, come to Manila, do merchandising over there," he said.

Then he told my wife, "I'm gonna take Moola some other place, I'm gonna take Moola to Manila," and he told me, "Sell this place, come to Manila."

She cried, she felt lonesome, my wife. She said, "You gonna leave me?"

I said, "Who told you I'm gonna leave you? You think I'm gonna leave my kids? No, I won't leave you, leave my kids."

She said, "No, don't go."

I'm not that kind of man, to leave my family here and go.

* * * * *

There's my mother's photo. She liked it here. I like my mother, see, I applied for her to come here. She was lonely. My brother went from Manila to stay with her, you know, and when he came here, with his family, I called my mama here. There weren't many other women from India here when she came, not then. She got sick here. . . . I became a citizen in 1962, and I brought my mother the same year. Didn't have to be a citizen but wanted to be legal. For my kids too, I married in 1962.

Religion and the new immigrants

(Susanna speaking) We brought up our children as Catholics, yes. There was no trouble, we married in the church, right here in Fowler. We picked a time, we thought about it. And then we married by Court too. In a Catholic church, I forget the name, in Fowler about seven years ago. We married because I wanted to get married in the Church. I said to my husband, "I don't want to live like that, I want to get married in the Church." He said, "Okay, if you like it." When I used to drive, I never refused, when he wanted to go to his church. I said, "Listen, I'm gonna call for the girls to take care of my kids," and I'd take him. I tried three days to fix it up, every place he wanted to go. He'd say, "I want to go to Stockton." I'd say, "Okay let's go early, stop where we need to." For lunch, I took a lot of food along. We had no problem about religion. Well, I'm a Catholic, you know, but I listen. Lots of people come over here, and they talk to me about religion. They know I'm a Catholic, but they never refused to come and talk to me. . . .Well, God gives a lot of different languages, you know, but I don't think so many Gods. (Moola speaking) Only one God.

* * * * *

(Moola speaking)   About our churches here, everybody went to the Stockton one, at least if they lived close by there, you know. Hindu, Muslim, everybody went. Afterwards, these days now, I don't know what they're doing. Chenchel Rai, I know him, he doesn't like that new group. I don't like people like that, I don't believe anything like that. The church started one way, it was for everybody, you just came and went to church. It belonged to everybody, the public, anybody could go. One thing I don't like, not for that new group, not everybody can go.

Before, the Hindu men married women here. You know, everybody married white women, everybody married Mexican women, everybody went to church. And our people, everybody went and sat on chairs. That was before, not now. Then, everybody could sit on a chair. And for food, they gave it on a plate, with a spoon, and paper to clean your hands. But after that, some Indian farmers and preachers have come. They want all the customs like India, and they've taken away the chairs, put people back on the floor again.

I went with my wife one time to Stockton, where they have lots of chairs in back. Me and my wife, we got a couple of chairs, we sat in the back.

"All right, man, sit on the floor, all right man, sit on the floor," someone said to me.

I don't care, people like that, people from India, why not have a church like other churches in this country? These India people are damn fools. Why have a church like before, why sit on the floor, why have no chairs, why have nothing? Today, it's different, twenty or fifty years have passed and today it's different.

"All kinds of people come here," I said to them. "I don't like the way you people do it. One woman over there, she's having a baby, you know, how's she gonna sit on the floor? How's she gonna get up with her stomach like that?"

They said to me, "That's the custom in India, people from India like customs like that."

Then they always want money. I got Bible (Granth Sahib), see, I believe that, but I say no, I won't go to the church if it's like that. This man came here, came by my home for money one day.

I said, "That's all right, if you want to make a church, put the chairs back. Everybody should sit on a chair, the women and kids and everybody, they can be on chairs. A woman sits on the floor, doesn't it shame you? Kids sit on the floor, doesn't it shame you people? Huh? You people are dirty," I said, "Don't you change your mind? Today, yesterday, don't you see the world, people, all changing; everything, everyday, it all changes. In this country, women and kids, they change their whole ways, you know. And you people hate women like that, they should sit on the dirty floor? You have no shame, you people? You're dirty, you people."

I gave money to the church, but I don't like it now. I told one man here, "Shave 'em up, shave 'em good. Let the hair, the beard go. What do they mean? Nothing. If you're dirty inside, having hair or beard won't help you. Shaving them off won't hurt you. You people don't understand anything."

The Hindustanis, these people come; they get a little bit of money, but money doesn't mean anything. Money doesn't make you good, it doesn't make you clean inside.

Relationship to the state

Only a few people, Hindustani, were here and they had no right to anything then. See, these countrymen, 1000, maybe 2000 Hindus here, they should have had rights together. Rights to live, hold a job, work. Most of our people lived by labor, you know. We were just farmers, common labor people. Some people, educated ones, they used to live in other places, they knew about the national movement, our country. They came here, made a corporation, made it with white men [to front for Punjabi farmers after the Alien Land Law went into effect].

The white men said, "I'll keep the records, let the Hindu people work and suffer." Who got the pistol, he got the law. Who got the power, he got the law. No power, no law.

* * * * *

There are records about the 1933 case [when an Imperial County Grand Jury indicted Moola, his father, and two other Punjabis along with five Anglos for conspiracy to evade the Alien Land Law by forming a corporation], they're in the big book, they kept them. They kept records in India too, and when India got free the records showed what they did. The Government always keeps records, when the time comes, they'll need them. Even Guru Gobind Singh kept records, he knew that someday they'd be needed. Always the Government keeps records.

Notes

1.   A larger number than that worked here for short periods of time. According to the 1930 Census, 1,873 men from India resided in California, while 1,476 did so in 1940.

2.   Sylvia Vatuk and Ved P. Vatuk, "Protest Songs of East Indians on the West Coast, U.S.A," *Thieves in My House: Four Studies in Indian Folklore of Protest and Change*, ed. Ved Vatuk (Varanasi: Vishwavidyalaya Prakashan, 1968), 63-80.

3.   These figures come from computer analysis of 111 first-generation couples for whom I found marriage licenses in County Clerk's offices in California.

4.   Only those sons (or Mexican stepsons) who worked in the fields with "Hindu" crews learned some Punjabi; Karen Leonard and B. LaBrack, "Conflict and Compatibility in Punjabi-Mexican Immigrant Families in Rural California: 1915-1965," *Journal of Marriage and the Family* 46 (1984): 527-37.

5.   H. S. Jacoby, "More Thind Against than Sinning," *The Pacific Historian* 11 (1958): 1-2, 8, succinctly summarizes the discriminatory legislation; while I have argued that most of the marriages were not motivated by a desire to put land in the wife's name, there is no doubt that a few marriages were so motivated (Karen Leonard, "Marriage and Family Life Among Early Asian Indian Immigrants," *Population Review* 25 (1982): 67-75).

6.   Karen Leonard, "Punjabi Farmers and California's Alien Land Law," *Agricultural History* 59 (1985).

7.   On the Ghadar party, see Harish K. Puri, *Ghadar Movement: Ideology, Organization, and Strategy* (Amritsar, India: Guru Nanak Dev University Press, 1983); Mark Juergensmeyer, "The Ghadar Syndrome: Immigrant Sikhs and Nationalist Pride," *Sikh Studies: Comparative Perspectives on a Changing Tradition*, ed. Mark Juergensmeyer and N. Gerald Barrier (Berkeley: Graduate Theological Union, 1979), 173-90; and Vatuk, "Protest Songs."

8.   Interview, Yolanda Singh, 1982.

9.   I tape recorded him for three days for about eleven hours, with his fourth wife Susanna Mesa Rodriguez Smith (and others at times) present.

10.   Richard A. Shweder and Edmund J. Bourne, "Does the Concept of the Person Vary Cross-culturally?" *Culture Theory*, ed. R. A. Shweder and R. A. Levine (New York: Cambridge University Press, 1984), 158-59.

11.   His antipathy to his Hispanic brothers-in-law in the U.S. is context-specific; he does not "know" that Punjabi brothers-in-law are not supposed to get along well because he has not experienced it. Another example of the skill with which he sketches context is shown by one word, the sarcastic "Daddy" used by Maria to address Judge Griffin. This captures exactly the relationship between Moola and the Judge--Griffin held land for him and posted bail for him in 1933--and between Moola and Maria as well.

12.   Material interests clearly played a major role in the three relationships as well. Carmen's family tried to seize his land. Maria did not even do the housework, much less help him farm (and in a segment not included here, he talked about how she got him to stop farming and set her up as proprietor of a town restaurant). Susanna, in contrast, has done field work with him from the beginning.

13.   This was not because he realized it was illegal to marry without first divorcing, or so I surmise from the inattention most of the immigrants paid to such details.

14.   Sylvia Vatuk, "South Asian Cultural Conceptions of Sexuality," *In her Prime: A New View of Middle-aged Women,* ed. Judith K. Brown (Mass: Bergin & Garvey, Inc., 1985), 136-52; Paul Hershman, "Virgin and Mother," *Symbols and Sentiments*, ed. I. M. Lewis (London and New York: Academic Press 1977), 261-291; Sudhir Kakar, *The Inner World* (Delhi: Oxford University Press, 1978).

15.   David Schneider, *American Kinship: A Cultural Account* (Englewood Cliffs, N.J.: Prentice-Hall, 1968).

16.   Material interest could explain this too, since the fact of marriage opened one up to divorce under community property provisions, with possibly unfavorable alimony and custody awards. But for such reasons Moola Singh should have divorced Maria much earlier.

17.   Bruce LaBrack, "The Sikhs of Northern California: A Socio-Historical

Study" Ph.D. diss., Syracuse University, 1980.

18.   J. A. B Van Buitenen, "On the Archaism of the Bhagavata Purana," *Krishna: Myths, Rites, and Attitudes,* ed. Milton Singer (Chicago: University of Chicago Press, 1966), 23-40.

19.   One could stress the closeness to Kabir's poems and Sufism here.

20.   Bruce LaBrack, "Immigration Law and the Revitalization Processes: the Case of the California Sikhs," *Population Review* 25 (1982): 59-66.

21.   Salim Khan told me that the reasons some early Muslim immigrants put Afghanistan as their birthplace in county documents was to distinguish themselves from the "Hindus." Khan's thesis is the best available source for the Punjabi Muslims.

22.   These were 66 women for whom I could compute "maternal fertility"; 24 of them brought children into their relationships with Punjabis.

23.   Hans Medick and David Warren Sabean, "Interest and Emotion in Family Kinship Studies: A Critique of Social History and Anthropology," *Interest and Emotion,* ed. Hans Medick and David Warren Sabean (New York: Cambridge University Press, 1984), 11; Alain Collomp, "Tensions, Dissensions, and Ruptures Inside the Family in Seventeenth and Eighteenth Century Haute Provence," *Interest and Emotion,* 146.

24.   Roy G. D'Andrade, "Cultural Meaning Systems," *Culture Theory,* ed. R. A. Shweder and R. A. Levine (New York: Cambridge University Press, 1984), 111-12.

25.   Obviously the reassertion of claims from the Punjabi families is responsible for some of these developments. Sources for this paragraph are primarily probate cases from Imperial County and interviews with Joe Mallobox, Anna Singh Sandhu, Mary Garewal Gill, Alfred Sidhu, and William Ewing (the last a lawyer for many Punjabis in El Centro).

26.   Robert A. Levine, "Properties of Culture: an Ethnographic View," *Culture Theory,* 86.

References

Collomp, Alain. "Tensions, Dissensions, and Ruptures Inside the Family in Seventeenth and Eighteenth Century Haute Provence." *Interest and Emotion.* Edited by Hans Medick and David Warren Sabean. New York: Cambridge University Press, 1984.

D'Andrade, Roy G. "Cultural Meaning Systems." *Culture Theory.* Edited by R. A. Shweder and R. A. Levine. New York: Cambridge University Press, 1984.

Hershman, P. "Virgin and Mother." *Symbols and Sentiments.* Edited by I. Lewis. London: Academic Press.

Imperial County, 1910 Probate Records, Civil Cases. Office of the County Clerk, 60 El Centro.

Jacoby, H. S. "More Thind against than Sinning." *The Pacific Historian* 11 (1958).

Kakar, Sudhir. *The Inner World.* Delhi: Oxford University Press, 1978.

Khan, Salim. "A Brief History of Pakistanis in the Western United States." Masters Thesis, Sacramento State University, 1981.

LaBrack, Bruce. "The Sikhs of Northern California: A Socio-Historical Study." Ph.D. dissertation, Syracuse University, 1980.

-----. "Immigration Law and the Revitalization Processes: The Case of the California Sikhs." *Population Review* 25 (1982).

Leonard, Karen. "Marriage and Family Life among Early Asian Indian Immigrants." *Population Review* 25 (1982).

Leonard, Karen, and LaBrack, B. "Conflict and Compatibility in Punjabi-Mexican Immigrant Families in Rural California: 1915-1965." *Journal of Marriage and the Family* 46 (1984).

Leonard, Karen. "Punjabi Farmers and California's Alien Land Law." *Agricultural History* 59 (1985).

Levine, Robert A. "Properties of Culture: An Ethnographic View." *Culture Theory*. Edited by R. A. Shweder and R. A. Levine. New York: Cambridge University Press, 1984.

Medick, Hans, and Sabean, David Warren. "Interest and Emotion in Family Kinship Studies: A Critique of Social History and Anthropology." *Interest and Emotion*. Edited by Hans Medick and David Warren Sabean. New York: Cambridge University Press, 1984.

Schneider, David. *American Kinship: A Cultural Account*. Englewood Cliffs, N.J.: Prentice-Hall, 1968.

Shweder, Richard A. and Bourne, Edmund J. "Does the Concept of the Person Vary Cross-culturally?" *Culture Theory*. Edited by R. A. Shweder and R. A. Levine. New York: Cambridge University Press, 1984.

Van Buitenen, J. A. B. "On the Archaism of the Bhagavata Purana." *Krishna: Myths, Rites, and Attitudes*. Edited by Milton Singer. Chicago: University of Chicago Press, 1966.

Vatuk, Sylvia. "South Asian Cultural Conceptions of Sexuality." *In Her Prime: A New View of Middle-aged Women*. Edited by Judith K. Brown and Virginia Kerns. Mass: Bergin & Garvey, Inc., 1985.

Vatuk, Sylvia and Ved P. "Protest Songs of East Indians on the West Coast, U.S.A." *Thieves in My House: Four Studies in Indian Folklore of Protest and Change*. Edited by Ved Vatuk, pp. 63-80. Varanasi: Vishwavidyalaya Prakashan, 1969.

Wolf, Arthur P. "Family Life and the Life Cycle in Rural China." *Households*. Edited by Robert McC. Netting, Richard R. Wilk, and Eric J. Arnold. Berkeley and Los Angeles: University of California Press, 1984.

Interviews

Ewing, William, 1981, lawyer in El Centro, Imperial County, California.

Mallobox, Joe, 1982, farmer in El Centro, Imperial County, California.

Resendez, Caroline Shine, 1981, businesswoman in Huntington Beach, Orange County, California.

Sandhu, Anna Singh, 1982, farmer in Calipatria, Imperial County, California.

Sidhu, Alfred, 1982, businessman in Sacramento, Sacramento County, California.

Singh, Moola and Susanna, 1982, 1983, farmers in Selma, Fresno County, California.

Singh, Yolanda, 1983, teacher in Santa Ana, Orange County, California.

The Role of Women in the Conservation of Culture: Gender Constraints in Tongan and Northern Ute Dance Forms[1]

Stephanie Reynolds

The early contacts between Tongans and Northern Utes and the West were cataclysmic, and both peoples are currently subject to Western cultural hegemony. The contribution of women to the persistence of traditional values in these two cultures is examined here within the context of women's dance behavior. Cultural meanings behind particular constraints in women's dance forms are analyzed in order to identify the general bases for gender constraints and their significance in the preservation of traditional culture.

In studies of women's art, a major theme is the role played by women as carriers of tradition, especially when cultures are under stress or in flux.[2] Researchers in women's art have proposed that women usually produce abstract forms rather than figurative images, and that they do not produce hieratic or religio-political art.[3] Women's progenerative powers have been postulated as a basis for the latter restriction which shields the continuation of the ancestral line from dangerous contact with the spirit world.[4] I shall analyze these theories on women's art as they apply to Tongan and Northern Ute dance forms.

The term "constraint" refers to a cultural imperative or limit, so that both the cohesion of a given culture and the significance of its cultural forms can be measured by the strength of the constraints which bind them. Thus, constraints are not treated in this discussion solely as negative limits on women's expressions but as a part of the form and substance of culture.

TONGA [5]

General Background

The South Pacific island-nation of Tonga has been somewhat insulated from industrial contact, due to its geographical isolation and a relatively benign British protectorateship. Many aspects of its traditional culture and complex social hierarchy were preserved following Western contact. Although the indigenous religion was abolished, the current king traces his ancestry back to the ancient gods. Initially, Methodist missionaries banned dance, but later it was smuggled back into missionary schools as hand-action enactments of religious stories.[6] Dance today is a secular hierarchical form which is used to mark ceremonial occasions and to communicate with visitors. In addition, dance performances for tourists are an important economic factor on the island.

Tongan women are allowed to rule and have higher ceremonial rank than men. However, Bott distinguishes between the Tongan systems of patrilineal authority and ceremonial rank, observing that while fathers and brothers control access to land, sisters have higher rank than brothers.[7] Women's higher status does not always translate directly into utilitarian power but is often implemented indirectly through persuasion. For example,

> The father's sister has ritual mystical power over her brother's children. Her curse can make a niece barren. Typically she names her brother's children. She used to choose their spouses. She is an honoured guest at their funerals. In the traditional system, if there were no immediately obvious heirs to a title, her wishes were taken into consideration in choosing an heir.[8]

Tongan women are noted for the dignity, grace, and restraint with which they apply their rank. The following statement by Tupou Posisi Fanua provides an excellent portrait of women's high status:

> The traditional status of women in Tonga is somewhat unique in the South Pacific. For while among our sister islands it seems that men regard women as only put on earth for the purpose of continuation of race, and also for providers for themselves, and a family that may follow. . . .

Not so for the Tongan woman. She expects her man to
bring food from the plantation and help her cook the family
meal, if there is a family. . . . Here in Tonga, the woman
always comes first within the family. The descendents of the
woman always have privileges that the descendents of a man
cannot claim, or expect . . . [These] *fahu* privileges can
always be claimed by the sister's children and grandchildren
. . . [But] the sister, the real one, cannot be *fahu* to her
brother's children. (Well she can, but it is not considered of
good taste to do so.) There is another one of our sayings:
"Open from the eye, the coconut." It means that because one
does not know a better way one takes the apparently easy
way. It denotes ignorance and selfishness. The older sister is
not the *fahu*, she is the "boss." She is the one who the
brother goes to and discusses with her what to do when
anything happens. And who should be the chief figure in it.
And what to give to who. But she never is the *fahu*, that is
if she has any knowledge or breeding.[9]

In addition to having high ceremonial rank, women in Tonga have
traditionally created ceremonial art. Many women's art forms (such as mats and
tapa) have persisted, while many traditional men's art forms (such as carving)
were discontinued following Western contact.[10] Today women compose both
poetry and dance.

Women As Carriers of Tradition

I shall test the theory that women uphold tradition in cultures
undergoing crises or transition by examining historical events as well as
contemporary values and practices. Western contact disrupted Tongan culture, as
evidenced by the temporary ban on dancing and the dissolution of the traditional
religion. Though women create formal dance and compose poetry today, men
were the producers of hieratic dance in the pre-contact period. Kaeppler writes
that two types of dance were described in the journals of Captain Cook's
voyages, the *me'etu'upaki*, in which men danced holding paddles, and the
me'elaufola, a hand-action dance performed by women or men.[11] The
me'etu'upaki was performed on formal occasions and was associated with the
inasi ceremony, when food was presented to the sacred king, the *Tui Tonga*, to
insure abundant harvests. The informal dance was the *me'elaufola*, which was

done by men or women, but not at the same time, and with different foot movements. Kaeppler proposes that the current formal dance, the *lakalaka*, evolved from the *me'elaufola* which was reintroduced, except both sexes now use the same foot movements, and both men and women dance the *lakalaka* in the same performance, although in separate groups. Thus, in pre-contact times only men participated in the hieratic form, while the current formal dance is performed by both men and women as a result of the disruption brought about by Western contact.

Currently, women's dancing embodies the quintessential characteristics of the Tongan dance: grace, subtlety, reserve, abstraction, and minimal spatial and torso movements.[12] Men's dancing, by contrast, is more literal and less subtle, characterized by clear vigorous movements which involve less use of the lower arms and hands. Often the men act out fighting with spears and wrestling, especially when dancing for tourists. Although it is impossible to describe the dance style of either gender as more distinctively "Tongan," the Tongan system of aesthetics is based upon distinctions which Tongans make between their dance form and the dances of other Polynesian societies. In their own view, the women's dance style more fully exemplifies the formal properties of the Tongan dance aesthetic.

Continuous pressure for Western adaptation has influenced the contemporary production of tourist dances. While all tourist dances have become faster and shorter than current traditional forms, the women's tourist style bears greater resemblance to their traditional style than does that of men. The men's tourist style is comparatively looser and rougher, diverging from the traditional men's dancing, which is graceful, dignified, and complex. There are more hand movements in men's traditional forms, adding range to the expressivity in the powerful masculine form. Men now perform war dances exclusively at tourist perfomances; and tourist dancing, with its pantomime fighting, is rougher than the traditional Tongan war dance. As men adopt more energetic and fierce movements from other islands, the difference widens between men's and women's styles.[13] Men have traditionally been freer in both movement and costume, and they have been less resistant than women to change. The greater reluctance to modify women's dance indicates that women are conservators of traditional values during periods of cultural change. The elimination of many functional aspects of men's war arts may explain why women's arts now embody the "traditional" aesthetic: once men's war arts were dismantled or reduced in significance, women's arts became more prominent.

Progenerative Constraints

Tongans frequently complain about women performing the Tahitian hip movement, which they have adopted as an exception to the women's traditional style. Western audiences expect hip movement from Polynesian dancers, but in Tonga to move the hips is the essence of rudeness.[14] Performances of Tahitian-type dancing are relatively rare, and female dancers always wear yards of cloth wrapped around their waists. As one Tongan choreographer put it:

> This is just to entertain the visitors. Here in Tonga we do not need the Tahitian movements, and the costumes: being almost naked. The King and the chiefs do not like that kind of dancing because it is not polite . . . You never do that kind of dancing in the palace or for the chiefs . . . It does not look well to move the hips. Then the police would come and take that man or woman away.*

These objections to hip movements limit women's adoption of movements from other islands, while the roughness of men's tourist dance does not offend Tongans. There is little, if any, Tahitian influence on traditional Tongan style, as women do not use hip movements in traditional dances.

The proscription against hip movements and other progenerative constraints--that is, rules relating to women's progenerative powers--indicate that Tongan sexual values influence what is considered appropriate behavior in dance. While progenerative constraints exist for both genders, some women's constraints are applied with greater rigidity; this may explain in part the greater conservatism in women's dance forms. Kaeppler notes that in the earliest accounts of Tongan dance, the dancers were said to be clothed only between the waist and the knee and that it is still considered in poor taste to expose or noticeably move this part of the body.[15] In Tongan dance terminology there is no word for the upper leg, and the traditional costume of a tightly wrapped skirt-like covering makes it difficult to move this part of the body. This restraint is relaxed in the dancing of young girls and of men. Also, in the Tongan version of sitting cross-legged, the upper legs are kept nearly parallel, especially for women. However, men and young girls need not keep their legs parallel.

---

*Quotes marked with an asterisk are from informants who prefer to remain anonymous.

Another aesthetic feature related to progeneration is the use of Tongan oil in the dance, which reflects the value Tongans place on virginity. Women dancers rub this shiny, fragrant oil onto the skin, and if it remains on the surface and does not soak in, this signifies that the woman is a virgin. Audiences enthusiastically acknowledge this feature during young women's solos. If the oil glistens and shines throughout the evening as the girl dances, even dripping off of her fingers, people cheer and sway, pressing and holding each other, so that large sections of the audience are lifted off the ground.

Progenerative constraints are also apparent in Tongan dance costumes. Although new design ideas are considered pleasing because they indicate cleverness and ingenuity, rigid rules control the shape of the Tongan dance costume. The women's costume must be down over the knee, up over the breasts, and must cover the torso completely, with a belt around the waist. Women who wore shorter skirts during the mini-skirt era were severely chastised. These rules dictate which parts of the body may be shown and are often based in sexual mores. For instance, the costume must be up over the breasts because it is *tapu* for a brother to see a sister's breasts.

In Tonga, where genealogical connections are critical to a complex social stratification, sex-related constraints play a central role in dance behavior. While many of these values apply to both genders, some constraints are more strongly applied or more explicitly expressed in the dance behavior of women.

Abstraction

Another principal feature of Tongan dance is its abstractness; the performers "scorn realism."[16] Men's movements in tourist dance are much more literal than women's movements because

> Our men have always been like that. See, if they try to demonstrate the word die, for instance, the girls would go just like this, or like that (she dipped her face, and her hands trembled faintly in front of her face)--just a little touch. But the boys, they would fall flat on the floor. And that, and get up. See, they demonstrate it. And women don't do that.[17]

Demonstration on the part of men and abstraction on the part of women fits the visual arts theory that women produce abstract images, while men produce figurative forms. Because dance is a form of behavior, the power of demonstrative, literal movements is emphasized.

More traditional designs in women's arts are always highly stylized so that there is very little potential for "rudeness." Tongans discourage rudeness by "keeping the suggestion of a real situation to a minimum"; they are especially sensitive about sexual rudeness.[18] The tendency towards abstraction in women's forms limits their potential for violating cultural norms and for making literal statements about the world.

The high value placed on abstraction in Tongan dance, and the greater embodiment of this quality by women dancers, may also be related to women's high ceremonial rank. The fact that women create the dance may explain its characteristic abstractness.

Tongan dance accompanies poetry and is not a central art form around which other arts are elaborated. Kaeppler considers poetry the leading part of a performance, with music as a rhythmic dimension and dance as a decorative element.[19] The function of dance as decoration contrasts with dance forms which are believed to bring about changes in the world directly, such as insuring good harvests or accomplishing divine possessions or initiations. The abstractness of Tongan dance and women's ability to create and perform it may both relate to its function as an accompanying form.

Finally, the fact that abstract forms do not appear to be subversive may facilitate their retention in a culture which is dominated by external forces. This may explain why women's art forms may persist longer under situations of domination.

Hieratic Constraints

While in pre-contact times men performed the sacred ceremonial dances, as a result of the disruption brought about by Western contact, both men and women now perform the formal dance. The participation of both genders in today's formal dance may have resulted from the breakdown of the traditional religion and the secularization of dance. However, though they can now participate, special religio-political constraints still exist for women.

For instance, only men can perform the formal *kava* ceremony, which differs from formal dancing in that it can accomplish tangible political changes. The *kava* movements are not considered a dance form by Tongans, as they do not accompany poetry, but gender constraints relating to *kava* movements are relevant in examining women's role in movement art. *Kava* is an essential feature in many ceremonies, as it "clenches the contract."[20] Status, while derived from genealogy, must be recognized by those holding political power. The royal family and nobility, who hold legally-defined status, may legitimize the legally undefined status of others by recognizing them during *kava* ceremonies.[21] Thus the *kava* ceremony can actively confer political power by status transformations. This ability to bring about ceremonially a "real" change may be a critical reason for limiting women's participation in hieratic dance.

Another important restriction on women's participation is that they do not play the dance drum which generates rhythm, the primary basis of Tongan dance. I was told that "rhythm is the boss" in dance, and that formerly chiefs beat the drums while their people danced, thus orchestrating all of the feelings which the dance brought about:

> The chiefs used to drum to keep time. The beat is like a heart, and when you come to something important like flowers or a pretty picture, you change so that there is the feeling there, that is kept in the feet by beating out the time. The feet beat the time that is in the song, so that they help create the mood with the rhythm and help create the picture and express the feelings that go with it.*

Thus, while women can compose both formal dance and dance poetry, the actuating force for movement lies exclusively within the domain of men.

Tongan dance movements are a persuasive element which decorates poetry, and this seems consistent with women's role. Bott, for instance, notes that women had the power to request favors of brothers, while men had the power to command.[22] The relationship between women's ceremonial and decorative function and their high rank is similar to the situation in Samoa, where, as discussed by Shore, high rank is associated with physical stasis and impulse denial, as opposed to impulse expression and utilitarian power.[23] Shore sees a parallel between men *versus* women and ceremonial rank *versus* political power. The high rank of Tongan women and their ceremonial, decorative function, combined with a relative physical stasis and constraint, is consonant with the general concept of rank in Tonga.

Another gender distinction in Tongan dance is that some women's dance forms are more detached from the literal meaning of the dance poetry. For instance, the *ula*, performed by one to eight women, does not interpret poetry, in contrast to other Tongan forms, but " . . . strives for beauty of movement and for displaying the beauty and dignity of the dancers."[24] The dancers of the *ula* are chosen for their skill in dancing, rather than according to social status, as in other Tongan dances. The *tau'o'lunga*, another women's dance, may interpret poetry, but need not do so.[25] Thus, some women's dance forms carry fewer religio-political implications than most Tongan dances: dancers are chosen for skill rather than rank, and the movements are more abstract and purely decorative.

NORTHERN UTE

General Background

Pre-contact Utes were nomadic hunter-gatherers who traveled in small family groups. Their fluid political structure centered around leaders chosen temporarily for specific purposes. Smith's 1936 ethnographic study of the Northern Utes described a relatively egalitarian relationship between the genders in the pre-reservation period of approximately 1845-1880.[26] Utes were loosely matrilocal and the most stable family unit was the mother and her children. Marriage was often a temporary bond; all of Smith's informants reported multiple marriages. Both genders had essential roles in arduous subsistence activities, and all bands in Utah experienced periods of great hunger.[27]

Contemporary Ute men and local white residents describe Ute women as courageous and tough. Some Ute men say they feel appreciative and proud of the support which women give the tribe during periods of crisis. The characterization of Ute women as vigorous and high spirited has historical precedents--witness Smith's description of marriage practices:

> It was not customary for a husband to fight with the man who took his wife, but he would take a horse belonging to the lover. This left the wife free to go with the other man. . . . It was customary for jealous women to take aggressive action against their rivals. . . . .A deserted wife might ride up to her former husband and stick her spear . . . in her husband's horse. . . . .If a man beat his wife, her family might interfere and kick him out.[28]

The relative equality of the sexes described by Smith is still practiced on the reservation today.[29] Ute women may serve on the tribal council and may be elected tribal chairman. Tribal monthly dividends, derived from oil money, are given out equally to men and women, with extra money going to the elders. Jorgensen describes how "[w]omen frequently manage the household budgets and serve as economic providers (a male responsibility) for their fathers, their sons, their brothers, perhaps even for their husbands."[30] Thus, in economic terms, women have, if anything, increased their range of responsibilities within an Anglo-influenced political economy.

The stability of the mother-child unit also has persisted. Some young women conceive children while attending dance events at other reservations and raise their children themselves, often with the help of their families. In the early reservation period, children of interband marriages were enrolled under the mother's band; later this was changed to enrollment under the father's band.[31] Northern Utes today are enrolled under their mother's band.

Menstrual taboos have always been practiced on the reservation. Traditional taboos were frequently broken, and although this was believed to cause harm, other actions could rectify this harm. Smith gives the following account of the somewhat lax attitude toward menstrual taboos:

> It was felt to be bad luck to see a menstruating woman, and women were isolated during their monthly periods. . . . All informants agreed that a man should not have intercourse with a menstruating woman, because it would endanger his "power" and might make him sick. However, this taboo was rarely observed, and many informants spoke of men visiting and sleeping with women in the hut. . . . Courtships took place in the hut, and many resulted in marriage. . . . This was the place for flirtations, and both single and married women used to receive their lovers there.[32]

Menstrual taboos today are more prevalent in dance behavior than in everyday life. Aspects of a modern Western lifestyle (many women are employed in tribal bureaucratic jobs, for instance) prevent seclusion and make other taboos (such as not touching one's face with one's hands) highly inconvenient. Current taboos surrounding dance behavior include proscribing menstruating females from coming into any dance circle, near a drum, or the Sun dance corral. These rules are rigidly prescribed but frequently broken, which provokes severe anxiety and vehement complaints.

Contemporary Northern Utes of the Uinta and Ouray Reservation in northeast Utah have been encroached upon by the dominant industrial society, and a religious dance form, the Sun dance, has developed in response to conditions of deprivation.[33] Practitioners dance for three days without food or water in order to obtain visions and spiritual power to benefit the community. In addition, one aboriginal dance form, the Bear dance, has survived. Bear dances are sponsored by communities each spring to celebrate the end of winter and to give couples a chance to congregate and pair off.

For the last eighteen years the Northern Ute reservation has held intertribal powwows. Two dance forms predominate: "traditional" and "fancy." These are pan-tribal forms in which both men and women participate, using different styles.[34] In traditional dance, people don outfits from earlier days, such as beaded buckskin dresses, leggings, porcupine quill roaches (worn on the head), and feather headdresses. The dance represents men and women in their traditional Indian roles. Fancy dance, on the other hand, provides a forum for innovation and is typically danced by younger men and women. (Children of all ages dance both forms.) Fancy dance is faster, more energetic, uses more space, and has higher elevation for men and a bouncier step for women. Brilliant colors rather than natural hues are used in fancy dance outfits. Powwow dance approximates Western representational performance more than other Ute dances.

Ute women now participate in all dance forms, but special limitations pertain to them. For instance, women travel to Fort Hall, Idaho, to dance in the Sun dance, because they are not allowed to participate in the Sun dance on the Northern Ute reservation. Men at Northern Ute act as Bear dance and Sun dance chiefs and sponsor these dance events, but women cannot. Also, only men act as masters of ceremonies at powwows.

Women have prerogatives of their own, however. All dances are occasions for sexual interaction, and Jorgensen describes how

> Women are always the aggressors, and the choice of dance partners is strictly up to them. This is a very good time for women to make advances towards more reticent men from their own and other reservations. . . . It is also a fact that teen-age girls generally introduce eleven- and twelve-year olds to coitus, and Sun dances are especially good times to carry out the lessons. . . . Women's dominance in social dancing and in introducing men to coitus, as well as their equality to--if not dominance over--men in initiating courtship may well bear on some of the resistance men have to dancing with women in the Sun dance rituals.[35]

The complaints which Ute men continually lodge against women's Sun dancing (as well as against their political and economic activities) are balanced by the appreciation and admiration they express for the strength that women bring to the tribe. Although Ute men genuinely object to women's Sun dancing, they nonetheless admire the spiritual and physical prowess of the women who dance. Men and women compete vigorously; the power of one gender is believed to augment that of the other. The excitement and satisfaction derived from this intergenderal competition are dependent upon the relative abilities of each.

Women as Carriers of Tradition

Northern Utes adopted new dance forms in response to the catastrophic effects of contact with whites, and women's participation involved trespass into men's domains. Paradoxically, while the increased range of women's activities confirms their role as carriers of tradition in times of crisis, it has generated vehement gender-related complaints. Predominant among these are objections to women's Sun dancing.

In pre-reservation times the Great Plains tribes and Wind River Shoshone performed the Sun dance to help them succeed in hunting and warfare. As such, the Sun dance belonged in men's province. During the 1880s Wind River shamans reshaped the dance to address illness and community misery: they dropped many features related to war and hunting (such as war-divining and ceremonial bison hunts) and integrated Christian concepts as the dance came to focus on communal welfare.[36] Northern Utes adopted this newer version of the Sun dance in 1889 or 1890.

Pre-reservation hunting and warfare rituals of the Northern Ute did not include the Sun dance, but the "fight dance" or "mean dance," done prior to war party excursions, was performed by men.[37] Jorgensen believes that the association of men's hunting and war activities with the Sun dance is one reason that Ute men resent women's participation as dancers.[38]

A precursor of the Sun dance on the Northern Ute reservation was the Ghost dance of 1870 and 1890. The Ghost dance was a transformative religious movement which prophesied the resurrection of dead Indians, the restoration of the Indian world, and the disappearance of whites.[39] The Ghost dance did not achieve its promise and was short-lived on the Northern Ute reservation. Northern Ute men and women participated equally in it, with no distinction in gender roles. According to Smith's informants, the dance movements were the same for men and women, no drum was used, and songs were contributed by both genders.[40]

The Ghost dance was a completely new dance form, so that identical participation by both genders did not constitute an invasion by women of men's domain. However, traditionally there were sexual divisions in religion and dance in Northern Ute society, so that full participation by women in this crisis-provoked hieratic dance was in fact an expansion of their normal range of behavior.

At contemporary powwows, women perform fancy dance which evolved from war dancing. The immediate precursor to powwows, show dancing, was also referred to as "war dancing"; it was an art form performed primarily by men following the termination of Sun dances.[41] Fancy dancing at powwows today is also called "war dancing," but it is performed by as many women as men, though women generally move less in and through space and have less dynamic range. Women keep their upper legs and knees together, although they kick up their heels to a fast beat (the girls' fancy dance resembles the Charleston). Fancy dancing provides a forum for innovation and is usually performed by children and very young men and women. It is less revered than traditional dance which embodies traditional culture. Fancy dancers dance to win contests and money prizes; thus women took up "war dance" after it was no longer related to war.

Men's war dances are usually spectacular and utilize great range with little constraint in movement. This is also true of men's fancy dance. In fancy dance men do level changes, spread their legs apart, do cartwheels with legs overhead, jump high in the air, land in splits, go from small still movements to great large movements and from very fast to very slow movements, and so on. Men's fancy dance is by far the freest and most colorful form of all Ute dances, in both movement and costume. Men use brightly dyed chicken feathers, and women use brilliant sparkling cutbeads on dance outfits.

While men's "war dancing" does not occupy a prominent cultural position today, war-related values do persist among the Northern Ute, and special honors and privileges are accorded veterans at powwows. For instance, in the feather ceremony, four traditional dancers, war veterans who have known action, pick up eagle feathers which have dropped from dance outfits. Retrieving the feathers symbolizes a preservation of the Indian ways; doing so corrects mistakes that could have brought serious harm to the Indian universe. Only male war veterans qualify for such special privileges and honors. Thus, while fancy dancing is referred to as "war dancing," values related to wars are implemented in a different forum which is reserved for men.

Intertribal powwows serve a vital cultural function, as they allow Indians to preserve their traditional way of life, or the Indian world, despite domination by the superordinate Anglo culture. Utes equate the survival of the tribe to the persistence of traditional life-ways which are believed to contribute to the harmony and balance of the universe.[42] As one war veteran at a 1982 Northern Ute Powwow put it:

I must fight for all Indian people who carry feathers, because

we must still carry on our traditional ways. Without our
feathers, what are we? Without our eagles to see over us, in
our ceremonies, what are we? Without our spiritual leaders,
without our singers, without our traditional dancers, what
are we? Are we just going to lay back, and let those people
who come from another shore destroy our ways and our
traditional values? I say no.*

As the 1981 Northern Ute powwow queen expressed it:

I think powwows are important because our old ways are
important, must not be lost or forgotten, important to
know, so we can maintain our ways and culture.*

At intertribal powwows, women are treated as carriers of tradition by
Utes and other Indians. They are called upon to settle arguments over matters of
tradition. Though their main role is to sit back and watch, they are consulted
about fine points of culture. As final arbiters of tradition, they serve as its
preservers.

Hieratic Constraints

Although Ute women now dance in the Sun dance, which is the
major hieratic dance form of the Northern Utes, they must travel to Fort Hall,
Idaho, to do so, because they are not allowed to Sun dance at any of the three
Ute reservations or at the Wind River Reservation. Women's Sun dancing
provokes extreme anxiety and resentment in Ute men.

Women are allowed to dance only at Fort Hall, and
Shoshone and Ute men do not encourage women to dance
even at Fort Hall. Sons and husbands are known to
discourage their mothers and wives from dancing; brothers
are known to discourage their sisters from dancing. Some
men refuse to dance with women, claiming that the women
press them into competition, thus destroying their
concentration. Other men dance with women, but work hard
not to be distracted by the female dancers, who often display
incredible stamina.[43]

Women are generally recognized as being able to dance harder and longer than men. Yet women may wait until they receive repeated spirit messages before deciding to dance. Jorgensen notes that perhaps "[t]hwarted by the economy, white polity and society, men want something of value for their own esteem. They want support from women in this endeavor, not competition from them."[44]

Ute men, in explaining their objections to women's Sun dancing, commonly discuss religious taboos regarding women in terms of a balanced, symmetrical process of nature, participated in by both genders. Men make sacrifices in order to pursue spiritual and literal life in the Sun dance; they also make sacrifices to ensure life in warfare and hunting. Men receive respect for these sacrifices, and domains which belong to them (such as the dance drum and Sun dancing) are based on their activities and contributions. Women participate in Nature's way of creating life, and since Indians emulate and revere nature, women are accorded considerable respect. According to Utes, women suffer while giving birth, and they suffer each month during menstruation. In addition, fearful negative powers, beyond the control of women, inhere in menstruation. Women receive respect, reverence, and gratitude for their contribution to the continuance of the tribe and for the suffering they endure. Matters related to birth are the natural domain of women; women usually initiate mating.

Because women already suffer in giving life, they are not required to suffer again in the Sun dance. They participate in critical auxiliary ways, by beading outfits, gathering brush, and bringing wet towels for the dancers. They spur the dancers on by singing and by standing up and exhorting them to dance harder. They call power into the dance corral.

There are many parallels between the Sun dance ideology and the process of giving life through birth. Jorgensen explains how male Sun dancers sacrifice to gain "power," which is equated with life and water, to ensure the continuation of the community.[45] Women also suffer by bearing children, again to ensure the community's continuance. The Sun dance itself is equated to a living being: "It's like a little child, who is still growing and learning and becoming itself." The dance, though transmitted from the spiritual world through men, is believed to have its own life force. The center pole used in the dance holds water for three months before passing its life (water, power) to others. Through the nest in the crotch of the center pole, water and life are channeled to others; the green branches and leaves at the top of the pole represent the "miracle of life."[46] Jorgensen describes how power (life) is synthesized by a fusion of opposing forces (hot-dry and cool-wet) which purge the dancer of evil spirit.[47] Menstruation represents a harmful negative force, which can dry out the dancers and make them sick. Menstruation is juxtaposed with birth: pregnancy stops menstruation and culminates in new life. Menstruation is women's hot-dry power which, if contained, can result in new birth; but when that hot-dry power leaves women without producing a child, it can cause harm.

Women with young babies and nursing mothers, as well as menstruating women are barred from the dance corral. It is believed the infants, just as the menstruating women, can dry out the dancers and singers and cause illness. Whereas menstruating women possess a hot-dry power, a harmful negative energy, infants contain cool-wet power which "attracts" power from the Sun dance corral. As Utes put it: "Those little babies will suck the water right out of those dancers." It is not the babies themselves who draw power, but rather, "something about those babies." The power drawn from the corral is believed to nourish the infants. A family with an ailing newborn child may take it to the Sun dance to restore its health, even though they will be criticized for doing so. Power, it is said, swirls in, under, and above the dance corral. Infants, who contain new life, are believed to have the ability to draw such power away from the corral and towards themselves. Women have drawn that power to create new life, and babies act as a magnet for the cool-wet power which the dancers seek.

Although women can now Sun dance, they do not usually get "knocked down" in a visionary experience as men do.[48]

> The ultimate form of a Sun dance religious experience is the vision. Dancers think that they have to be literally knocked down by the buffalo, or the eagle, or the center pole to receive a vision. A vision is not a prerequisite to the acquisition of power and good health, however, for both come from participation alone, whether or not the dancer is knocked down. Moreover, to fall in a Sun dance does not necessarily mean that a dancer has received a vision, or even a dose of power that he can control, but it does mean that he has been hit with a jolt of power. The dancer's body should be so upended that it is raised parallel, four feet or so above the ground. The dancer should then land on the back of his neck and shoulders. The body goes stone cold as it is filled with cool water. During his vision the recipient may talk to one or more spirits, perhaps Buffalo, perhaps "That Man." He will then be instructed by the spirit(s) about the extent and meaning of his power and the way in which it is to be

controlled . . .[49]

Although women have not been reported to "go down" in the dance, they do gain spiritual power from dancing. But the tendency for women not to be hit by jolts of power is a notable limit on their participation as dancers.

As in Tonga, Northern Ute women are prohibited from sitting around any dance drum. The drum's rhythm acts as a socializing agent; rhythm initiates the dance; the drum molds and sustains the dance's dynamic course; frequently, the drum indicates the close of a dance. Adherence to the beat of the drum is a critical criterion in judging powwow dancers. The drum has a spirit and life force; Utes speak of the drum as the heartbeat of the people. (In a sense, women's biological power to generate new heartbeats within themselves is balanced by men's cultural power to create and control the heartbeat of the people.)

The powwow drum's heartbeat is a collective heartbeat, which can at times transform a dance ground and transport those on it to another spiritual level.[50] When people feel this happenning, they often experience tremendous rushes of emotion--at such times a group of people standing around a powwow drum may burst into tears. Some say that their thoughts are filled with their "relations" and the Indian world. The drum communicates with the Creator, carrying the people's messages and prayers. The dance drum brings people closer together as they become more in tune with the basic harmony of universal forces; they are drawn into harmony with each other, as all forces in the universe are interrelated.

An additional hieratic constraint is that men utilize magic at powwows more than women. Magic is often carried out as private behavior outside of the dance genre; people from various reservations come together and compete for prizes, and some may work magic on others in order to win. Others will perform counter-measures to protect themselves. Women wear protective articles but tend not to actively wield spiritual power against other dancers.

Abstraction

Contemporary powwow dancing is the only Ute form in which women's movements are notably more abstract. In traditional dance, men often imitate animal qualities and hunting and war activities, such as the "sneakup." Women in traditional dance often enact a stillness to portray waiting for their men to return from hunting or war.[51] Women's powwow dance movement is characterized by the same movement qualities that mark Tongan women's dance: grace, order, greater inhibition of movement, control, formality, dignity, constraint, stasis, permanence of form, and accord. Men use greater movement and dynamic range in both traditional and fancy dance.

Although women use less movement and demonstration than men in powwow dancing, there is no evidence that women's dancing was more abstract in earlier Ute forms. For instance, in the Scalp dance " . . . women would bite the scalps and spit on them: 'some of their own people might have been killed by the enemy, and this would make the women feel mean toward the scalps'."[52] In the Bear dance, a man and a woman used to don bearskins and imitate the actions of two bears. Both men and women imitated coyote cries in the Coyote dance.[53] The Lame dance was a women's dance, in which the leading dancer wore a war bonnet and carried a scalp stick; the women danced in a line, with "pretend" crutches, limping as if lame in one leg.[54]

The greater abstraction used by women in powwow forms may be due to the type of representation involved. Indigenous forms made no distinction between representation and direct action. Some actions might express feelings (such as in the Scalp dance); imitation of animal qualities is often considered a form of spiritual and physical activity in which animal spiritual and physical powers are broached. But the purpose of traditional dance at powwows is to present Indians in their proper traditional roles, as men and women. As one person said: "It shows the other people that we are still carrying on." In this portrayal, women use less demonstration and direct action and a more limited movement range.

The use of abstraction rather than direct action in women's dance represents the introduction of a new gender constraint which can be analyzed within a larger context of cultural change occurring under Anglo domination. Northern Ute women's political-economic status has remained the same (if not risen) during the reservation period, and in some instances women now participate in activities (such as Sun dancing) which were previously the domain of men. At the same time, new gender constraints have evolved. These include more abstraction and a more limited movement range relative to men in powwow and Sun dancing, which were not indigenous Ute forms. In contrast, movements in the Bear dance are the same for both genders. Since the Bear dance was the major indigenous Ute dance form,[55] and the Sun dance is currently the Northern Utes' major religious dance form, gender constraints in these two dances may be compared.[56]

The Sun dance imposes severe limits on women's participation: women's progenerative powers are seen to be antithetical to the acquisition of power through Sun dancing. In contrast, the Bear dance has more equal gender roles: while men organize and orchestrate the dance, women choose their partners, and men are obligated to dance. Menstrual huts, commonly used for trysts, were erected near the dance corral.[57] Jorgensen describes how the Bear dance (in contrast to the Sun dance) was related to both hunting prowess (for men) and sexual prowess (for both genders):[58]

> [They] believed that a Ute hunter once saw a bear dancing outside a cave in the spring. The bear instructed the Ute hunter that he would gain sexual and hunting prowess if he propitiated bears by performing the dance.[59] It seems clear that the aboriginal Ute dance was performed to propitiate bears, to make Ute hunters more successful, and to make men and women successful in their sex lives. It was also used as the public announcement of the completion of the girls' puberty ritual. Utes equate the dance with the girls' puberty ceremony of the Apache.[60]

The association of the dance with girls' puberty and women's initiation of coupling activities demonstrates that women's progenerative powers were not taboo in the Bear dance as they are in the Sun dance but instead, were propitiated and celebrated.

One might ask why the Utes introduced the new redemptive Sun dance rather than alter the indigenous Bear dance to address community misery. Jorgensen describes how the Utes did, in fact, refashion the Bear dance after becoming disillusioned with the Ghost dance.[61] The altered form, which centered on the pursuit of good health, was performed for approximately fifteen years during the 1870s and 1880s. The Utes restored the dance to its original form in the 1890s. Rather than developing their Bear dance into a full-fledged redemptive movement, the Utes adopted the Sun dance.

It is not clear why the Utes chose the Sun dance over the Bear dance as a vehicle for their new redemptive religion. But a parallel between Tongans and Northern Utes suggests an hypothesis for further investigation. Jorgensen points out that the Wind River Shoshones had refashioned the Sun dance ritual in the 1880s, following their last big bison hunt and last warfare with other Plains tribes, at a time when they had lost access to subsistence resources.[62] Hunting and warfare were men's activities, and men's disempowerment in these realms coincided with the reshaping of their hunting and war ritual into a spiritual quest for power (life) in a male-dominated redemptive religious movement. In Tonga, formal rank was to some degree divorced from political power and was associated with stasis, dignity, restraint, subtlety, and control.

Qualities associated with rank (and with women, who outrank men) comprise the Tongan system of dance aesthetics. Thus, perhaps disestablished forms of power are given new ritual or ceremonial shape when a people loses its autonomy and is dominated by others.

Progenerative Constraints

Constraints relating to women's progenerative powers in the Sun dance have already been discussed in relation to heiratic constraints. I shall now describe progenerative constraints in the Bear dance. While Bear dances are initiated and orchestrated by men, these dances are an occasion for couples to consort, and women are always the aggressors. It is said that if a man refuses to dance, or jumps over the corral fence and runs away, he may be crippled, his hunting abilities may be impaired, or he may be killed by a bear while hunting. It behooves a woman to persist to the point of unreasonableness in the face of male resistance; if a man or his relatives try to buy her off, she may nevertheless still stand fast in her selection. The dance is thus a vehicle for celebrating women's procreative powers and sexual prowess.

In earlier times, young girls who had had their first menses during a given year might be danced to exhaustion and received their first sexual experience at the annual Bear dance.[63] The bashfulness of some men and the forwardness of women at Bear dances is a great source of humor and intersexual teasing.

A major source of disgruntlement at recent Bear dances was the wearing of slacks by women. People (especially women) complained that women in slacks looked like two men dancing together. The Colorado Utes specified on their Bear Dance poster than women wearing pants would be turned away. (No similar limitation for men's wear was included.) Given the function of the Bear dance as an occasion for spontaneous mating, it is possible that the wearing of pants by women is disapproved of because it would hinder courtship.[64]

An additional factor may be that people regret that the Bear dance does not have the cultural prominence it enjoyed in former times. The Bear dance used to provide a unique opportunity for couples to get together, but this is no longer the case. Today's Bear dances have an air of solemnity and reverence, in which people show respect for their only remaining indigenous dance celebration. Women who do not wear traditional skirts acknowledge the loss of an important function of the dance, and some may find this regrettable.

While greater conservatism exists in Tonga toward changes in women's versus men's dance movements, conservatism in American Indian dance forms differs for the two genders. Because Indian men have a greater range of participation in religious dance, there are countless interdictions which apply to them only. Many of these are transient and cannot be generalized readily. Permanent prohibitions do exist, such as not drinking water while Sun dancing, but men as a group do not usually violate this rule. In contrast, women commonly violate some traditional rules, such as breaking menstrual taboos, sitting at the drum, dancing in Sun dances, or wearing slacks at Bear dances.

In examining the conservation of traditional culture, because women have expanded their participation to domains that traditionally were the prerogative of men (such as economic suppport of families, or dancing in Sun dances), we see that while they are appreciated, on the one hand, for perpetuating traditional culture, on the other hand, they have been criticized for special gender-related changes in behavior.

Conclusion

The Tongan and Ute cultures differ radically in social structure, the use of dance, and the role of women. But in both cultures dance is a central and powerful feature, and there are strong gender constraints in the dance behavior of females. Theories of gender constraints in visual arts also apply to dance. While the specific rules vary, between the two cultures and between the two art forms, general bases for gender constraints are apparent. Both societies have been subjected to cultural hegemony, and women have begun to perform in hieratic or hierarchical dance forms which were previously the domain of men. However, special limits on women's participation in religio-political movement forms persist in both cultures, and these are associated with the intervention of spirits in worldly affairs (in the Northern Ute Sun dance) and the initiation of tangible political changes (in the Tongan *kava* ceremony). Women's movements in both cultures are more abstract, and this associates with representational performance dance (Tongan dance movement ornaments poetry in performances for people of rank or for tourists; powwow dancing represents Indians in their traditional roles). Similar gender differences in movement qualities exist in both cultures: men's movements are freer and use more range; women's movements are characterized by grace and control. Women's progenerative powers are a critical basis for dance constraints in both cultures, and these constraints vary greatly in content according to social structure and cultural context. (In Tonga, progenerative constraints arise from sexual mores, in a culture where genealogical ties are closely regulated. Among the Ute, women's procreative powers, rather than their virginity, are celebrated, and progenerative constraints exist in the form of birth and menstrual taboos. While Teilhet suggests that progenerative constraints shield the genealogical line from spirit contact--dance entails contact with a spirit world--the powers of Ute male dancers are shielded from powerful natural processes which result in progeneration.) In both cultures women have penetrated men's domains and this ingression constitutes a supporting element. At the same time, acute criticisms are leveled against women. Despite the contradictory reaction to their changing role, women, by providing essential support and by energizing traditional values, occupy a central place in the preservation of traditional culture.

Notes

1.   Fieldwork on the island of Tongatapu in Tonga was carried out under a University of California Grant for Humanities and Interdisciplinary Studies in the summer of 1981 and in the fall of 1983. All research in Tonga was performed in the company of Dr. Jehanne Teilhet, who I wish to thank for her valuable support and guidance. Field trips to the Northern Ute Reservation were made in the summer of 1982, winter of 1982-83, summer of 1984, and spring through fall of 1985. The first two trips were funded by a University of California grant given to Dr. Joseph G. Jorgensen to conduct a comparative study of Indian and Anglo responses to energy development on or near the Ute Reservation in Utah and the Crow Reservation in Montana; I was the senior researcher in Utah. I would like to express my appreciation to Dr. Jorgensen for his continuing support and counsel, for his critical reading of this paper, and for his many substantive contributions to my analysis of Ute culture.

2.   Jehanne Teilhet, Lectures in Art History, Visual Arts Department, University of California, San Diego.

3.   Jehanne Teilhet, "The Equivocal Role of Women Artists in Non-Literate Cultures," *Heresies* 4 (1978): 96-102.

4.   Ibid.

5.   For a more detailed analysis of gender differences in Tongan dance, see Stephanie Reynolds, "Imperatives and Persuasion in the Conservation of Culture: Gender Constraints in Tongan Dance," *Proceedings of the Third International Symposium of the Pacific Arts Association, September 1984* (New York: Metropolitan Museum of Art, forthcoming).

6.   Adrienne Kaeppler, "Tongan Dance: A Study in Cultural Change," *Ethnomusicology* 14 (1970): 266-77.

7.   Elizabeth Bott, "Power and Rank in the Kingdom of Tonga," *The Journal of Polynesian Society* 90 (1981): 7-81.

8.   Ibid., 18.

9.   Toupou Posesi Fanua, taped essays on Tongan culture, 1983. Toupou Posesi is a researcher for the Tonga Traditions Committee and a past Research Fellow at the University of Auckland, New Zealand.

10.   Jehanne Teilhet, personal communication.

11.   Adrienne Kaeppler, "Preservation of Evolution and Function in Two Types of Tongan Dance," *Polynesian Culture History,* ed. Genevieve Highland, et al. (Honolulu: Bishop Museum Special Publication 56, 1967), 503-36.

12.   Adrienne Kaeppler's analysis of Tongan dance supports this observation. Kaeppler was criticized by Jennifer Shennon for basing her descriptions of Tongan dance primarily on women's forms ("Approaches to the Study of Dance in Oceania: Is the Dancer Carying an Umbrella or Not?" *Journal of Polynesian Society* 90, no. 2, [1981], 193-208). My research demonstrates that both Kaeppler and Shennon are right: Kaeppler's analysis of Tongan dance emphasizes qualities in women's dancing because the women's dancing does embody the formal properties of Tongan dance aesthetics.

13.   Futa I. Helu, personal communication. Futa is founder and director of the Atenisi Cultural Institute on Tongatapu and has published numerous articles on Tongan arts. I attended his lectures on Tongan dance.

14.   Adrienne Kaeppler, "Method and Theory in Analyzing Dance Structure with an Analysis of Tongan Dance," *Ethnomusicology* 16 (1972): 173- 217.

15.   Ibid.

16.   Adrienne Kaeppler, "Aesthetics of Tongan Dance," *Ethnomusicology* 15 (1971): 175-85.

17.   Posesi, personal communication.

18.   Futa I. Helu, personal communication.

19.   Adrienne Kaeppler, "Melody, Drone and Decoration: Underlying Structures and Surface Manifestations in Tongan Art and Society," *Art and Society: Studies in Style, Culture and Aesthetics*, ed. Michael Greenhalgh and Vincent Megaw (London: Duckworth, 1978), 261-74.

20.   Futa I. Helu, personal communication.

21.   George Marcus, "Contemporary Tonga: The Background of Social and Cultural Change," *Friendly Islands: A History of Tonga,* ed. Noel Rutherford (Melbourne: Oxford University Press, 1977), 210-27.

22.   Bott, "Power and Rank."

23.   Bradd Shore, *Sala'ilua: A Samoan Mystery* (New York: Columbia University Press, 1982).

24.   Kaeppler, "Tongan Dance," 274.

25.   Ibid.

26.   Anne M. Smith, "Ethnology of the Northern Utes," *Papers in Anthropology* 17 (New Mexico: Museum of New Mexico Press, 1974).

27.   Ibid.

28.   Ibid.

29.   No comprehensive analysis of the status of Northern Ute women has been published. For status indicators proposed in recent cross-cultural studies, see Karen E. Paige and Jeffery M. Paige, *The Politics of Reproductive Ritual* (Berkeley and Los Angeles: University of California Press, 1981); Peggy R. Sanday, *Female Power and Male Dominance: On the Origins of Sexual Inequality* (Cambridge: Cambridge University Press, 1981); Martin K. Whyte, *The Status of Women in Pre-Industrial Society* (Princeton: Princeton University Press, 1978); Martin K. White, "Cross-Cultural Codes Dealing with the Relative Status of Women," *Ethnology* 17 (1978): 211-37; and William N. Stephens, *The Family in Cross-Cultural Perspective* (New York: Harper Colophon, 1963). Stephens, for example, proposes a domestic deference dimension which includes such indicators as: a) wife kneels or bows to husband; b) wife rarely disputes husband; c) wife doesn't call husband by name; and d) husband dominates decision-making. For an analysis of the status of women on the Northern Ute Reservation based on variables such as the above, see Reynolds, "A Comparative Examination of Dance Efficacy" (Ph.D. Diss., University of California, Irvine, 1988). Further cross-cultural research should

be carried out for the present study in order to control for the relatively high status of Tongan and Northern Ute women; the author is currently performing field research with Mixtec Indian groups (who are rigidly patrilocal, and women commonly defer to men) on the U.S.-Mexico border.

30.   Joseph G. Jorgensen, *The Sun Dance Religion: Power for the Powerless* (Chicago: University of Chicago Press, 1974), 254.

31.   Smith, "Ethnology of the Northern Utes."

32.   Ibid., 147-48.

33.   Jorgensen, *The Sun Dance Religion.*

34.   The different gender styles in powwow dances will be discussed in the section "Abstraction."

35.   Jorgensen, *The Sun Dance Religion,* 301.

36.   Dimitri B. Shimkin, "The Wind River Shoshone Sun Dance," *Anthropological Papers* 41, Bureau of American Ethnology Bulletin 151 (1953): 397-494.

37.   Smith, "Ethnology of the Northern Utes."

38.   Jorgensen, personal communication.

39.   James Mooney, *The Ghost Dance Religion and the Sioux Outbreak of 1890* (Chicago: University of Chicago Press, 1965).

40.   Smith, "Ethnology of the Northern Utes."

41.   Jorgensen, *The Sun Dance Religion.*

42.   Stephanie Romeo (Reynolds), "Concepts of Nature and Power: Environmental Ethics of the Northern Ute," *Environmental Review* 9 (1985): 150-70.

43.   Jorgensen, *The Sun Dance Religion,* 253.

44. Ibid., 254.

45. Jorgensen, *The Sun Dance Religion.*

46. Ibid., 206-11.

47. Ibid., 288.

48. Jorgensen, personal communication.

49. Jorgensen, *The Sun Dance Religion,* 212-15.

50. An essential difference between Western and Northern Ute art forms is that Ute art is metaphoric in a way that is literal. It is not possible to fully explicate this feature of Ute art, because once any spiritual system is abstracted from its specific life form, no language exists to describe it. But Ute metaphors are necessarily "literal" in part because to them, the entire universe is animate and interrelated; all things, including thoughts, are considered alive and real; and art is animate, with spirit. Thus "literal" here means "real"; there can be nothing which is purely "abstract" in the Western sense, because everything has spirit. Utes have an inclusive worldview which allows them to believe in everything; contradictions are sustained and resolved as the universe continues in its process of creation. Religious ideology manifests itself in tangible experiences: the drum really is alive, and its beat really enters the observer's body and transforms him or her.

51. Bird-like movements are commonly used by both sexes. But women tend to use more generic movement qualities, such as smooth leaning turns reminiscent of a bird's soaring flights. Men tend more actually to imitate particular birds. Men wear feathers and they may walk and move their heads exactly as a bird would to gain access to the bird's specific spiritual powers for religious purposes. There is much more specificity and therefore more variety in men's utilization of bird-like movements.

52. Smith, "Ethnology of the Northern Utes," 223.

53. Ibid.

54. Ibid.

55. Verner Z. Reed, "The Ute Bear Dance," *American Anthropologist* 9 (1896): 237-44; Robert H. Lowie, "Dances and Societies of the Plains Shoshone," *Anthropological Papers of the American Museum of Natural History, New York* 11 (1915), 803-35; Leslie Spier, "Havasupai Ethnography," *Anthropological Papers of the American Museum of Natural History, New York* 29 (1918): 81-392; Julian H. Steward, "A Uintah Bear Dance, March 1931," *American Anthropologist* 34 (1932): 263-73.

56. Jorgensen, *The Sun Dance Religion.*

57. Smith, "Ethnology of the Northern Utes."

58. Joseph G. Jorgensen, "Ghost Dance, Bear Dance, and Sun Dance," *Handbook of North American Indians*, ed. Willian C. Sturtevant. Volume 11, Great Basin 1986, ed. Warren L. d'Asevedo.

59. Joseph G. Jorgensen, "The Ethnohistory and Acculturation of the Northern Ute" (Ph.D. diss., Indiana University, 1964).

60. Joseph G. Jorgensen, 1969 fieldnotes on the Bear Dance at the Southern Ute, Ute Mountain, Ute, and Northern Ute reservations, and Memorial Day Ceremonies at the Wind River Shoshone Reservation, April 19-June 30.

61. Jorgensen, "Ghost Dance, Bear Dance."

62. Jorgensen, *The Sun Dance Religion.*

63. Jorgensen, personal communication.

64. Jorgensen, personal communication.

References

Bott, Elizabeth. "Power and Rank in the Kingdom of Tonga." *The Journal of Polynesian Society* 90 (1981).

Fanua, Toupou Posesi. Taped essays on Tongan culture (1983). Toupou Posesi is a researcher for the Tonga Traditions Committee and a past Research Fellow at the University of Auckland, New Zealand.

Fusitu'a, 'Eseta, and Noel Rutherford. "George Tupou II and the British Protectorate." *Friendly Islands: A History of Tonga.* Edited by Noel Rutherford. Melbourne: Oxford University Press, 1977.

Jorgensen, Joseph G. "The Ethnohistory and Acculturation of the Northern Ute." Ph.D. dissertation, Indiana University, 1964; 1969 fieldnotes on the Bear Dance at the Southern Ute, Ute Mountain, Ute, and Northern Ute reservations, and Memorial Day Ceremonies at the Wind River Shoshone Reservation, April 19-June 30.

-----. *The Sun Dance Religion: Power for the Powerless.* Chicago: University of Chicago Press, 1974.

-----. "Ghost Dance, Bear Dance, and Sun Dance." *Handbook of North American Indians.* Edited by Willian C. Sturtevant. Volume 11, Great Basin 1986, edited by Warren L. d'Asevedo.

Kaeppler, Adrienne. "Folklore as Expressed in the Dance in Tonga." *Journal of American Folklore* 80 (1967).

-----. "Preservation of Evolution and Function in Two Types of Tongan Dance." *Polynesian Culture History.* Edited by Genevieve Highland, et. al. Honolulu: Bishop Museum Special Publication 56, 1967.

-----. "Tongan Dance: A Study in Cultural Change." *Ethnomusicology* 14 (1970).

-----. "Aesthetics of Tongan Dance." *Ethnomusicology* 15 (1971).

-----. "Method and Theory in Analyzing Dance Structure with an Analysis of Tongan Dance." *Ethnomusicology* 16 (1972).

-----. "Melody, Drone and Decoration: Underlying Structures and Surface Manifestations in Tongan Art and Society." *Art and Society: Studies in Style, Culture and Aesthetics*. Edited by Michael Greenhalgh and Vincent Megaw. London: Duckworth, 1978.

Lowie, Robert H. *Dances and Societies of the Plains Shoshone, Anthropological Papers of the American Museum of Natural History* 11. New York, 1915.

Marcus, George. "Contemporary Tonga: The Background of Social and Cultural Change." *Friendly Islands: A History of Tonga*. Edited by Noel Rutherford. Melbourne: Oxford University Press, 1977.

Mooney, James. *The Ghost Dance Religion and the Sioux Outbreak of 1890*. Chicago: University of Chicago Press, 1965.

Paige, Karen E. and Paige, Jeffery M. *The Politics of Reproductive Ritual*. Berkeley and Los Angeles: University of California Press, 1981.

Reed, Verner Z. "The Ute Bear Dance." *American Anthropologist* 9 (1896).

Reynolds, Stephanie. "Imperatives and Persuasion in the Conservation of Culture: Gender Constraints in Tongan Dance." *Proceedings of the Third International Symposium of the Pacific Arts Association, Metropolitan Museum of Art, New York, New York, September, 1984*, forthcoming.

Reynolds, Stephanie. "A Comparative Examination of Dance Efficacy in Traditional, Urban Industrial, and Trasitional Societies." Ph.D. dissertation, University of California, Irvine, 1988.

Romeo (Reynolds), Stephanie. "Concepts of Nature and Power: Environmental Ethics of the Northern Ute." *Environmental Review* 9, no. 2 (1985): 150-170.

Rutherford, Noel, ed. *Friendly Islands: A History of Tonga*. Melbourne: Oxford University Press, 1977.

Rutherford, Noel. "George Tupou II and Shirley Baker." *Friendly Islands: A History of Tonga.* Edited by Noel Rutherford. Melbourne: Oxford University Press, 1977.

Sanday, Peggy R. *Female Power and Male Dominance: On the Origins of Sexual Inequality.* Cambridge: Cambridge University Press, 1981.

Shimkin, Dimitri B. "The Wind River Shoshone Sun Dance." *Anthropological Papers* 41, Bureau of American Ethnology Bulletin 151 (1953).

Shore, Bradd. *Sala'ilua, A Samoan Mystery.* New York: Columbia University Press, 1982.

Smith, Anne M. "Ethnology of the Northern Utes." *Papers in Anthropology* 17, New Mexico: Museum of New Mexico Press, 1974.

Spier, Leslie. "Havasupai Ethnography." *Anthropological Papers of the American Museum of Natural History New York* 29 (1918).

Stephens, William, N. *The Family in Cross-Cultural Perspective.* New York: Harper Colophon, 1963.

Steward, Julian, H. "A Uintah Bear Dance, March 1931." *American Anthropologist* 34 (1932).

Teilhet, Jehanne. "The Equivocal Role of Women Artists in Non-Literate Cultures." *Heresies* 4 (1978).

Teilhet, Jehanne. "The Role of Women Artists in Polynesia and Melanesia." *Art and Artists in Oceania.* Edited by Sidney Mead. Palmerston Norther: Dunmore Press Limited, 1983.

Whyte, Martin K. *The Status of Women in Pre-Industrial Society.* Princeton: Princeton University Press, 1978.

-----. ""Cross-Cultural Codes Dealing with the Relative Status of Women." *Ethnology* 17 (1978).

Reflections on White Feminism:
A Perspective from a Woman of Color

Aida Hurtado

It is an intriguing question why women of color and white women have very serious differences even though they both do women's work--bearing and rearing children and doing housework--and such tasks are equally devalued regardless of the women's race or ethnicity. Why haven't women of color joined the white feminist movement *en masse?* The question is especially perplexing since a larger percentage of black women than white women support the formal goals of the women's movement.[1] Moreover, rising divorce rates, single parenting, and changing employment patterns are affecting all women in similar ways.[2] Thus, it would seem that there should be enough superordinate goals to unite an otherwise diverse population.

I shall examine feminist theory written by women of color as well as by white women in the United States to see why the former have not flocked to the contemporary women's movement.[3] I shall focus mainly on two crucial differences between them: the dissimilar way in which sexist oppression is imposed on each group and the different relationship each group has to white men. I contend that the male domination of women of color is enforced through *rejection* rather than through *seduction*. White middle-class women are groomed from birth to be the lovers, mothers, and partners (however unequal) of white men. It is a seductive situation because of the economic and social benefits attached to those roles.[4] White upper- and middle-class women are supposed to be the biological bearers of those members of the next generation who will inherit positions of power in society. Women of color, on the other hand, are groomed from birth to be primarily the lovers, mothers, and partners (however unequal) of men of color, who are also oppressed by white men. As bearers of the next generation of people who will mainly be workers, women of color are not perceived to be as desirable as, or equal to, white women, even by men of color. For most working-class women of color, the possibility of marrying a white middle-class male is rather remote. The avenues of advancement open to white women, if they conform to prescribed female roles, are not even a theoretical possibility for most working-class women of color. I am not arguing that one form of sexist oppression is harsher than the other, but rather, that the very way of enforcing oppression produces different political and social responses and skills in the two groups of women. At times, such a difference in skills causes the two groups to clash. I shall propose some ways in which these differences can be bridged, even though they cannot be completely obliterated. I also conclude that the intimacy white middle-class feminists share with white men hampers their efforts to organize effectively against the *status quo*. Such intimacy does not exist between feminists of color and white men; therefore, their perceptions of and actions toward the latter tend to be quite different from those of white, middle-class feminists.

What Binds Us Together and What Sets Us Apart: Similarities and Differences between White Feminist and Minority Scholarship

The academic writings of white feminists share many characteristics with the academic writings of minority scholars, specifically Chicano scholars.

1. Both groups reject the dominant paradigms which exist in academia.

2. Both groups try to describe a reality which has been ignored in traditional academic writings, or if described at all, has been stereotyped and distorted. Consequently,

  a) both groups question the construction of social categories "to justify the unfair treatment of women and people of color." While feminists question the biological basis of gender; minorities challenge the notion that race is a biological category with corresponding differences in intellectual potential.[5]

  b) Both groups want to develop new methods of describing reality which are not entirely based on the white-male-rational-king-of-the-universe model.

c) Both groups advocate a multi- disciplinary approach that transcends traditional academic boundaries. The most experimentation has occured in the arts and the humanities, through poetry, like that of Lorna Dee Cervantes, through theater, such as the productions of Teatro Campesino, and through films, such as *El Norte*.

3.   Feminist scholarship produced by white women and Chicano scholarship have a rather short history, because the participation of white women and minorities in integrated major universities is a recent phenomenon.

4.   Both feminist and minority scholars are activists. Their goal is not only to understand a reality which has been excluded from mainstream scholarly writings, but ultimately to change the existing power arrangements in academia. They have doubtlessly proposed different strategies to bring about change, but both groups produce works that criticize the existing paradigms and power arrangements.

But there are also differences between feminists and minority scholars. Many women of color have written very eloquent critiques of the white women's movement since the late 1960s and they continue to do so.[6] However, these critiques have had little impact, until very recently, on the thinking of white feminists. The recent focus on racism is not the result of a profound change in feminist theory; rather, as Gloria Joseph comments with regard to Adrienne Rich's article on feminism and racism, "She reiterates much that has been voiced by black female writers, but the acclaim given her article shows again that it takes whiteness to give even blackness validity."[7]

Published feminist theory, for the most part, has been written by white, middle-class, educated women because from its very beginning, the women's movement in the United States has been led by these women.[8] Consequently, the experience of working-class white women has also been blatantly left out in much of white feminist theory.[9] This is not surprising because academic production requires time and financial resources. Ethnic and racial minorities and white working-class people have historically lacked both.

Poverty hampers the ability of all working-class people, especially racial and ethnic minorities, to participate in higher education; without financial assistance, few low-income and minority students can attend universities; without higher education, few working-class and minority intellectuals can become professors; and among the working-class and the minority scholars, only a miniscule number care to write feminist theory. White women, in contrast, especially those from upper- and middle-class backgrounds, have had some access to higher education, although many white women scholars, like minority scholars, also got hired only as a result of the political movements of the 1960s. The crucial difference in the class orgins of the participants in the white feminist and the racial and ethnic movements sets the stage for the conflict between them in the contemporary women's movement.

Explanations for Women's Oppression: White Feminist Theory

Feminist theory written by white women, although middle-class in origin, is by no means homogeneous. Alison Jaggar, in her book, *Feminist Politics and Human Nature*, identifies four different strains of feminist theory.[10] Each of them has a different explanation for why women are oppressed and proposes a different solution for liberation. Each makes different assumptions about female human nature and holds different aspects of this society's patriarchical system responsible for women's oppression. Accordingly, the appropriate political avenues proposed for changing women's subordinate status also vary. The four strains identified by Jagggar are liberal feminism, Marxist feminism, radical feminism, and socialist feminism.

Liberal feminism derives its philosophical assumptions about human nature from liberal political theory which emerged with the growth of capitalism and provided the justification for individual autonomy and self-fulfillment. One of the central tenets of liberalism is the right of individuals to own private property. Liberal feminists attempted to extend the "inalienable rights" of men to women as well. The philosophical and political project of liberal feminism is to prove that there are no innate, biological differences between men and women in their potential for rational thought or action. Liberals believe women are capable of doing any job as well as men. The source of oppression is a patriarchal system which, being socially constructed, can therefore also be socially deconstructed. The solution to women's oppression is to get women to assimilate fully into male culture. This is the rationale behind the Equal Rights Amendment. Liberal feminists argue for equal opportunity for all, including the right of women to join the army. In many ways, liberal feminists play interest-group politics. For example, there are women's professional organizations which mirror men's professional organizations, and there are magazines that teach women executives how to "dress for success" and to "network" to better infiltrate the work world.

Liberal feminism has been a politically progressive movement: its adherents have played a crucial role in changing marriage laws, fighting for the legalization of abortion, and lobbying for laws to provide equal wages to both genders. This particular strain of feminism has been responsible for major changes in society which have benefited all women, including working-class women and women of color. Liberal feminism, however, is not a politically radical movement: it is not usually concerned with issues of race and class, and when it is, it does so only tangentially.

Marxist feminism bases its notion of women's nature on the Marxist conception of human nature. Whereas liberal political theorists argue that the human species is different from other species because of its capacity for rational thought, Marxists view humans as different because of their ability to consciously and purposely manipulate the nonhuman world for survival. Marx called this ability "praxis." Men and women are different because their praxis are different, and that, in turn, gives them different consciousnesses or world-views. According to Marxists, since productive activity in a capitalist society is more differentiated by class than by gender, middle-class women have more in common with middle-class men than with other women, while working-class women's allegiance also tends to be with their male counterparts.

Marxist feminists argue that women's subordination is but one form of general class oppression that serves the interests of capital. Women are considered useful particularly for the reproduction of labor. According to Marxist feminists, because consciousness is determined by commodity production outside the home, working-class women who enter the labor force are more "liberated" than non-wage earning middle-class women; therefore feminism is more likely to flourish among the latter as a form of "false consciousness." Women's liberation will come about only when the capitalist system is destroyed, and women *en masse* can join the public realm of social production. As with male Marxists, Marxist feminists have not analyzed the role of race or ethnicity in the dynamics of oppression.

The third strain of feminist theory discussed by Jaggar is radical feminism. Although radical feminists do not adhere to a single view of human nature, they have favored one particular view which has underpinned many of their theoretical writings. Radical feminists postulate that the source of women's oppression is men's biology, or their innate capacity to be violent.

They believe that women are superior biologically because of their potential capacity to give birth, which in turn engenders other psychological characteristics such as nurturance, warmth, emotional expressiveness, endurance, and practical common sense:

> Women's special closeness with nature is believed to give
> women special ways of knowing and conceiving the world.
> Radical feminists reject what they see as excessive
> masculine reliance on reason, and instead emphasize feeling,
> emotion and nonverbal communication.[11]

The solution, therefore, to women's oppression is to affirm women's natural capacities even if it is done at the expense of becoming entirely separate from men.

Radical feminists also do not provide a specific analysis of race or class. Their assumption is that universal sisterhood is possible because of the apparent universality of women's subordination and because

> the differences of national culture . . . are the superficialities
> that cover up the fundamental similarity of all national
> cultures the world over. This fundamental similarity is the
> split between male culture and female culture . . .[12]

Socialist feminists overlap with both Marxist and radical feminists. They agree with the Marxists that productive activity (praxis) determines social relationships and that women have been oppressed because their economic activity is not valued. However, socialist feminists expand the Marxist category of productive activity to include "women's work," such as housework and childrearing. Unlike Marxists who consider the class struggle to be the primary political struggle, or radical feminists who believe that women's liberation should take precedence over the fight to end all other kinds of oppression, socialist feminists do not rank oppressions into a hierarchy; rather, they claim that

> capitalism, male dominance, racism and imperialism are
> intertwined so inextricably that they are inseparable;
> consequently the abolition of any of these systems of
> domination requires the end of all of them.[13]

A socialist revolution will not solve women's oppression until gender-specific productivity is reevaluated and the accompanying ideology debunked. Therefore the goal of socialist feminism is

> to abolish the social relations that constitute humans, not only as workers and capitalists but also as women and men. Whereas one version of radical feminism takes the human ideal to be a woman, the ideal of socialist feminism is that women (and men) will disappear as socially constituted categories.[14]

Each of these feminist strains offers a sophisticated analysis of women's condition and, to a certain extent, explains the position of all women in the United States. However, they all fail to address the unique position of women of color in any comprehensive manner. Jaggar believes that women of color have not developed a "distinctive" perspective and therefore fails to accord them any philosophical space. She notes that "a very few [black feminists] are radical feminists, although almost none seems to be a lesbian separatist,"[15] but she does not discuss why this is so. In fact, most black feminists adhere to a socialist feminist rather than a radical feminist perspective, because the former is the only theoretical perspective which gives class and gender equal importance in explaining the subordination of women. However, black socialist feminists recognize that the socialist perspective subsumes racial and ethnic identity under gender and class, and consequently, it minimizes the significance of racial oppression.

Although Jaggar thinks black feminist theory fits within the scheme she proposes, I disagree with her because of some important exceptions that she glosses over that, to me, highlight the crux of the differences between feminists of color and white feminists. She also claims that feminists of color other than blacks have not developed "a distinctive and comprehensive theory of women's liberation."[16] According to her, whatever writings exist are "mainly at the level of description." Unfortunately, Jaggar fails to recognize that the same statement is made about feminist writings in general (and is mostly made by male academics). Her failure to analyze what feminists of color have written either shows enormous wisdom on Jaggar's part (because she concedes that she lacks the understanding to present the perspective of these women), or it is blatant negligence which borders on racism. If Jaggar's stance is representative of white feminists, little wonder, then, that feminists of color feel alienated from white feminists.

The Wedge that Cuts: Differences between White Feminists and Feminists of Color

Frances D. Gage, writing about the Akron, Ohio, Women's Rights Convention, held in May of 1851, described Sojourner Truth, an early black feminist and ex-slave, as follows:

> The leaders of the movement trembled on seeing a tall, gaunt black woman . . . march deliberately into the church, walk with the air of a queen up the aisle, and take her seat upon the pulpit steps. A buzz of disapprobation was heard . . . When, slowly from her seat in the corner rose Sojourner Truth . . . At her first word there was a profound hush . . .

> "That man over there say that women needs to be helped into carriages, and lifted over ditches, and to have the best place everywhere. Nobody ever helps me into carriages, or over mud-puddles, or gives me any best place!" And raising herself to her full height, asked, "And ain't I a woman? Look at me! Look at my arm!" (and she bared her right arm to the shoulder, showing her tremendous muscular power). "I have ploughed, and planted, and gathered into barns, and no man could head me! And ain't I a woman? I could work as much and eat as much as a man--when I could get it--and bear the lash as well! And ain't I a woman? I have borne thirteen children and seen them most all sold off to slavery, and when I cried out with my mother's grief, none but Jesus heard me! And ain't I a women?"[17]

This passage captures the crux of the differences between white middle-class feminism and the issues that women of color have to face when addressing the question of gender. Sojourner Truth highlighted the two basic differences between white feminists and feminists of color which have persisted to the present day: the different way sexist subordination has been imposed[18] and class differences.[19] In the rest of this essay, I shall focus at length on the first difference and comment breifly on the second.

A. Differences in Gender Subordination: Rejection versus Seduction

"Ain't I a woman?"

The dual construction of female gender

If the definition of what a woman is, is differentially constructed for white women and women of color, and gender is the marking mechanism through which sexist subordination is imposed,[20] then the two groups of women must experience different forms of subordination. As Sojourner Truth pointed out, while white women were considered to be too fragile to cross puddles by themselves and required the best places everywhere because of their special status as weak creatures, black women were forced to plough and work side by side with black men. Yet both were considered women. Why this difference in the social construction of gender?

White women are persuaded to become the partners of white men for the purpose of biological reproduction and are seduced into acccepting their subservient role in meeting the needs of white men. In contrast, women of color who work outside the home are often indistinguishable from the unskilled male laborers who meet the economic needs of an industrialized society.[21] White men only notice the sex of women of color when it is necessary to reproduce workers or when they want sexual satisfaction without the emotional entanglements of, and the rituals that are required in, relationships with women of their own group.[22] Simultaneously, while women of color are *rejected*, white women are being persuaded to submit:

> . . . White women face the pitfall of being seduced into
> joining the oppressor under the pretense of sharing power.
> This possiblity does not exist in the same way for women
> of color. The tokenism that is sometimes extended to us is
> not an invitation to join power; our racial "otherness" is a
> visible reality that makes it quite clear. For white women
> there is a wider range of pretended choices and rewards for
> identifying with patriarchal power and its tools.[23]

White women who reject the rewards of seduction, however, may be severely punished. Those who dare to rebel are accused of not being "feminine"[24] and are stripped of their gender status by the "ultimate threat" of banishment to the restricted social space of lesbians.[25] White women have to be convinced to be white men's accomplices because as John Stuart Mill has observed,

> It was not sufficient for women to be slaves, they must be willing slaves, for the maintenance of patriarchal order depends upon the consensus of women. It depends upon women playing their part . . . voluntarily suppressing the evidence that exposes the false and arbitrary nature of man-made categories and the reality which is built on those categories.[26]

The dual conception of gender based on race--"white goddess/black she-devil, chaste virgin/nigger whore, the blonde blue-eyed doll/the exotic 'mulatto' object of sexual craving"--in many ways has freed women of color from the distraction of being offered the rewards of seduction in exchange for conforming to established gender role expectations.[27] Women of color have been *degenderized* by the dominant society where they "do not receive the respect and treatment--mollycoddling and condescending as it sometimes is--afforded to white women."[28] The worst jobs, often categorized as "unfit for women," are given to women of color who are considered the"mules of the world."[29]

> *These hands fight back. The police, a battering husband, white men who would rape us and the land we live on . . . We drive the trucks to the demonstrations, we tie the sashes of our children, dancing for the first time in the circle of the drum. We weave the blankets. We keep us culture . . . Our hands live and work in the present, while pulling on the past. It is impossible for us not to do both.[30]*

Identity invention versus reaffirmation of cultural roots

White feminists emphasize the process of *deindividuation* from authority figures in order to recover the ability to develop their own definition of what it means to be female.[31] Radical feminists who reject the patriarchical definition of gender have been absorbed with a woman-centered identity-building process. Deindividuation from the oppressor is very similar to the task of decolonization or regrouping that minority groups undertook in the 1960s.[32] In both instances, socially stigmatized groups reacquire their history and take previously denigrated characteristics and turn them into positive affirmations of self.[33] For example, radical feminists glorify menstrual blood as a symbol of women's capacity to give birth, while blacks use skin color in the slogan "Black is Beautiful" as their rallying cry.[34]

White women are at a greater disadvantage than other minorities in attempting to reacquire their identity--perhaps it is more accurate to say, in inventing their identity--because, unlike minorities who can refer to a specific event in history (e.g., slavery, military conquest) as the beginning of their subordination, women

> . . . have always been subordinated to men, and hence their dependency is not the result of a historical event or a social change--it was not something that occurred. The reason why otherness in this case seems to be an absolute is in part that it lacks the contingent or incidental nature of historical facts. A condition brought about at a certain time can be abolished at some other time, as the Negroes of Haiti and others have proved; but it might seem that a natural condition is beyond the possibility of change.[35]

Oppressed minorities in the United States "retained at least the memory of former days; they possessed in common a past, a tradition, sometimes a religion or culture."[36]

White women have had the arduous task of reacquiring themselves while simultaneously trying to define what it is they wanted to become, with no former template to follow. They were ill-prepared both academically and experientially to achieve the redefinition of gender in adulthood when patriarchical ideology was so deeply ingrained in them and they have had so little experience with political activism in general.[37] The existing academic paradigms, emanating from male culture and distorting women's experience, are virtually useless. With no academic, historical, or cultural path to follow, white women nevertheless undertook the task of redefining gender. It speaks well of white women that they have achieved such enormous success in building feminist theory and in obtaining concrete political results when they started literally with nothing more than an intuitive dissatisfaction with their subordination.[38]

As part of their subordination, white women have been denied equal participation in public discourse with white men. Ardener argues that white women are socialized in the "art of conversation" while men are trained in the more formal "art of rhetoric" or the "art of persuasion."[39] The unequal access to different modes of discourse gives white women no structured medium through which to voice and to define their oppression.[40] Freidan called this the "problem that has no name"[41] because what women were voicing "did not fit into the same categories as the problems which had already been given names (by males)."[42] In the 1960s, consciousness-raising groups were used not only to delineate women's concerns but to develop a discourse as well.[43]

In contrast, women of color have not been groomed to be the "parlor conversationalists" white women are expected to be. Working-class women of color, in particular, come from oppressed cultures which have been barred from the oral public discourse as well as from the written discourse of society at large. Minority people in the United States, therefore, have often excelled in verbal performance among their own peers. They have embraced speech as one of the few, if not the only, medium for expression. Older women are especially valued as story tellers who have the responsibility to preserve the history of the group from generation to generation.[44] The oral tradition, coupled with not having to meet white standards of feminine discourse, has freed women of color verbally. Women of color can be bawdy, rowdy, and irreverent, because, after all, they are the "she-devils" and "objects of sexual cravings." The only white women given such verbal freedom are glorified prostitutes. Women of color can be "mouthy" enough to voice unutterable truths to white males because what else can one expect from the whores/slaves/mules of the world?

The verbal ability of women of color is a form of power almost equal to masculine power. As Davis points out, only Sojourner Truth could single-handedly rescue the Akron Convention for women's suffrage from the sneers and jeers of hostile white men: "Of all the women attending the gathering, she alone was able to answer aggressively the male supremacist arguments of the boisterous provocateurs" because "there were very few women in those days who dared to 'speak in meeting'."[45] This incident poignantly underscores the fact that differential access to various forms of discourse paradoxically gave a black ex-slave woman an advantage over the educated, middle-class women in the meeting who stated, "She [Sojourner Truth] had taken us up in her strong arms and carried us safely over the slough of difficulty, turning the whole tide in our favor."[46] The masculine imagery in this statement further highlights how women of color have been degenderized from traditionally-conceived feminine roles.

*"Nobody ever helps me into carriages,
or over mud-puddles, or gives me any
best place!"*

The private versus the public sphere as the catalyst for political consciousness

White women gained gender consciousness by examining their personal lives. They realized that what happens in the intimacy of their own homes is exempt from the political forces that affect the rest of society.[47] Family life is supposed to be the safe haven where men retreat from the fierce competitive public world and receive love and nurturance from women. The cry of feminists has been "The personal is political." But the public/private distinction is an artificial one that allows men literally to have absolute power and no accountability for any abuses committed in the personal sphere. The private/public distinction also devalues "women's work" done in the home and arbitrarily assigns a higher status to work performed in the public sphere.[48]

Women of color, however, do not enjoy the economic conditions that allow the private/public distinction to be made. The state constantly intervenes in their private sphere, so that the racial/ethnic/gender consciousness of women of color grew from the awareness that the *public is political*.[49] When welfare agencies have life-and-death decision-making power over minority people's family life, when sterilization programs are targeted at minority populations, when the army is more likely to recruit minority men and more likely to send them to the front lines of whatever wars are in progress, then all of these and many other interventions make it clear that there is no such thing as a "private" sphere for people of color, most of whom are entirely at the mercy of the state.[50] Not only is the public political but the private sphere (whatever is left of it) must be placed on hold.

It is not surprising that there are tensions and differences between women of color and white women when their respective political consciousness has been generated by opposite forces. The concern of white feminists with physical appearance (such as weight in the form of bulimia and anorexia nervosa),[51] the division of household labor, and identity formation,[52] seem trivial or secondary to women of color. For example, Joseph quotes a black lesbian who said:

> There is no logical comparison between the oppression of Third World women on welfare and the suppression of the suburban wife and her protests about housework. This is exemplified in the situation of the welfare mother who does

not know where the next meal is coming from and the suburbanite who complains about preparing and serving meals.[53]

For many white women, the concerns of affirmative action for all people of color, activism against racism at home and abroad, school desegregation, prison reform, voter registration, union organization, all seem to hover too closely to *male-identified* causes. The solidarity between women and men of color seems incomprehensible from the white feminist perspective which views patriarchy as a system that confers equal privilege to all men by virtue of their gender. To most white feminists, the commitment of women of color to class and racial struggles has the semblance of "false consciousness" because, with the exception of socialist feminists and Marxist feminists, they believe that the most basic oppression is based on gender and not on race or class.

> *"I have ploughed and planted, and gathered into barns, and no man could head me! . . . I have borne thirteen children and seen them most all sold off to slavery . . . "*

Differences in social skills and political socialization

Oppressed through rejection, women of color are a marginal group in U.S. society from the time they are born. It is not a status conferred on them as they step outside the confines of the ascribed roles for women. As Audrey Lorde poignantly describes, women of color are hated from birth.[54] Their sheer presence is a reminder of much that is denigrated in this society--femaleness and darkness. The consciousness of being hated begins in childhood:

> I don't like to talk about hate. I don't like to remember the cancellation and hatred, heavy as my wished-for death, seen in the eyes of so many white people from the time I could see. It was echoed in newspapers and movies and holy pictures and comic books and Amos 'n' Andy radio programs. I had no tools to dissect it, no language to name it.

The AA subway train to Harlem. I clutch my mother's

sleeve, her arms full of shopping bags, christmas-heavy. The wet smell of winter clothes, the train's lurching. My mother spots an almost seat, pushes my little snowsuited body down. On one side of me a man reading a paper. On the other, a woman in a fur hat staring at me. Her mouth twitches as she stares and then her gaze drops down, pulling mine with it. Her leather-gloved hand plucks at the line where my new blue snowpants and her sleek fur coat meet. She jerks her coat closer to her. I look. I do not see whatever terrible thing she is seeing on the seat between us--probably a roach. But she has communicated her horror to me. It must be something very bad from the way she is looking, so I pull my snowsuit closer to me away from it, too. When I look up the woman is still staring at me, her nose holes and eyes huge. And suddenly I realize there is nothing crawling up the seat between us; it is me she doesn't want her coat to touch. The fur brushes past my face as she stands with a shudder and holds on to a strap in the speeding train. Born and bred a New York City child, I quickly slide over to make room for my mother to sit down. No word has been spoken. I'm afraid to say anything to my mother because I don't know what I've done. I look at the sides of my snowpants, secretly. Is there something on them? Something's going on here I do not understand, but I will never forget it. Her eyes. The flared nostrils. The hate.[55]

Experiences such as the above force women of color to acquire survival skills in childhood, sometimes at the tender age of five or six.[56] For example, many children of color have acted as the official translators for their monolingual relatives at the gas company, at the telephone company, and in disputes with bureaucrats unresponsive to poor, working-class people. The early interaction of women of color with the public has helped them to develop a public identity and public discourse and the political skills to fend off state intervention.[57] Women of color do not have to struggle to establish their ego boundaries because they have not been taken care of by an oppressive patriarchical system. Relatively few get a high school diploma, even fewer finish college, and only an infinitesimal number obtain graduate degrees.[58] Despite the odds against them, they are not ambivalent about getting an education, acquiring economic independence, and practicing their professions.[59]

Poverty had been feminized long before middle-class white women fell from grace as a result of the rising divorce rate. Women of color were born out of grace. Their deprived, marginal status has forced them to acquire survival skills which include developing informal networks of support,[60] alternative forms of health care,[61] and political activism. Those who are the products of the struggles of the 1960s enter the work force with a long history of student activism.[62]

Unlike women of color, white middle-class feminists often had guarded childhoods in which they were protected from the harshness of sexism, classism, and racism. Many white feminists did not acquire their gender consciousness until they were adults.[63] When white feminists and women of color unite for political action, the former's reactions to oppression frequently seem immature to the latter. White women often are surprised at the harshness with which the power structure responds to threat; they do not have well-developed defenses to fend off the attacks. Women of color, on the other hand, are not startled at all at the punitiveness of those who maintain the status quo. Women of color think to themselves, "If you only know the cruelty the oppressor is capable of inflicting! But if we tell you, you won't believe us, because you have to experience such brutality from birth to see clearly our scars."

In political action, white feminists tend either to follow the male blueprint they unconsciously acquired from their early socialization or they reject it totally. If they adopt the former approach, they are quite effective because they make use of the bureacratic language and socio-political rules that govern the power structure in this country.[64] Liberal feminists have had such a big impact at the macro-level for precisely this reason. Radical feminists, on the other hand, have followed the latter path and have been successful mainly at the micro-level by developing modes of decision-making which are not logic-driven or hierarchical in nature.

The political skills that women of color developed as they dealt with state intervention are neither the conventional masculine political skills that white liberal feminists have adopted nor the free-spirited approaches that radical feminists experiment with. Instead, women of color are trained through everyday battle with the state apparatus to be urban guerrillas.[65] As such, their fighting capabilities are not codified anywhere for others to learn from and are often not understood by white middle-class feminists. For example, many women of color treat anger as a weapon:[66] "My anger has meant pain to me but it has also meant survival, and before I give it up I'm going to be sure that there is something at least as powerful to replace it on the road to clarity."[67] Most white women, on the other hand, fear anger, because it is the mighty father unleashing his wrath:

> For women raised to fear, too often anger threatens
> annihilation. In the male construct of brute force, we were
> taught that our lives depended upon the good will of
> patriarchal power. The anger of others was to be avoided at
> all costs because there was nothing to be learned from it but
> pain, a judgment that we had been bad girls, come up
> lacking, not done what we were supposed to do. And if we
> accept our powerlessness, then of course any anger can
> destroy us.[68]

The automatic response of white women to anger is guilt--crippling guilt
which does not allow them to create or to function as free individuals. But for
women of color, "Guilt is not a response to anger; it is a response to one's own
actions or lack of action."[69] This difference is the source of much of the
conflict between white feminists and feminists of color:

> When women of color speak out of the anger that laces so
> many of our contacts with white women, we are often told
> that we are "creating a mood of hopelessness," "preventing
> white women from getting past guilt," or "standing in the
> way of trusting communication and action." . . . One
> woman wrote, "Because you are Black and Lesbian, you
> seem to speak with the moral authority of suffering." Yes I
> am Black and Lesbian, and what you hear in my voice is
> fury, not suffering. Anger, not moral authority. There is a
> difference.[70]

Another difference between white women and women of color is that
though the former have been socialized to be the nurturing caretakers of the
world, relatively few of them have had to cope with the loss of children.
Sojourner Truth's words, "I have borne thirteen children and seen them most all
sold off to slavery," have a contemporary ring to them. Substitute drugs,
prison, discrimination, poverty, or racism for slavery and women of color have
lost their children at alarming rates in contemporary U.S. society. It is the
immediate loss of children and the continuing threat to the survival of future
generations that often separates white feminist concerns from those of feminists
of color.

Some problems we share as women, some we do not. You

fear your children will grow up to join the patriarchy and
testify against you, we fear our children will be dragged from
a car and shot down in the street, and you will turn your
backs upon the reasons they are dying.[71]

The loss of children as well as the loss of human potential sustain the anger of
women of color at a pitch incomprehensible to white women:

Women of color in America have grown up within a
symphony of anger, at being silenced, at being unchosen, at
knowing that when we survive, it is in spite of a world that
takes for granted our lack of humanness, and which hates our
very existence outside of its service. And I say symphony
rather than cacophony because we have had to learn to
orchestrate those furies so that they do not tear us apart. We
have had to learn to move through them and use them for
strength and force and insight within our daily lives. Those
of us who did not learn this difficult lesson did not survive.
And part of my anger is always libation for my fallen
sisters.[72]

B. Freedom through Distance: Different Degrees of Intimacy with White Males

Being shut out of mainstream U.S. society, women of color do not
have the same relationship to authority figures and structures as white feminists
do. White midde-class feminists have been socialized to revere and support
authority figures, most of whom are male and some of whom are their fathers,
brothers, or husbands. The authority figures within white middle-class families
are the same authority figures venerated outside the family, and therefore the
stage is set for an almost unconscious loyalty to them. White feminists have
spent much of their energy trying to disengage themselves from seeking
patriarchal approval in order to feel that their existence is worthwhile. It is such
an invidious need and so deeply ingrained that even when there is an
intellectual committment to women's liberation, visceral responses are attuned
to what men think, specifically to what white males with status and power
think.

Most women of color, however, live in working-class environments
where many households are headed by women or by men who have authority

only within the family, and where a large proportion of the minority men have less education than their spouses or daughters or sisters. The authority figures who rule such families are not the same as the authority figures who rule U.S. society. The latter, particularly the policeman, the foreman, the lawyer, the physician, the teacher are often disdained, resented, and mistrusted. Hence, women of color are not wired to respond kindly to white male authority figures. When women of color become activists on behalf of women's liberation, they feel no ambivalence towards taking action against persons with whom few have had a personal relationship. They have not experienced any failed attempts to be a white authority figure's wife or lover. On the contrary, fully conscious of the sources of their oppression, they come to appreciate their fathers' strength and gain a deeper understanding of their failings.

Lesbians, too, have an easier time building solidarity with other women, especially other lesbians, because they have also rejected, at least in one sphere, intimacy with the defenders of the status quo. Lesbians are disengaged enough not to entertain the white men's ideas and feelings. For many white women, lesbianism is a political choice. This is not to say women of color are unaffected by the sexism of men of color. However, for most of them, the sexism within their own group is not what limits and subordinates them outside their still largely segregated communities.

Their degree of intimacy with white males has an impact not only on how white women experience subordination but also on the political actions they take to end it. Because seduction implies consent on the part of the seduced and benevolence on the part of the seducer, guilt is the natural outcome when the yoke of domination is broken by white women. White feminists have had to come to terms with the distracting "benefits" of being seduced into subordination. They are constantly reminded that women of color have far greater disadvantages and that if they do not conform to expected female norms, they too will suffer accordingly. When economic and social status can be obtained through marriage to white men, especially those in positions of power, then most white women would hesitate to lose this avenue for success through unacceptable behavior. As Lorde points out:

> Today, with the defeat of ERA, the tightening economy, and
> increased conservatism, it is easier once again for white
> women to believe the dangerous fantasy that if you are good
> enough, pretty enough, sweet enough, quiet enough, teach
> the children to behave, hate the right people, and marry the
> right men, then you will be allowed to co-exist with
> patriarchy in relative peace, at least until a man needs your

job or the neighborhood rapist happens along. And true, unless one lives and loves in the trenches it is difficult to remember that the war against dehumanization is ceaseless.[73]

White women, if they live with white men, enjoy no respite because they are under the direct duress of sexist subordination day and night. Working white women are especially at risk. They are fighting sexism in the trenches at work all day long, and when they come home they have to fight yet other forms of sexism. And, because they live dispersed among white males, they have no sanctuary where they can get together to interpret their daily experiences. Even in those instances when they can get together, they often find it difficult to cooperate because they grew up in a capitalist society which promotes competitiveness. To combat such situations, white feminists have concentrated on redefining the meaning of success for women, so that broader goals of community advancement and individual socioeconomic status attainment are deemed more important than gaining vicarious satisfaction through their husband's accomplishments or their children's success.

Oppression through rejection, however, creates a bond of solidarity among women of color.[74] They seldom have the carrot of marriage-to-white-men-in-power dangling in front of them to distract them. Consequently, they try to carve out an existence within the confines assigned to their group and to find refuge among others like themselves. Having their own group to retreat to, they can reaffirm their view of reality after interacting with the white power structure in the world of work. Such tightly knit groups of women periodically help each other to exorcise the pain they feel.[75] Because women of color, for the most part, do not know the intimate details of white men's lives, such "ignorance" allows them to engage in political action aimed at changing the socioeconimc conditions of society at large, rather than transforming just the personalities of individual white men.

Women of color are many-headed seers who can reveal different facets of our identities, depending on who we are interacting with.[76] And we have full knowledge that very few people will ever know all parts of ourselves. How many times do I remember my mother, my sister, my friend, my colleague, saying, *"Déjalo hablar"* [let him (the lover, the father, the brother, the white boss) talk/blab] and *then* we proceeded to do what we wanted to do and to believe what we wanted to believe. Women of color know how to use a wall of silence to retain our sense of identity and our view of the world--a wall that is impenetrable and which salvages our essence from destruction. As the slaves before us, we know when and how to yield in order to survive not only oppression but also the oppressor. When we are out of the presence of the oppressor, we celebrate our sense of self, we poke fun at and mimic him, and we restore the balance robbed from our souls.[77] Women of color do not have to compete with one another; instead we embrace each other to enable all of us to endure our daily injuries.

Conclusion

What, then, is the solution for bridging the differences between white women and women of color? Are we condemned to stand on the separate shores of understanding because neither group wants to take the responsibility for building the bridge of communication? Are we to have the same problems that men and women in general are having in constructing a language in common? I do not believe that has to be the case. If anything, the feminist struggle and the class and race struggles have taught both groups of women some important lessons, including the necessity to unify and to dismiss the kind of competition promoted by a patriarchal system.

There is an important study that illuminates the path of common understanding possible between different groups of women. Using longitudinal survey data, Gurin and Rubin found that white feminists who were conscious of racial inequities differed markedly from those who were critical only of gender disparity.[78] White feminists who were more aware of the oppressed status of blacks in U.S. society had had more interracial experience in both their work and home environments. I believe this study confirms what we as women have intuitively known for a while: for understanding to develop and for muted groups to be heard, the dominant group has to renounce its privileges.

I believe women of color have something to teach white women, if only the latter can set aside their own pain and preconceptions or erroneous notions of what it is to be female and of color in U.S. society. In a patriarchal society which functions on a system of hierarchy, oppression is very well defined. There is no doubt that a black lesbian, who does not meet society's stereotypical definition of femininity, has insights which are unavailable to a fair-skinned, heterosexual Chicana who is shaped like a Barbie doll. That is why Audrey Lorde's writing is so powerful. She has been corraled on the fringes of society and has survived to share with us her wonderful, painful, and empowering insights. She is a survivor who refuses to conform at any level. But there are very few survivors, and even fewer who are strong enough to tell about their ordeals. Yet, if we shut someone like Lorde out because she is "too angry," "too unfeminine," "too lesbian," or too far removed from our conception of reality, then are we really interested in changing society? If we are committed to changing the basis of all oppression, we have to question everything, including ourselves. If we want to redistribute privilege in a more egalitarian way, it means we have to give up our own individual gains wrested from the crumbs the oppressor throws at the oppressed. If the women's movement is to grow, thrive, and last, differences among women cannot be ignored, because it is precisely on an understanding of these differences that the women's movement in the United States and in the world must be built.

Notes

1.   Phyllis Marynick Palmer, "White Women/ Black Women: The Dualism of Female Identity and Experience in the United States," *Feminist Studies* 9, no. 1 (1983): 151-76.

2.   Beatriz Pesquera, "Work and Family: A Comparative Analysis of Professional, Clerical, and Blue-collar Chicana Workers" (Ph.D. diss., University of California, Berkeley, 1985); Denise Ann Segura, "Chicanas and Mexican Immigrant Women in the Labor Market: A Study of Occupational Mobility and Stratification" (Ph.D. diss., University of California, Berkeley, 1986).

3.   Women worldwide share commonalities; however, there are very important cultural and economic differences which should not be ignored. I focus on the writing of women in the U.S. in order to understand the differences between white women and women of color in this country. What the implications of my analysis are for women elsewhere is for them to decide.

4.   Simone de Beauvoir, *The Second Sex* (New York: Random House, 1952); Audrey Lorde, *Sister Outsider* (Trumansburg, N.Y.: The Crossing Press, 1984).

5.   Gloria Joseph and Jill Lewis, *Common Differences: Conflicts in Black and White Feminists' Perspectives*, ed. Jill Lewis (New York: Anchor Press, 1981).

6.   Florynce Kennedy, "Institutionalized Oppression vs. the Female," *Sisterhood is Powerful*, ed. R. Morgan (New York: Vintage Books, 1970), 438-46; Toni Morrison, "What the Black Woman Thinks about Women's Lib," *New York Times Magazine,* 22 August 1971; Gloria Joseph, "The Incompatible Menage a Trois: Marxism, Feminism, and Racism," *Women and Revolution*, ed. Lydia L. Sargent (Boston: South End Press, 1981); Lorde, *Sister Outsider;* Bell Hooks, *Feminist Theory from Margin to Center* (Boston: South End Press, 1984).

7.	Joseph, "Incompatible Menage a Trois"; Adrienne Rich, *Of Lies, Secrets and Silence: Selected Prose, 1966-1978* (New York: W.W. Norton and Co., Inc., 1979).

8.	Angela Davis, *Women, Race, and Class* (New York: Vintage Books, 1983).

9.	Joseph and Lewis, *Common Differences.*

10.	Alison M. Jaggar, *Feminist Politics and Human Nature* (Totowa, N.J.: Rowan & Allanheld Publishers, 1983), 95. I find Jaggar's scheme for feminist writings helpful, although I agree with her assessment that it is not definitive because of the natural evolution of feminist theory generally and in response to changing social realities particularly.

11.	Ibid., 95.

12.	Barbara Burris, "The Fourth World Manifesto," *Radical Feminism,* ed. Ellen Levine and Anita Rapone (New York: Quadrangle Books, 1973), pp 337-38.

13.	Jaggar, *Feminist Politics,* 124.

14.	Ibid., 132.

15.	Ibid., 11; One of the reasons for black women's lack of participation in the radical feminist movement may be that "radical feminism . . . was sparked by the special experiences of a relatively small group of predominantly white, middle-class, college-educated, American women in the later 1960s . . . Today, those who are attracted to radical feminism still tend to be primarily white and college-educated" (Ibid., 83-84).

16.	Ibid., 11.

17.	Davis, *Women, Race and Class.*

18.	Lorde, *Sister Outsider;* Hooks, *Feminist Theory.*

19.	de Beauvoir, *The Second Sex.*

20.   Candace West and Don Zimmerman, "Doing Gender," *Gender and Society* 1 (June 1987).

21.   Gloria Joseph, "White Promotion, Black Survival," *Common Differences;* Tomás Ybarra-Fraustro, "When Cultures Meet: Integration or Desintegration?" Stanford University, Unpublished ms., 1986; Lorde, *Sister Outsider.*

22.   Rich, *Lies, Secrets and Silence;* Hooks, *Feminist Theory.* Limitations of space preclude a discussion of the relationship between women of color and men of color. Female scholars of color have started to portray eloquently the solidarity as well as conflict between minority women and minority men. For especially insightful data and analysis on Chicanas, see Pesquera, "Work and Family," Segura, "Chicanas and Mexican Immigrant Women," and Patricia Zavella, *Women's Work and Chicano Families: Cannery Workers of the Santa Clara Valley* (Ithaca: Cornell University Press, 1987). Suffice it to say that men of color are also influenced by the different conceptions of gender which depict women of color as "less feminine" and "less desirable" than white women (Joseph, "White Promotion,"; Hooks, *Feminist Theory).* This is a form of internalized oppression that different segments of minority groups have to deal with--one which I believe has been belabored in the last twenty years. It must ultimately be resolved by men of color rather than by women of color. A. Memmi, *The Colonizer and the Colonized* (New York: The Orient Press, 1965); Eldrige Cleaver, *Soul on Ice* (New York: McGraw Hill, 1968).

23.   Lorde, *Sister Outsider*, 118-19.

24.   Dale Spender, *Man Made Language* (London: Routledge and Kegan Paul, 1980), 94-95.

25.   Lorde, *Sister Outsider*, 121.

26.   Spender, *Man Made Language*, 101-2.

27.   Rich, *Lies, Secrets and Silence;* Hooks, *Feminist Theory.*

28.   Joseph, "White Promotion," 27. This is Joseph's analysis of the position of black women, but I believe it applies to all women of color in the United States.

180

29.   Zora Neale Hurston, *Dust Tracks on a Road* (New York: Arno Press, 1969).

30.   Beth Brant, ed., *A Gathering of Spirit: Writing and Art by North American Indian Women* (Montpelier, Vt.: Sinister Wisdom Books, 1984), 14.

31.   Nancy Chodorow, *The Reproduction of Mothering: Psychoanalysis and the Sociology of Gender* (Berkeley and Los Angeles: University of California Press, 1978); Nancy Friday, *My Mother/My Self: The Daughter's Search for Identity* (New York: Delacorte Press, 1977).

32.   Erika Apfelbaum, "Relations of Domination and Movements for Liberation: An Analysis of Power between Groups," *The Social Psychology of Intergroup Relations*, ed. W. G. Austin and S. Worchel (Monterey, Calif.: Brooks/Cole Publishing Company, 1979).

33.   H. Tajfel, "Social Identity and Intergroup Behavior," *Social Science Information* 13 (1974): 65-93; Apfelbaum, "Relations of Domination."

34.   Jaggar, *Feminist Politics*.

35.   de Beauvoir, *The Second Sex*, xxi.

36.   Ibid.

37.   Hooks, *Feminist Theory*.

38.   Betty Freidan, *The Feminine Mystique* (New York: Penguin Books, 1963).

39.   Shirley Ardener, *Perceiving Women* (New York: John Wiley, 1975).

40.   Spender, *Man Made Language*.

41.   Freidan, *The Feminine Mystique*.

42.   Rowbotham, *Woman's Consciousness*.

43.   Spender, *Man Made Language*.

44. Ybarra-Fraustro, "When Cultures Meet."

45. Davis, *Women, Race, and Class.*

46. Cady Elizabeth Stanton, Susan B. Anthony, Matilda Joslyn Gage, *History of Woman Suffrage, Vol. 1 (1848-1861)* (New York: Fowler and Wells, 1881).

47. Freidan, *The Feminine Mystique.*

48. Joseph and Lewis, *Common Differences.*

49. Candace West crystallized my understanding of this difference.

50. Joseph, "White Promotion."

51. Susie Orbach, *Fat is a Feminist Issue* (New York: Paddington Press, 1978).

52. Chodorow, *The Reproduction of Mothering;* Spender, *Man Made Language.*

53. Joseph, "White Promotion," 22.

54. Lorde, *Sister Outsider.*

55. Ibid., 147-48.

56. Cherrie Moraga and Gloria Anzaldua, eds, *This Bridge Called My Back: Writings by Radical Women of Color* (Watertown, Mass: Persephone Press, 1981; Joseph, "White Promotion."

57. Spender, *Man Made Language.*

58. Segura, "Chicanas and Mexican Immigrant Women."

59. Pesquera, "Work and Family."

60. Hooks, *Feminist Theory.*

61.   Robert T. Trotter III and Juan Antonio Chavira, *Curanderismo: Mexican American Folk Healing* (Athens, Ga.: University of Georgia Press, 1981); Aida Hurtado, "Preliminary Study of Midwife Practices in Hidalgo County, Texas: A Needs Assessment for a Midwife Training Program," Unpublished ms.

62.   Pesquera, "Work and Family."

63.   Freidan, *The Feminine Mystique.*

64.   Spender, *Man Made Language.*

65.   Moraga and Anzaldua, *This Bridge Called My Back.*

66.   Lorde, *Sister Outsider;* Hooks, *Feminist Theory;* Moraga and Anzaldua, *This Bridge Called My Back.*

67.   Lorde, *Sister Outsider*, 132.

68.   Ibid., 131.

69.   Ibid., 130.

70.   Ibid., 131-32.

71.   Ibid., 119.

72.   Ibid., 129.

73.   Ibid., 119.

74.   Lorde, *Sister Outsider;* Hooks, *Feminist Theory;* Brant, *A Gathering of Spirit.*

75.   Brant, *A Gathering of Spirit.*

76.   Ibid.

77.   Ibid.

78.   Patricia Gurin and Mary Rubin, "Building Bridges: White Feminists Consider Racism and Poverty," Unpublished ms., 1985.

184

References

Acuña, Rodolfo. *Occupied America: a History of Chicanos*. 2nd. ed. New York: Harper and Row, 1981.

Ardener, Shirley. *Perceiving Women*. New York: John Wiley, 1975.

Apfelbaum, E. "Relations of Domination and Movements for Liberation: An Analysis of Power between Groups." *The Social Psychology of Intergroup Relations*. Edited by W. G. Austin and S. Worchel. Monterey, Calif.: Brooks/Cole Publishing Company, 1979.

Barrera, M. *Race and Class in the Southwest: A Theory of Racial Inequality*. Notre Dame: University of Notre Dame Press, 1979.

Brant, Beth, ed. *A Gathering of Spirit: Writing and Art by North American Indian Women*. Montpelier, Vt.: Sinister Wisdom Books, 1984.

Burris, Barbara. "The Fourth World Manifesto." *Radical Feminism*. Edited by Ellen Levine and Anita Rapone. New York: Quadrangle Books, 1973.

Chodorow, Nancy. *The Reproduction of Mothering: Psychoanalysis and the Sociology of Gender*. Berkeley and Los Angeles: University of California Press, 1978.

Cleaver, Eldrige. *Soul on Ice*. New York: McGraw-Hill, 1968.

Davis, Angela. *Women, Race, and Class*. New York: Vintage Books, 1983.

de Beauvoir, Simone. *The Second Sex*. New York: Random House, 1952.

Friday, Nancy. *My Mother/My Self: The Daughter's Search for Identity*. New York: Dell Books, 1981.

Freidan, Betty. *The Feminine Mystique*. New York: Penguin Books, 1963.

Hooks, Bell. *Feminist Theory from Margin to Center.* Boston: South End Press, 1984.

Hurston, Zora Neale. *Dust Tracks on a Road.* New York: Arno Press, 1969.

Hurtado, Aida. "Preliminary Study of Midwife Practices in Hidalgo County, Texas: A Needs Assessment for a Midwife Training Program." Unpublished ms.

Jaggar, Alison M. *Feminist Politics and Human Nature.* Totowa, N.J.: Rowan & Allanheld Publishers, 1983.

Joseph, Gloria. "The Incompatible Menage a Trois: Marxism, Feminism, and Racism." *Women and Revolution.* Edited by Lydia L. Sargent. Boston: South End Press, 1981.

-----. "White Promotion, Black Survival." *Common Differences: Conflicts in Black and White Feminists' Perspectives.* Edited by Jill Lewis. New York: Anchor Press, 1981.

Joseph, Gloria and Lewis, Jill. *Common Differences: Conflicts in Black and White Feminists' Perspectives.* Edited by Jill Lewis. New York: Anchor Press, 1981.

Kennedy, Florynce. "Institutionalized Oppression vs. the Female." *Sisterhood is Powerful.* Edited by R. Morgan. New York: Vintage Books, 1970.

Lorde, Audrey. *Sister Outsider.* Trumansburg, N.Y.: The Crossing Press, 1984.

Memmi, A. *The Colonizer and the Colonized.* New York: The Orient Press, 1965.

Morrison, Toni. "What the Black Woman Thinks about Women's Lib." *New York Times Magazine,* 22 August 1971.

Orbach, Susie. *Fat is a Feminist Issue.* New York: Paddington Press, 1978.

Pesquera, Beatriz. "Work and Family: A Comparative Analysis of Professional, Clerical, and Blue-collar Chicana Workers." Ph.D. dissertation, University of

California, Berkeley, 1985.

Rich, Adrienne. *Of Lies, Secrets and Silence: Selected Prose, 1966-1978*. New York: W.W. Norton and Co., Inc., 1979.

Rowbotham, Sheila. *Woman's Consciousness: Man's World*. New York: Penguin Books, 1973.

Shanley, Kate. "Thoughts on Indian Feminism." *A Gathering of Spirit: Writing and Art by North American Indian Women*. Edited by Beth Brant. Montpelier, Vt.: Sinister Wisdom, 1984.

Showalter, Elaine. *A Literature of their Own: British Women Novelists from Bronte to Lessing*. Princeton: Princeton University Press, 1977.

Segura, Denise Ann. "Chicanas and Mexican Immigrant Women in the Labor Market: A Study of Occupational Mobility and Stratification." Ph.D. dissertation, University of California, Berkeley, 1986.

Spender, Dale. *Man Made Language*. London: Routledge and Kegan Paul, 1980.

Stanton, Cady Elizabeth; Anthony, Susan B.; and Gage, Matilda Joslyn. 2nd. ed. 1889. *History of Woman Suffrage, (1848-1861)*. Vol. 1 of 4. New York: Fowler and Wells, 1881.

Tajfel, H. "Social Identity and Intergroup Behavior." *Social Science Information* 13 (1974).

Trotter III, Robert T., and Chavira, Juan Antonio. *Curanderismo, Mexican American Folk Healing*. Athens, Ga.: University of Georgia Press, 1981.

West, Candace, and Zimmerman, Don. "Doing Gender." *Gender and Society* 1 (1987).

Zavella, Patricia. *Women's Work and Chicano Families: Cannery Workers of the Santa Clara Valley*. Ithaca: Cornell University Press, 1987.

Challenge and Counter-Challenge:
Chicana Literary Motifs

Alvina E. Quintana

Many feminist scholars argue that the problem with feminist theory today is that it focuses primarily on the differences between men and women, rather than on the differences among women. As the feminist preoccupation with male/female differences develops and expands, the gap between Anglo feminists and feminists of color widens. Although much of feminist thought claims to encompass diverse perspectives and to speak of universals, many women of color believe that feminist discourse is, in fact, only white in perspective, with little concern for issues of ethnicity, culture, and class. Marilyn Strathern contends that feminists are in constant debate:

> The fact of debate maintains a connection between them. It looks as though we have an impossible array of theoretical positions: 'here we are speaking in many voices' [Haraway 1981:481]. But it is a phenomenon of feminism that the positions are held, often very explicitly, in relation to one another.[1]

In light of the diversity of feminist theorists writing today, Strathern's point is well taken, but how does it apply to women of color, who (in most cases) do not write theory?

Language has been dominated by male discourse and ideology, and therefore, it reflects the influence that men have over the roles and status of both women and men in our society. In an effort to rectify this imbalance, feminist theorists have appropriately begun to develop a discourse that addresses issues related to the subordination and control of women. Since the voices of women of color are generally not represented in this "array of theoretical positions," they, as a group with their own particular issues and concerns, become the suppressed text[2] and remain on the margins of feminist discourse.

The experience of being marginal is nothing new to Chicanos and Chicanas. The sociological concept of the "marginal person" categorizes a person caught between two cultures, such as the Mexican American.[3] For a Chicana, marginality is more complex because she not only experiences a conflict between the competing values of Mexican and American cultures, but she often also feels ambivalent towards ethnicity and gender in general. It is precisely this ambivalence, this tension between race and self, that has contributed to Chicana apathy towards the women's movement and feminist theory. Strathern's essay on the relationship between feminism and anthropology discusses the tension between these two fields created by the challenge and counter-challenge implicit in their approaches to knowledge. I shall carry Strathern's discussion a little further, in the spirit of the Ortner and Rosaldo studies,[4] and look at the issue of challenge and counter-challenge between Anglo and Chicana feminist thought. In particular, I shall focus on some of the differences among women.

Because of the absence of theoretical writings about Chicanas, it is necessary to examine other forms of writing as theory.[5] For Chicanas, literature provides a medium in which to voice female concerns, much as the dominant ideology of the United States provides the medium for male discourse.[6] As Adrienne Rich points out:

> A radical critique of literature, feminist in its impulse,
> would take the work first of all as a clue to how we live,
> how we have been living, how we have been led to imagine
> ourselves, how our language has trapped as well as liberated
> us; and how we can begin to see--and therefore live--afresh.[7]

One of the problems with feminist theory today is that many theorists have fallen prey to the notion that science and art are separate. When feminist theorists move away from their dualistic way of compartmentalizing literature as false and abstract theories as true, and instead, examine more closely the relationship between literature and theory, they will open the doors to more comprehensive theorizing about cultures and individuals. Susan Krieger's ideas regarding social scientists' methods are interesting:

> Our models are not only abstract, but also out of touch. I
> think that descriptive explanations, with their primary
> faithfulness to data and detail, are one way to break out of
> this pattern, to show more of what is "really" going on.
> They require a combination of the novelist's and the social

scientist's mind: a willingness to construct a representation
as a novelist might, yet at the same time a desire to think
like a social scientist.[8]

Krieger is calling for an interdisciplinary emphasis. Knowledge should be applied across the disciplines, intertwined and woven into life experiences, if it is ever to move beyond intellectual calisthenics or amount to more than compartmentalized, bite-sized bits of information for the exclusive consumptiom of a particular academic audience.

Krieger's concerns regarding the standard approach to theory are not new by any means; they merely represent yet another voice in what has been an on-going debate over the value of scientific observation versus the value of descriptive interpretation. Although Clifford Geertz's work on the interpretation of cultures effectively excludes any discussion or consideration of women, with a few minor modifications his discussion can be used to support Krieger's position, since he does provide a convincing and eloquent argument for using "thick description" to move anthropology beyond subjective abstract data and analysis to the type of semiotic interpretation employed by literary critics. Terry Eagleton is another critic who has contributed to this discussion on the relationship between science and art:

Science gives us conceptual knowledge of a situation, art
gives us the experience of that situation, which is equivalent
to ideology. But by doing this, it allows us to "see" the
nature of that ideology, and thus begins to move us towards
that full understanding of ideology which is scientific
knowledge.[9]

Studying the social sciences and literature (actual human behavior and symbolic representation) together sets the stage for more inclusive theorizing, which will eventually eliminate the ineffective, outdated, and, above all, inaccurate analysis which holds women hostage today. Women's literature provides the voices to express, and the rituals to enact, the experience of growing up female. Chicana writers, like ethnographers, focus on microcosms within a culture, unpacking rituals in the context of inherited symbolic and social structures of subjugation. These writers are acting as their own ethnographers, using the word for self-representation.

Self-representation provides an indispensable mechanism for deconstructing the Chicana cultural experience, because it effectively eliminates the possibility of outsiders misinterpreting cultural symbolic systems and allows the Chicana to express her own ambivalence towards her ethnicity and gender. In this way, marginal individuals become the subjects of their own discourse. Once a female child is born to Mexican parents living in the United States, she is more than just her parents' daughter; she, like other female babies, is her *mother's* daughter. Gender determines how this child will be socialized. At the same time, when females are born into this world they are not just their mother's daughters: they are more accurately the daughters of the ideology of their times.[10] They are Mexicans first, and individuals second--female manchilds of the world in which they live, destined to search for identification and meaning because of their gender. Freud asked "What do women want?" Women continue to ask in various ways, "Who are we?" Women exist in a vacuum within a male-defined world, but as they grow and question, their consciousness changes. New questions arise, and new developments occur, every time the familiar question regarding identity resurfaces. In universities, through feminist and other scholarly theories, women learn that they are historical creatures.[11] This realization should not be dismissed as insignificant or obvious, for once women examine their historicity in terms of the fashioning of a specific identity, they are well on the way to challenging the limitations that have maintained their subordinate status.

Chicana literature, when viewed, in the Jamesonian sense, as an ideological production mirroring the Chicana collective mind and confronting the cultural limitations placed on women by history, provides an essential key to unlocking the mysteries surrounding the Chicana experience and builds the necessary foundation to bridge the political gap between mainstream and marginal feminist theory. In this sense, the literature can be viewed as an allegory of the social dilemma Chicanas face regarding race and gender. Chicana literary voices resemble the feminist voices of their Anglo-American counterparts in that their political perspectives often appear to be, in Marilyn Strathern's words, "in constant debate." To understand the relationship among these seemingly different Chicana positions, it is necessary to look first at the literature as an apparatus in itself.

The Chicana literary text is analagous to a musical fugue because of its use of the polyphonic vocal principle of separate voices maintaining unified integrity throughout the musical (or literary) composition.

> A fugue begins with a theme, or "subject," on which each voice enters in turn, as if 'imitating' the preceding one. Each voice follows the subject with a "countersubject." The opening, called the "exposition," introduces the main material and all the voices. Then comes a "development," in which there are many "episodes," introducing new material,

playing the voices against each other in various combinations, transforming the themes rhythmically and harmonically, taking the music far from the opening key or tonality.[12]

The Chicana literary text opens in an apologetic chord, relying heavily on the pitch set by cultural or religious ideologies. Once this tonality has been established, setting the mood as it questions and clearly outlines how Chicanas position and identify themselves in cultural terms, it is followed by the counterpoint of the voices of rage and opposition. An exchange of these two modes introduces new material which transforms the original theme, moving Chicana discourse along in search of a knowledge of "self" in oppositional terms. Once the oppositional tone has been established, new themes emerge which change the tone yet again, as the literature of struggle and identification adapts to variation and looks at the contemporary Chicana from different angles as a "woman" in her own right, a woman at the center. But the rhythms and counter-rhythms do not stop here; rather they grow and move, dialectically, into the self-critical terrain of the literature of new-vision.[13] This final mode, which focuses on broader issues concerning the survival of the species and of culture, as well as on issues related to a concept I shall call the "universal woman," is not final in the sense of closure; it simply represents another layer in the quest for critical understanding. The literature at this stage is self-conscious and self-critical, oftentimes providing more questions than answers, thus taking on a hermeneutic quality as it draws from and parodies the earlier modes in the literary discourse. The stage of "new-vision" functions as the opening or springboard of another, more global, discussion of the gender-race dichotomy, as it attempts to make sense of the Chicana's need for cultural and feminist identification.

"Universal woman" is a notion I extract from Helene Cixous' essay, "The Laugh of the Medusa," in which she speaks of the need for women to develop a discourse: "Woman must put herself into the text--as into the world and into history--by her own movement."

I've seen them, those who will be neither dupe nor domestic, those who will not fear the risk of being a woman; will not fear any risk, any desire, any space still unexplored in themselves, among themselves and others or anywhere else. They do not fetishize, they do not deny, they do not hate. They observe, they approach, they try to see the other woman, the child, the lover--not to strengthen their own narcissism or verify the solidity or weakness of the master, but to make love better, to invent.[14]

On a political and philosophical level, this passage addresses the issues with which many women of color have repeatedly been concerned. For the most part, Chicanas have criticized the tendency to improve oneself by denigrating others. Cixous' discussion outlines an all-embracing approach to issues involving sexism. Her utopian vision moves all women towards a universal concept of womanhood. It exemplifies a consciousness to which many women aspire, but at the same time, by failing to acknowledge race as a variable, it excludes a significant number of women. Her efforts thus represent a step towards a final resolution of the confict between white women and women of color because of its paradoxical nature. But unfortunately, the kind of movement or consciousness Cixous suggests can only be achieved after women begin to look at the implicit paradox in her argument. We cannot speak in universals until we first acknowledge our differences. The problems she raises are therefore essential, in the final analysis, to the development of a more global type of feminist discourse.

I have listed the literature of Chicanas that resonates with Cixous' utopian perspective under the new-vision phase, since it moves beyond culturally-bound analyses to more transformative, universal issues dealing with the subordination of women in general. My concern is with how meaning is produced in Chicana literature: how do the stories and poetry of Chicana writers develop a new framework within which to view women? Does Chicana literature present a new view? And if so, is it the kind of view Annette Kuhn calls cultural intervention, because it subverts and challenges the masculine and the feminist "mainstream text"?[15]

Tomás Ybarra has divided the Chicano literary process into three stages: a) genesis, b)subversion, and c) regeneration. The four modes of Chicana literature I have delineated--apology, rage and opposition, struggle and identification, and new-vision--differ from Ybarra's because they do not represent a linear/historical reading of the literary text. His final stage does, however, include what he calls the evolution of Chicana feminist thought based on the politics of language and colonization. Only in the late 1970s and early 1980s did women's views begin to appear *en masse* in the literature on the politics of language and colonization. The provocative question regarding this stage, or rather, this historical moment, concerns the relationship between literary form and modes of production, because as Fred Jameson has argued, "aesthetic objects can only come into existence through a process of alienation and estrangement within human society."[16]

The literature of apology is liberal in the sense that it argues that women were held back from developing to their full potential by traditions and cultural values. Although Ybarra has included the literature of this interval in his final regenerative stage, it is more accurately described by the term reappropriation, since it concerns a reclamation of history, as opposed to a rebirthing of a literature that has been virtually non-existent. Contemporary Chicana writings represent a significant feminist reappropriation of history as they subvert the Chicano historical text through justifications or radical explanations. Literature in this mode underscores the linguistic subordination of Chicanas. By accepting the need to assimilate through suppressing their own language and culture, Chicanas have been subordinated.[17]

This realization is expressed in Lorna Dee Cervantes' poem, "Refugee Ship":

> Like wet cornstarch, I slide
> past my grandmother's eyes. Bible
> at her side, she removes her glasses.
> The pudding thickens.
>
> Mama raised me without language.
> I'm orphaned from my Spanish name.
> The words are foreign, stumbling
> on my tongue. I see in the mirror
> my reflection: bronzed skin, black hair.
>
> I feel I am a captive
> aboard the refugee ship.
> The ship that will never dock.[18]

Cervantes describes the alienation process, which begins with her feelings of isolation due to being "orphaned from [her] Spanish name," a process that ultimately robs many Chicanos of a crucial part of their identity, reducing the language of a people to foreign words, "stumbling on my tongue."[19] The literature of apology attempts to demolish myths and dominant codes in order to liberate women. Once the theme has been set, as in the musical fugue, additional voices enter, resonating with the initial theme as well as introducing different, sharper intervals or counter-rhythms by constructing new definitions of womanhood, and reinterpreting the history which has held women captive. Chicanas now challenge openly the virgin/whore dichotomy imposed by the male interpretation of ideology, history, and language. Sylvia Gonzales attacks the pervasive quality of masculine historical discourse in her poem "Chicana Evolution":

I am Chicana
But while you developed
in the womb,
I was raped again.
I am Chicana
In a holocaust of sperm,
bitter fragments of fertilization
mankind's victim,
humankind's burden.[20]

In language that directly associates men with genocide, "Chicana Evolution" alludes to the "original sin"--the rape of the Chicana archetypal mother, la Malinche, who is considered a traitor to Mexico in the male interpretation of history. The poem also challenges masculine cultural imperialism and its by-product, the Chicana legacy of betrayal. The literature of apology is filled with this kind of feminist reappropriation of historical figures which have dominated masculine discourse.

The literature of rage and opposition is characterized by its confident bold tone, no longer apologizing or rationalizing away women's inequality, but rather, challenging and demanding equal rights for women. The ideals of this radical feminism correspond with the emphasis of the new left Alison Jaggar describes in *Feminist Politics and Human Nature*.[21] Numerous Chicanas have passionately denounced the Chicano's use of *la mujer*, and even the *movimiento*, for his own ends. This literature reflects the rage Chicanas feel about the sexual domination and exploitation of women in the name of tradition. Lorna Dee Cervantes decries the way *Raza* rhetoric has glossed over this fact:

"You Cramp My Style, Baby"

You cramp my style, baby
when you roll on top of me
shouting "Viva La Raza"
at the top of your prick.

You want me como un taco,
dripping grease,
or squeezing maza through my legs,
making tamales for you out of my daughters.
You "mija"
"mija" "mija" me

until I can scream

and then you tell me,
"Esa, I LOVE
this revolution!
Come on Malinche,
gimme some more!"[22]

The Chicanas producing the literature of rage and opposition are revolutionaries who use their sharp words to confront rather than encircle issues of female exploitation. Their writings renounce and overthrow masculine domination in order to move the Chicana from subjugation to liberation. Although the Chicana has experienced economic, social, and racial oppression, the literature of rage and opposition concerns itself almost exclusively with sexual oppression.

Cherrie Moraga is a writer and social activist, whose writing falls well within the mode of rage and opposition. Her work (essays, poems, and short stories) has a cutting edge, as it openly questions the role of men in Chicano culture. Her essay, "Lo Que Nunca Paso Por Sus Labios," reads like a radical feminist manifesto, since all the radical feminist concepts are highlighted in her discourse. She writes of the institution of heterosexuality and its side effect, heterosexism. Although her work is primarily concerned with sexuality in its radical feminst form, it is fresh because she adds new dimensions of ethnicity and culture:

> Women of color have always known, although we have not
> always wanted to look at it, that our sexuality is not merely
> a physical response or drive, but holds a crucial relationship
> to our entire spiritual capacity. Patriarchal religions--whether
> brought to us by the colonizer's cross and gun or emerging
> from our own people--have always known this. Why else
> would the female body be so associated with sin and
> disobedience? Simply put, if the spirit and sex have been
> linked in our oppression, then they must also be linked in
> the strategy toward our liberation.[23]

Moraga's work should be recognized as an important, provocative contribution to feminist literature in general, and specifically as an important contribution to Chicana literature, because it makes a serious attempt to free Chicanas from the phallo-centric literature of the 1960s. Her work ruptures some of the myths and taboos that up until recently have remained unchallenged and tucked away under a very intricate cultural cloak. Cherrie Moraga's writings place her in the front ranks of other radical writers because she writes of protest and liberation. She uses her skill with language to help bridge the gap between the literature of apology and the literature of struggle and identification. As Terry Eagleton points out:

> Literary works are not mysteriously inspired, or explicable simply in terms of their author's psychology. They are forms of perception, particular ways of seeing the world; and as such they have a relation to that dominant way of seeing the world which is the social mentality or ideology of an age.[24]

The literature of struggle and identification carries forth the political implications of Marxist theory. In this mode, the writers are concerned with bringing women to the forefront. They are not preoccupied with the definition by negation of the literature of apology nor the definition by reversal of the literature of opposition; rather they focus on women as productive, self-sufficient, and complex human beings in their own right.

Gina Valdes' *There are no Madmen Here* offers a wonderful example of the kind of literature that focuses on women as resourceful human beings. Her story is about the life of Maria Portillo, who is introduced as a stereotypical married Mexican woman, exploited by her husband, living a life of loneliness, insecurity, and frustration in her traditional role of wife and mother. Maria has feelings and emotions that often leave her questioning:

> She had not done what she wanted for so long that she was not sure of what she really wanted, but she knew that it was something other, better than what she had. She felt tired of thinking, of looking for work, of not finding it, of trying to figure out her husband's moods and whereabouts, of waiting for him. At night, lying on the edge of the double bed, she often felt alone, more so than when she had been a single woman.[25]

Maria finds herself caught in a dilemma of either playing her traditional role, feeling lonely and unfulfilled, or pulling out, taking control of her own life, and raising her children without the help of her husband. She decides to take her life into her own hands by leaving Mexico and moving to the United States with her three daughters. The novel makes a strong statement about the will and determination of this mother as she confronts all the frustrations of a foreign country and alien tongue. It is a story about oppression and Maria's struggle for survival, but in a larger perspective, it is a story about the marginalization of a people. Valdes also develops a subversive subtext that emphasizes the tension between tradition and modernity that many Third World novelists have grappled with.[26] Maria watches as her family begins to sway between cultures. Valdes poses a riddle that focuses the issue:

> "Did you hear what she said? She's ten years old and she can't speak English." "Why should I speak English? I'm Mexican." "You live in the United States, you should speak English." "I don't live here, I'm visiting." "Visiting? You've been visiting for three years." "At least I speak English better than you speak Spanish. What kind of Mexican are you?" "I'm not Mexican, I'm American, and so are you, we were born here." Maria saw her young niece running to her mother. "Mama! Louie says that I'm American because I was born here. Is that true?" "Tell me, mihijita, if the kittens are born in the oven, are they kittens? Or are they biscuits?"[27]

Madmen focuses on Maria as head of household, managing her life, working so that her daughters will have a better life. In one sense, this is a success story, as Maria abandons her role of subordinate wife when she leaves her husband. But on another level, Maria's liberation leaves a lot to be desired, because as she soon discovers in the United States, she will always be subordinated because of her race, class, and gender. Maria takes a job in a sewing factory but finds it necessary to supplement her income by working in the family tequila-smuggling business. The author makes an effective commentary on the exploitation inherent in the segmented labor market in this country, as well as on the oppression brought about by organized religion. Maria has escaped one man but still hangs on tightly to Saint Anthony, Saint Jude, the Pope, and, of course, the Almighty Father. She remains powerless, not because of her macho husband, but because of the capitalistic system of production and corruption, which is directly related to the religious system that subordinates her. Both institutions trap Maria in a life of iron-clad inequality. In short, Maria's oppression and exploitation have little to do with being married. Gina Valdes' novel forces women to take a look at the broader picture and to question what is at stake when considering levels of exploitation and discrimination; her novel also questions the social reproduction of organized religion within a culture.

Valdes is a powerful writer who challenges the exploitation of

workers in the United States in many forms. Her poem, "Working Women,"
reiterates some of the same issues that appear in *Madmen:*

> Mi amigo, un cholo transplantado,
> anda todo alocado con su Monte Carlo
> amarillo con swivel bucket seats,
> sun roof y quadrophonic sounds.
> Me lleva low riding por El Cajon
> a mirujear a las rucas on display
> this working night, una con sus
> tight red pants boogying on the curb,
> fast gone, una gordita con su little
> skirt hasta el ombligo y su fake fur,
> otras dos waiting sentadas for a trick,
> y el chota con sus two fast guns
> acercándoseles a otras dos, y ahí into
> Winchell's Donuts entra el pimp con
> sus red pants, white shirt y su
> cocked felt hat, y yo no sé que ando
> aqui cruising so low, mirujeando
> this working women's scene, thinking
> of what rucas and rucos do to pay
> their rent and eat, I, a poet hustling
> hot verbs, a teacher selling brainwaves
> in the S.D. red light school district,
> feeling only un poco mejor than these
> rucas of the night, a little luckier,
> just as worn, my ass grinded daily
> in this big cathouse U S A, que a
> todos nos USA, una puta mas in this
> prostitution ring led by a heartless
> cowboy pimp.[28]

"Working Women" emphasizes the untenable position Chicanas find
themselves in as they maneuver between two cultures: Mexican and
Anglo-American. Although the negative side of this experience sometimes
leads (as in Lorna Dee Cervantes' poem "Refugee Ship") to feelngs of isolation
and alienation from the Spanish language, on the more positive side of the
bicultural experience lies the very real opportunity to experiment with two
language systems. The Chicano's marginal position between cultures requires
him to work within two code systems. Valdes' poem beautifully illustrates how

code-switching is a verbal interaction characteristic of bilingual populations in the midst of social change. But her poem moves far beyond code-switching as it demonstrates the irony and limitations of a system which either subordinates or reifies its subject population.

My final category, the literature of new-vision, opens itself up to a multiplicity of voices and perspectives as it extracts elements of all other forms of Chicana literature. I call it the literature of new-vision because of its broader transformative view. Rather than limiting itself to issues related to an isolated form of oppression, it addresses a number of social problems without taking on an authoritarian tone or dictating a particular perspective. The Chicana voices in this mode are varied, and yet speak, as Strathern states, "in relation to one another." These voices point to an "array of theoretical positions." Together they hold the real possibility for social change and transformation.

Although the late Tomás Rivera divided Chicano literature into the following three stages--conversation which records and preserves deeds and people, rebellion and conflict, and invention and creation--a quick survey of Chicana literature reveals that his categories apply only to Chicano (but not Chicana) writings. Juan Felipe Herrera recognizes Chicana feminist literature as "the most visible and vital branch in contemporary Raza writing."[29] He contrasts their work with the conservative tendencies of Chicano writers, who have received recognition and whose works consequently have been included in college curricula. Having become very comfortable, they have "opted for the cool intellectualism typical of the North American literary voice, with hopes of accommodation by East coast publishing centers." What we are witnessing here is the institutionalization of Chicano literature. The process Herrera has described can be understood by taking another look at Jameson's dialectical analysis. Chicano writers have received recognition by shutting out the feminine interpretation of history. In this sense, their acceptance by academia becomes a vehicle for the containment of Chicana writers. Since Chicana writers are running up against the limits imposed on them by the Chicano interpretation of history, they are still writing with desire, still struggling against oppression. Theirs is a literature of passion and rebellion, and they are becoming more visible through their language.

For Chicanas, writing brings power and change. Cherrie Moraga speaks of the importance of language in "It's the Poverty":

> I lack imagination you say
> No. I lack language.
> The language to clarify
> my resistance to the literate.

Words are a war to me.
They threaten my family.
To gain the word
to describe the loss
I risk losing everything.
I may create a monster
the word's length and body
swelling up colorful and thrilling
looming over my mother, characterized.
Her voice in the distance
unintelligible illiterate.
These are the monster's words.[30]

It is very clear in the above poem just what is at stake when Chicanas speak out. Moraga unmasks the rewards as well as the penalties that come with the articulation of ideas. The poem shows the duality the oppressed must confront. This is undoubtedly a point of conflict. Paolo Freire explains how the conflict lies in

> the choice between being wholly themselves or being divided; between ejecting the oppressor within or not ejecting him; between human solidarity or alienation; between following prescriptions or having choices; between being spectators or actors; between acting or having the illusion of acting through the action of the oppressors; between speaking out or being silent, castrated in their power to create and re-create, in their power to transform the world.[31]

Cherrie Moraga's words are of the utmost importance in this context. Like Freire, she raises questions about the pedagogy of the oppressed, but more importantly, she raises her questions by piercing through the limitations of the masculine discourse Freire aligns himself with, a discourse which equates testicles with power.

Sandra Cisneros has considered power in a different way. She writes about the relationship of writing, power, and liberation in *The House on Mango Street:*

> She listened to every book, every poem I read her. One day I read her one of my own. I came very close. I whispered it into the pillow:

I want to be
like the waves on the sea,
like the clouds in the wind,
but I'm me.
One day I'll jump
out of my skin.
I'll shake the sky
like a hundred violins.

That's nice. That's very good, she said in her tired voice.
You just remember to keep writing, Esperanza. You must
keep writing. It will keep you free, and I said yes, but at that
time I didn't know what she meant.[32]

The literature of new-vision brings Chicanas full circle as it breaks
through the source of their initial alienation from language. It breaks the bonds
of religious and cultural oppression as it uses the word to press forward in the
search for self-identification, while also providing a predominantly unrecognized
form of self-representation of the "other"--the kind of self-representation
experimental ethnographers are striving for. It is this kind of representation,
this kind of critical reading of the text, which leads to the self-awareness
necessary for transformation. Teresa de Lauretis' work makes it clear just how
important critical reading is for change:

But a critical feminist reading of the text, of all the texts of
culture, instates the awareness of that contradiction and the
knowledge of its terms; it thus changes the representation
into a performance which exceeds the text. For women to
enact the contradiction is to demonstrate the non-coincidence
of woman as text, as image, is to resist identification with
that image. It is to have stepped through the looking
glass.[33]

In closing, let me again stress that the four modes of Chicana
literature I have outlined are not necessarily sequential. The intervals or modes
of expression should be viewed as interdependent. Their correlation and
movement, which are marked by a regulated succession of strong and weak
elements, representing opposite or different conditions, in turn produce the
whole musical score. Some writers compose in all four categories, while others
may limit themselves to one. In Lydia Camarillo's poem, "Mi Reflejo," it

becomes clear how a single poem can include all four modes of expression.

The poem begins by asking the question "Who goes there?" and responding "It is I." This question and its response are repeated throughout the poem, and are used to evoke the spirits and stories of women in Mexican history. Camarillo uses her poetry to reappropriate and reinscribe history in female terms, using both Spanish and English to develop a new discourse on *identidad*. She therefore begins with the conquest:

> Conquistaste y colonizaste mi gente.
> You alienated me from my people.
> Me hiciste la 'Vendida.'
> Ya no te acuerdas de me?
> I am Malinche.[34]

The poem moves on to include Sor Juana Ines de la Cruz, Frida Kahlo, and la Virgen de Guadalupe in a chant-like form. As Camarillo's poem progresses in dialectical terms, she moves through the mode of rage and opposition as she also establishes Mexican women's history in a chronological sequence, setting the foundation for the representation of a point of view which, for the most part, has either been forgotten or suppressed. She closes her poetic/political discourse by stating that women today are reflections of the past:

> Si somos espejos de cada una,
> Soy Malinche,
> Soy la Virgen de Guadalupe,
> Soy Sor Juana Ines de la Cruz,
> Soy Frida Kahlo
> Soy Mujer.[35]

Camarillo's "Mi Reflejo" draws from all four modes of expression, though not in the sequence outlined in this essay. She reverses the final two modes, first stressing the mode of new-vision as she deduces that to be a woman is to be a combination of the historical and the present. Camarillo ends her discourse in the mode of struggle and identification, stating that as reflections of the past, women represent half of the struggle against oppression, and asserting that together with our *compañeros*, "We are the Revolution."

Chicana literature provides the voices, identifies the issues, and performs the rituals necessary for including Chicanas in the ongoing debate among other feminists. It bridges the gaps in thinking between masculine and feminine interpretations of history. It resembles music because it concerns itself with a combination of positions and it thus functions as the kind of ethnographic representation for which some anthropologists strive but which most feminist theorists have, unfortunately, overlooked. Women's literature in general, and Chicana literature in particular, provides one possible solution to the problem of challenge and counter-challenge between mainstream and marginal feminist theories for dealing with issues of marginality within feminist research. But beyond this, looking at literature as the articulation of history or as ethnographic documentation of culture and female experience effectively opens the door to a new kind of interdisciplinary, but more importantly, intergenderal (a form that takes into account both male and female ideas) approach to knowledge.

For helpful criticism of this paper I would like to thank Marta Morello-Frosch, Hayden White, Jose Saldívar, and May Diaz.

Notes

1.   Marilyn Strathern, "Dislodging a World View: Challenge and Counter-Challenge in the Relation Between Feminism and Anthropology," Lecture at the Research Center for Women's Studies, University of Adelaide, 4 July 1984. To be published in *Changing Paradigms: The Impact of Feminist Theory upon the World of Scholarship*, ed. Susan Magarey (Sidney: Hale and Iremonger, forthcoming).

2.   Fredric Jameson, *The Political Unconscious: Narrative as a Socially Symbolic Act* (Ithaca, N.Y. : Cornell University Press, 1981).

3.   I can still remember the shock I felt when I first discovered in an undergraduate Sociology class that I was a "marginal person." It is interesting to note that the discipline of anthropology has also coined a term for individuals operating within two cultural systems: "cultural broker."

4.   Sherry Ortner, "The Founding of the First Sherpa Nunnery and the Problem of 'Women' as an Analytic Category," unpublished ms.; Michelle Rosaldo, "The Use and Abuse of Anthropology," unpublished ms.

5.   Here I am alluding to Terry Eagleton's ideas regarding silences in the text which not only reveal the presence of ideology, but also the relationship of specific writers to the modes of production.

6.   Alvina Quintana, "Language, Power & Women: A Hermeneutic Interpretation," *Critical Perspectives: Women, Race & Class in a Cultural Context* (University of California, Berkeley: Department of Ethnic Studies, Fall 1984), 10-20.

7.   Adrienne Rich, "When We Dead Awaken: Writing as Revision," *Of Lies, Secrets and Silence: Selected Prose, 1966-1978* (New York: W.W. Norton and Co., Inc., 1979), 35.

8.   Susan Kreiger, *The Mirror Dance* (Philadelphia: Temple University

Press, 1983), 196.

9. Terry Eagleton, *Marxism and Literary Criticism* (Berkeley and Los Angeles: University of California Press, 1976), 18.

10. Nancy Hartsock, *Money Sex and Power* (Baltimore: Johns Hopkins University Press, 1983).

11. Here I am alluding to Marxist theory in general and Fredric Jameson's Marxist criticism in particular, as it relates to the fashioning of identity in terms of the historical moment in question. The fact that the women's movement was reactivated in the 1960s is of particular relevance to the questions women ask regarding gender differences.

12. Sidney Finkelstein, *How Music Expresses Ideas* (New York: International Pubs. Co., 1970), 135.

13. Hayden White, *Tropes of Discourse* (Baltimore: Johns Hopkins University Press, 1978) has been especially helpful for me in developing my modes of poetic discourse. His discussion of Kenneth Burke's "master trope" irony has become particularly relevant to my analysis of the "New Vision" stage in Chicana literature.

14. Helene Cixous, "The Laugh of the Medusa," *New French Feminisms* (Boston: University of Massachusetts Press, 1980).

15. Annette Kuhn, *Women's Pictures* (London: Routledge & Kegan Paul, 1982), 13-18.

16. William C. Dowling, *Jameson, Althusser, Marx: An Introduction to the Political Unconscious* (Ithaca: Cornell University Press, 1984), 21.

17. *Chicano* here refers to the entire race rather than to just men.

18. Lorna Dee Cervantes, *Emplumada* (Pittsburgh: University of Pittsburgh Press, 1981), 41.

19. See Norma Alarcon's discussion regarding the bicultural experience of Chicanas in, "What Kind of Lover have You Made Me, Mother?: Towards A Theory of Chicanas' Feminism and Cultural Identity Through Poetry,"

Women's Studies Anthology, Indiana University Press, forthcoming.

20.   Sylvia Gonzales, "Chicana Evolution," *The Third Woman: Minority Women Writers of the U.S.*, ed. Dexter Fisher (Boston: Houghton Mifflin Co.), 418.

21.   Alison M. Jaggar, *Feminist Politics and Human Nature* (Totowa, N. J.: Rowman and Allanheld Pub., 1983).

22.   Lorna Dee Cervantes, "You Cramp My Style, Baby," *El Fuego de Aztlan* 1 (1977): 39.

23.   Cherrie Moraga, *Loving in the War Years* (Boston: South End Press, 1983), 132.

24.   Terry Eagleton, *Marxism and Literary Criticism*, 23.

25.   Gina Valdes, *There are No Madmen Here* (Colorado Springs, Co.: Maize Press, 1982), 48.

26.   Here I am referring to Elliott Evans' discussion of subversive subtext in his unpublished ms., History of Consciousness Program, University of California, Santa Cruz.

27.   Valdes, *There are No Madmen Here*, 72.

28.   Gina Valdez, *Comiendo Lumbre* (Colorado Springs: Maize Press, 1986), 58.

29.   Juan Felipe Herrera, "The Califas Movimiento," *Poetry Flash*, March 1984, 1-5.

30.   Moraga, *Loving in the War Years*, 62-63.

31.   Paolo Freire, *Pedagogy of the Oppressed*, trans. Myra Bergman Ramos (New York: Continuum Pub. Co., 1984), 33.

32.   Sandra Cisneros, "Born Bad," *The House on Mango Street* (Houston: Arte Publico Pr., Revista Chicano-Riquena, University of Houston Press, 1984).

33.   Teresa de Lauretis, *Alice Doesn't* (Bloomington: Indiana University Press, 1982), 36.

34.   Lydia Camarillo, "Mi Reflejo," *La Palabra* (Tucson: Post Litho Press, 1980), 73.

35.   Ibid.

The Union League and Agricultural Change in the Deep South during Reconstruction

Michael W. Fitzgerald

A large body of work has been published on the evolution of the post-Civil War South. Many historians, in particular, have examined the emergence of sharecropping in cotton. Some scholars have stressed the rational economic reasons for the breakdown of the centralized plantation, while others have seen such changes as the result of black laborers pressuring for greater autonomy. The tumultuous politics of the era were, however, also relevant to this process. By examining the impact of the first political organization among blacks, the Union League, on agriculture in Alabama and Mississippi, we can better understand the forces at work. The League, I shall argue, was formed in response to the crisis of the plantation system, and it grew out of intense conflict in agriculture. Its development influenced economic trends of critical long-term significance in Southern history.

In order to understand the unrest which accompanied the rise of the League, it is necessary to discuss the situation in the countryside from which it emerged. During Presidential Reconstruction from April 1865 to March 1867, southern cotton planters shared a common vision of the future. As James Roark has pointed out in *Masters Without Slaves*, they hoped to maintain as many aspects of slavery as possible. Specifically, the planters wanted gang labor, overseers, whipping, women and children in the work force, and intrusive oversight of the freedmen. The Black Codes enacted by the various planter-dominated state legislatures enabled planters to carry out these objectives. The codes generally included harsh vagrancy statutes and the creation of a pass system. They often deprived freedman of the right to own or rent land. In practice, this represented an attempt to rebuild agriculture along coercive lines, using the power of the state to bolster the authority of the planter. Most acknowledged that reimposition of slavery *per se* was unlikely, given the presence of the Freedmen's Bureau and the army, but they thought they could maintain much of slavery's substance without interference.[1]

This, of course, was unsatisfactory to the freedmen. The experience of bondage had left them with an intense distaste for anything associated with it. As it gradually became clear that they were expected to work under much the same conditions as before, the ex-slaves became increasingly restive. At first, their dissatisfaction manifested itself in rumors of land redistribution: the "forty acres and a mule" of legend. As the likelihood of realizing such expectations declined, freedmen became more assertive in their dealings with employers. One north Alabama planter's complaints were typical:

> My hands are beyond my control. Yesterday all men but four refused to take care of mules--would not even feed them and Saturday noon did not get back to work on time by a long ways. This morning I called them to work at 5 minutes before 5 o'clock. The first hand got to work 8 minutes after 6 o'clock, the last one . . . 11 minutes after 7 o'clock. I can't get but part work at a time.[2]

His laborers, on the other hand, complained that conditions were worse than under slavery and were unacceptable to freed blacks.[3] Their behavior was typical of freedmen throughout the South, who shortened their hours of work, shirked traditional chores, and sent their children to school. Many women stopped cultivating cotton. The critical issue for the freedmen, however, was access to land--if not by confiscation, then by rental or purchase.

But southern planters were determined to deny land to freedmen, seeing any sort of independent farming by blacks as tantamount to anarchy. One northern reporter noted that the feeling against landownership by Negroes was so strong that the man who should sell to them would be in danger of his life. Even renting them land would make one a pariah, he noted. Those few freedmen who succeeded in gaining access to land faced still more hostility, as an Alabama freedman discovered: his neighbors drove him from his home by threatening to blow his brains out.[4]

An impasse emerged as planters continued to farm with gang labor but were no longer able to force blacks to work like slaves. This stalemate contributed to the poor harvests reported throughout the region in 1865, 1866, and 1867. Of course, there were other factors besides the freedmen's behavior--declining cotton prices, unusually heavy rainfall, and insect infestations all added to the agricultural depression. But the freedmen's work habits were a substantial cause, and poor crops in turn increased dissatisfaction among the laborers who seldom received much beyond food and board for their work. In sum, the planters blamed the freedmen for all their economic woes--which were substantial--and the freedmen thought the planters were cheating them, as many were. This contributed to an economic disaster of large proportions, as many plantations neared bankruptcy. During the immediate postwar period freedmen were angry and restive, but were unable to force significant changes in plantation management. This deadlock is critical to understanding the politicization of the freedmen with the onset of Military Reconstruction. It set the social context for the rise of the Union League movement among vast numbers of rural freedmen.

The Union League (also known as the Loyal League) was the first Radical Republican organization in the South. It originated in the North during the war as a patriotic organization; after Appomattox, it spread into the South among white yeoman Unionists. The League's members were bound by oath to secrecy, and they used rituals reminiscent of the Masons. Once Military Reconstruction began, Congressional Republicans used this organization to evangelize among the newly-enfranchised freedmen. Paid organizers traveled through the southern states, initiating freedmen into the order. The response to the League was dramatic: vast numbers of freedmen joined within weeks. Intense conflict spread through the plantation regions, as drilling and mass activities by freedmen became commonplace. To a striking degree, the League mobilization let freedmen use the threat of force to advantage, creating an immediate impact on planters' control over their labor force.[5]

Perhaps the best way to understand this social upheaval is to examine one area and its plantations in detail. Hale County in the rich Alabama cotton belt was demographically typical of the plantation region. It offers a paradigm of the changes occurring during Military Reconstruction. In April 1867 black political activities commenced, and four thousand freedmen attended a huge rally at the county seat of Greensboro. To the intense alarm of the planters, League organizers began meeting weekly with the freedmen in private. In June, a leading freedman was assassinated, and in response thousands of armed freedmen descended on Greensboro, some threatening to burn it to the ground. Bands of freedmen roved the countryside for days. Soon thereafter, the freedmen formed an organized militia in preparation for the next outbreak.[6]

Escalating political strife had a direct impact upon the plantations of Hale County. According to a Democratic source, every black laborer for ten miles around had joined the League. One planter complained that the freedmen were seizing their share of the crop, another that they were coming and going when they chose, entirely ignoring his orders. Landowners all across the region made similar complaints. An extraordinary indication of the League's influence was provided by a planter some thirty miles away:

> I have recently had a good deal of trouble with the hands . . .
> it seems that certain parties in or near Greensboro has [sic]
> been telling them that they ought to receive forty five
> dollars per month instead of ten, that neither the present crop
> or the lands belonged to the planters, but that they belonged
> to the Government. . . . Such talk has demoralized them
> very much & has very seriously impaired what was three
> weeks ago a beautiful prospect for a crop . . . [7]

A great many planters complained that agitation was rendering the freedmen restless and sassy, undercutting their own authority as employers. The local Bureau agent confirmed the effects of political agitation upon the ex-slaves. He reported that "without great caution difficulty with the freedmen will be inevitable."[8] He, too, blamed League agitators for the likelihood of violence.

The papers of two Hale County landowners show how these changes affected individual plantations. Political upheaval encouraged by the League helped force agricultural change in the area. On the large Watson plantation, the owner had farmed since the war with gang labor and tight supervision, but now an impending "war of races" threatened. The League agitators were telling his freedmen to "ignore the Southern white man as soon as possible [;] not to work with him, or for him, or be controlled by him, but to set up for themselves."[9] Setting up for themselves, of course, meant farming independently of white control. Faced with this unrest among the work force, Watson at first decided that planting would never pay again, and he therefore intended to let the land lie idle. By the beginning of 1868, however, he decided to abandon gang labor and to rent land instead to groups of freedmen working under their own supervision. Satisfactory results were soon apparent; his manager wrote that "the negroes are working very well this year," a condition he ascribed to the fact that they were now working in small squads.[10]

A similar situation developed some miles away on the Cameron plantation. Cameron's overseer had farmed after the war along familiar lines, but here, too, conditions changed with the beginning of Radical agitation. After his hands registered to vote, they all expected to "have the lands and the growing crop upon it, one or two said they understood such things, they all belong to the Union League." By October, the overseer decided that a restructuring of his operation was essential: he would henceforth use families to work the land. By 1868 improved work habits were reported among the freedmen on the Cameron place as well.[11] According to press accounts, this pattern was typical of the region, as large numbers of freedmen became tenant farmers soon thereafter.[12]

League-related turbulence was equally evident in Bullock County, located in the eastern Alabama cotton belt, where an apparent League uprising occurred largely in response to agricultural grievances. The League began operations in the area in the early summer of 1867, and one planter complained of the "demoralizing tendency" of League drilling.[13] The freedmen left their work at every rumor and, as a result, failed to gather a crop after raising it. The changed temper of the freedmen became more evident in July, when one planter found occasion to "correct by whip" a freedwoman in his employ.[14] An angry mob of freedmen gathered that evening, burst in the planter's door, and prepared to take him to the local authorities for punishment. Alarmed white neighbors arrived in force, and a standoff ensued through the night. The stalemate was only broken the following morning when one freedman seized a horse and summoned reinforcements from the surrounding area. The freedmen bound their captive and bore him to the county officials, who, doubtless intimidated, incarcerated the unhappy planter.

There followed months of rural unrest. In September, the League's state secretary, John C. Keffer, gave a speech at the county seat and was bushwacked on his way out of town. Upon news of the shooting, three League militias from the countryside marched on the county seat, besieging it for two days while negotiations proceeded. Some activists threatened to burn the town but were dissuaded by news that Keffer had survived and his assailant had been captured.[15]

All of this tension culminated in the Perote disturbances of November 1867. The details of what happened in this rural neighborhood are somewhat vague, but it seems that the catastrophic harvest that season had left the laborers unusually restive. A black adventurer named George Shorter persuaded some freedmen that he had permission from military authorities to set up a League government. He reportedly had a falling out with some of his comrades over funds and ordered several of them seized by the League. County officials heard rumors of Shorter's activities, and they ordered his arrest. In response, the Leaguers, still believing him a representative from the federal government, determined to resist further arrests. An arsonist then torched the local black church, whereupon Leaguers besieged the village of Perote for several days. Panic-striken whites informed the army that sixty armed blacks were threatening "disorder, riot, insurrection and bloodshed."[16] Only when federal troops arrived several days later and disarmed the freedmen did quiet finally return.It is most significant that several local newspapers portray the

Perote upheaval as a labor conflict. One, for example, made this quite explicit:

> We have heard from a reliable source of some very bad
> conduct on the part of some of the freed people near Perote
> in Bullock County. It seems in several instances not
> satisfied with the settlement as made by their employers and
> unwilling to call in anyone else, although the Bureau agent
> was proposed, they proceeded to help themselves to what
> they thought they ought to have, regardless of the rights of
> others, and threatening with death any one who might
> interfere to prevent them . . . We fear that this is but the
> beginning . . . [17]

Immediately afterward, a county officeholder noted a concerted refusal by freedmen to contract for another year's work.[18]

Regardless of whether the Perote affair was explicitly a labor upsurge, it was in the midst of this unrest that planters in Bullock County decided to rent land to freedmen. The local newspaper stated that "Southern farmers are compelled to change their old routine system of farming and try some other."[19] The paper reported that many farmers were renting land to freedmen with satisfactory results.

The League insurgency was thus, in part, a labor revolt with marked implications upon planters' capacity to manage their holdings.[20] The argument here is not that the League was solely responsible for the emergence of sharecropping; many economic and social factors combined to place gang labor under intense strain. The point is that the politicization of the freedmen was both an agrarian economic insurgency *and* a political mobilization. This movement undermined the planters' already tenuous control. The political turmoil of Radical Reconstruction served as a catalyst of change, causing landowners to realize that production could no longer be carried out along familiar lines. By mid-1868, decentralized tenant farming had become the predominant form of agricultural organization in the area.

All over Alabama, the ex-slaves became much more assertive in other ways as well. One white lawyer's complaints were typical. He claimed that before the League organizers came, a "good feeling" prevailed between the races.[21] After the Leaguers arrived, though, the freedmen became suspicious of the whites. They would not get off the sidewalk for a white man, or even a white woman. The Leaguers even dared to come into town armed on various occasions. The impudence which this lawyer noted was real, even if its causes were somewhat different from what he believed. Such changes obviously had their most significant implications on the plantations, where they challenged the whole ethos of subordination based upon slavery.

The organization's mostly white leadership was primarily interested in electoral activity, but freedmen in local councils often had wider concerns. At Uniontown, for example, the Freedmen's Bureau agent complained that political meetings were rendering blacks worthless as laborers. No one, he thought, could miss the changed attitude of the ex-slaves. At Talladega, a labor strike immediately followed creation of the League, and near Selma, agricultural strikes grew out of electoral activities. Throughout the state, League and other Republican activists frequently spoke of the desirability of escaping gang labor, recommending renting and purchasing land. In fact, most of the prominent black activists in the League were later involved in creating an agricultural labor organization, the Alabama Labor Union, in the early 1870s.[22] In essence, the League functioned in Alabama as a vehicle for expressing a diverse array of grievances.

In Mississippi, the evidence also indicates that the League was closely involved in agricultural unrest, though the process seemed to have moved more slowly than in Alabama. Though the League's spread was gradual in Mississippi, the basic trend of events was similar. One newspaper reported that the League urged freedmen not to contract with whites, or to pay a rent of more than $1.50 an acre for land. Another paper reported that the League had told freedmen not to work for whites in any capacity. In Natchez, a "Loyal Labor League" reportedly had determined that "hands would not work the coming year except as lessees of land . . ."[23] One white in a League stronghold observed that the blacks had acquired some exalted ideas since they had received the vote. They frequently discussed the notion of renting land and used phrases like "'If we contract' & c."[24] In Mississippi, as in Alabama, the League served as a channel for the expression of labor insurgency, complicating planters' efforts to maintain control over their labor force.

A striking example of this occurred in Vicksburg, where Leaguers undermined the process of contracting gang laborers. According to the local Bureau agent, black League leaders prevented freedmen from contracting in early 1868, and as late as May large numbers of idle freedmen remained in Vicksburg. This reportedly caused a severe labor shortage on the farms. The Bureau agent thought that the Leaguers were trying to keep them in town in order to gain their votes in the coming election, but his own account suggests a different motive. Large numbers of planters were "giving up to the freedmen" and renting them land, and the evidence suggests that this was the freedmen's basic objective in refusing to contract as laborers. As one local black leader earlier asked, "what if we should compel them to lease us lands?"[25] Whatever the motive might have been, this was in fact what the League boycott helped to accomplish.

The level of mass activity in both states during 1867 would have been difficult to sustain for long, but several factors combined to accelerate the breakup of the League movement in the following years. One was that the attainment of tenant status tended to dampen black discontent, at least temporarily. Now that large numbers of freedmen were gaining greater day-to-day independence for themselves and their families, some of the resentment feeding the League insurgency dissipated. While sharecropping proved to be an economic trap in the long-run for blacks, it initially lessened conflict between them and their landlords. The immediate grievances behind the League upsurge became less acute with the decline of gang labor.

The changing attitude of the landowners indicates the effectiveness of using sharecropping as a safety valve. As the freedmen's work habits improved, production increased, as did, fortuitously, the price of cotton. Consequently, both planters' profits and the price of land went up. Virtually overnight, white resistance to land rental collapsed, as planters realized that decentralized sharecropping was in their best interest. As one Mississippi Klansman later commented, "I greatly prefer the renting system and get along very well with it. The negro likes it better and I like it better."[26] An Alabama planter recalled some years later that the changes made blacks more resistant to political agitation. The abandonment of gang labor by planters actually proved to be financially advantageous, and planters soon realized that more money could be made through usury than farming. Sharecropping coopted blacks and enabled planters to stabilize a plantation regime that had been in danger of collapse.

Another factor in the decline of League activities was the Ku Klux Klan. In the spring of 1868 the Klan spread across Alabama and across Mississippi gradually thereafter. The Klan offered whites a potent instrument of repression with minimal risk; the freedmen, now dispersed across the plantations, were unable to devise effective countermeasures to meet the nightriders. The rural Leagues were crushed in a matter of months, the weekly meetings soon ceased, and mass activities by freedmen became far more dangerous--and desperate.

While the Klan's overt goal was political, it had a direct effect on agriculture as well. With the arrival of the Klan, planters were once again able to rely on preponderant physical force in their dealings with workers. Many rejoiced in the effectiveness of the Klan in disciplining laborers. As one planter observed of the Mississippi-Tennessee border region, "had it not been for their deadly fear of the Ku Klux, I do not think we could have managed them as well as we did."[27] Another stated that planters simply could not get along without the Klan. This emphasis on the advantages of terror seems plausible in view of the fact that planter families led and directed the Klan in the black belt, at least during its initial phase, and the terror had a direct influence on conditions in the countryside. The existence of the Klan, along with the concession of sharecropping to the freedmen, stabilized the rural regime. Southern agriculture took on the basic shape that it would hold for the next seventy years or so, though its coercive character grew more overt only after Redemption.[28]

What, then, is the overall significance of the League movement? At the most obvious level, a study of its history demonstrates the futility of discussing economic changes without consideration of politics. Some recent economic historians have argued that sharecropping emerged as a result of market forces, but given the circumstances, it seems misleading to discuss such changes without reference to the aspirations of the freedmen. The shift to sharecropping occurred during intense labor strife, and abstracting economic changes from their social context is misleading, because labor revolt, under some circumstances, clearly can become a market force. In social terms, the politicization of the freedmen through the League was a culmination of their resistance to slave-like conditions in agriculture. This resistance eventually doomed gang labor and tight supervision throughout most of the cotton South.

The Union League clearly represented a labor revolt as well as a political upsurge: it helped pressure planters towards a major restructuring of the plantation system. Though ultimately repressed by Klan terror, the League served as a means to compel the plantation system to change. It politicized freedmen during several years of struggle against slave-like conditions of work. Their resistance eventually forced plantation owners to concede to the blacks' desire for autonomy. By channeling black dissatisfaction into a powerful political movement, the League encouraged the transition from the centralized model of plantation production derived from slavery to one characterized by decentralized tenant farming.

Notes

1.   James L. Roark, *Masters Without Slaves: Southern Planters in the Civil War and Reconstruction* (New York: Norton, 1977), 141-42. See also Michael W. Fitzgerald, "The Union League Movement in Alabama and Mississippi: Politics and Agricultural Change in the Deep South during Reconstruction" (Ph.D. diss., University of California, Los Angeles, 1986), 182-88.

2.   E. G. Black to Callis, 12 May 1866, Letters Received by the Sub Assistant Commissioner [hereafter SAC] Huntsville, vol. 58, Records of the Bureau of Refugees, Freedmen, and Abandoned Lands [hereafter RG 105], National Archives [hereafter NA].

3.   Ibid.

4.   Whitelaw Reid, *After the War: A Southern Tour* (Reprint; New York: Harper and Row, 1966), 564; Complaint Book, entry for 4 March 1867, SAC Demopolis, vol. 141, RG 105, NA.

5.   Fitzgerald, "The Union League," 14-21.

6.   S. G. Spann to Pierce, 12 April 1867, Letters Received SAC Demopolis, box 27, RG 105, NA; Carrollton *West Alabamian*, 21 August 1867, quoting Greensboro *Beacon*. For a detailed discussion of the situation in Hale County, see Fitzgerald, "The Union League," 189-98.

7.   E. B. Perrin to Pierce, 26 July 1867, Letters Received SAC Demopolis, Box 27, RG 105, NA.

8.   G. A. Farrand to Pierce, 2 December 1867, Letters Received by the Assistant Commissioner for Alabama [hereafter M809], RG 105.

9.   Parrish to Watson, 28 May 1867, Watson Papers, Duke University.

10.   G. Hugins to Watson, 5 June 1868, Watson Papers, Duke University.

11.   O'Berry to Cameron, May 1867, 11 August and 20 October 1867, 30 January 1868, 6 April 1868, Cameron Papers, University of North Carolina [hereafter UNC].

12.   Mobile *Register,* 30 May 1869.

13.   E. A. Broly to Swayne, 7 August 1867, Swayne Papers, ADAH. For a more detailed treament of the events in Bullock County, see Fitzgerald, "The Union League," 203-11.

14.   W. Ivay to McCall, in McCall to Swayne, 26 July 1867, M809, RG 105.

15.   Union Springs *Times*, 25 September 1867.

16.   Citizens of Perote to Swayne, 30 November 1867, M809, RG 105.

17.   Carrollton *West Alabamian*, 11 December 1867, quoting Eufaula *News.*

18.   McCall to "Asst. Comm. of the Bureau," 10 January 1868, M809, RG 105.

19.   Union Springs *Times*, 18 September and 30 November 1867, 2 May 1868.

20.   Union Springs *Times*, 18 September 1867, 2 May 1868.

21.   U.S. Congress, *Testimony Taken by the Joint Select Committee to Inquire into the Condition of Affairs of the Late Insurrectionary States* (Washington: Government Printing Office, 1872); *House Reports*, 42nd cong., 2nd Sess., no. 22, vol. 10, 1623 [cited hereafter as *KKK*].

22.   Fitzgerald, "The Union League," 211-23.

23.   Raymond *Hinds County Gazette*, 15 September 1869; Forest *Register*, 8 October 1870, quoting Goodman *Star;* Jackson *Clarion*, 14 October 1870; Natchez *Democrat*, 23 December 1869.

24.   J. C. Caruthers to R. L. Caruthers, 13 November 1867, Caruthers Papers, UNC.

25.   J. C. Chapman to S. C. Green, 6 May 1868, Letters Sent SAC Vicksburg, vo. 274, RG105, NA; J. T. Trowbridge, *The South: A Tour of Its Battle-Fields and Ruined Cities, A Journey Through the Desolated States, and Talks with the People* (Hartford: n.p., 1866), 196, 193-94.

26.   *KKK* 2, no. 11, 223.

27.   Robert Philip Howell Memoir, UNC.

28.   Fitzgerald, "The Union League," 294-303.

Authoritarian Populism and Code Words:
Race and the New Right

Michael Omi

At the end of World War II, Henry Luce's designation of the coming period as "the American century" hardly seemed an exaggerated vision of things to come. The United States found itself with an unparalleled ability to develop and extend its economic and commercial position, to institutionalize its political and military power globally, and to project its vision of democracy and social justice as the model for the "free world" to emulate.

The "American century" proved to be short-lived. By the 1970s, people in the United States had experienced the fall of Saigon, the fall of a President, and the fall of Keynesianism and the political alignment which sustained it. Over the past two decades, Americans have exhibited a profound shift in mood, from an optimistic outlook of limitless upward mobility to a foreboding sense of economic decline, cultural disintegration, and political crisis.

The New Right operates in this political atmosphere and offers an alternative to the perceived moral and existential chaos which racks the present social order. It is a contemporary attempt to create an authoritarian, right-wing populism--a politics fueled by *resentment:*

> Collecting millions of dollars in small contributions from blue-collar workers and housewives, the New Right feeds on discontent, anger, insecurity, and resentment, and flourishes on backlash politics. Through its interlocking network, it seeks to veto whatever it perceives to threaten its way of life--busing, women's liberation, gay rights, pornography, loss of the Panama Canal--and promotes a beefed-up defense budget, lower taxes, and reduced federal regulation of small business. Moreover, the New Right exploits social protest

and encourages class hostility by trying to fuel the
hostilities of lower-middle-class Americans against those
above and below them on the economic ladder. [1]

Observers have discussed the emergence and growth of right reaction,[2]
but few, if any, have highlighted and analyzed in detail the importance of *race*
as a defining issue of this reaction and as a key feature of New Right
mobilization. The above quote speaks of "class" antagonism, whereas leftist
and progressive analyses have argued that the defining project of the New Right
is the reassertion of "patriarchy."[3] While, for the most part, this is true, such
analyses understate the importance of race by subsuming it under some other
supposedly more "fundamental" category of political life, such as class or
gender. By contrast, I shall argue that race was crucial in the initial reaction
against the progressive gains of the 1960s (then known as "backlash," e.g.,
anti-busing movements),[4] was central to the electoral perspective of the New
Right (the "southern strategy"), and that it continues to be a major, if at times
disguised, issue for the New Right today.

In many ways, the New Right incubated and developed in the
political setting created by the racial minority movements of the 1960s; its
agenda was framed in opposition to the politics and ideology of those
movements. As Allen Hunter notes, the New Right "seeks to regain control of
America for the white middle strata of America, 'the people' who felt that they
were bypassed and put down by the changes of the 1960s."[5] The emergence of
"new social movements" (black, Chicano, feminist, gay, etc.)[6] in the 1960s
appeared to "balkanize" the nation politically. These movements invoked a
bewildering array of new social and political values, which created
unprecedented political fragmentation and left the "mainstream" with no clear
notion of the "common good." Commonly-held notions of family, community,
and nation were challenged, discarded, and/or transformed, and no principle of
cohesion or new cultural center emerged to replace them.

In the face of these challenges, traditional conservatism seemed to
have little to offer--society and politics, and the conventional way in which
they were understood, had already been radically transformed. Only the
appearance of the New Right in the mid-1970s gave the beleaguered ranks of
the "silent majority" any glimmer of hope--the projection of a clear, pragmatic,
and, perhaps most importantly, *comforting* vision.

The New Right

The term "New Right" was introduced into the national vocabulary by political analyst and New Right figure Kevin Phillips. Gillian Peele defines the New Right as "a loose movement of conservative politicians and a collection of general-purpose political organizations which have developed independently of the political parties."[7] It rose to national prominence during electoral campaigns in the early 1970s with a flurry of dramatic political activity--from the promotion of controversial social issues to "smear campaigns" aimed at ousting liberal opponents from political office.

While the New Right's political agenda includes substantive economic issues, it is better known for its focus on *social* issues. This, in part, derives from its evolution into a coherent network from a range of disparate, grass-roots, single-issue groups. Allen Hunter observes that these groups

> . . . included local anti-busing groups that developed from the mid-1960s on; local and nationally coordinated efforts to oppose sex education which began in 1968/1969; the anti-abortion movement which got its start in the late 1960s and leapt forward in 1973 with the Supreme Court decision legalizing abortion; the anti-ERA movement begun in 1972; and the anti-gay campaigns that date from the mid-1970s.[8]

Aside from a host of single-issue groups, typical New Right affiliates include the American Conservative Union, the National Conservative Political Action Committee (NCPAC), the Conservative Caucus, the Young Americans for Freedom, and a group of fundamentalist Protestant sects with millions of adherents. Leading figures of the New Right are fundraiser/publisher Richard A. Viguerie, Paul Weyrich (Committee for the Survival of a Free Congress), Howard Phillips (Conservative Caucus), and John T. Dolan (NCPAC), as well as activist Phyllis Schlafly (Eagle Forum, Stop-ERA), and fundamentalist evangelist Rev. Jerry Falwell (Moral Majority). Periodicals identified with the New Right are the *Conservative Digest, Policy Review, Human Events,* and *New Guard.* [9] The key New Right think tank is the Heritage Foundation, founded by brewer Joseph Coors and Paul Weyrich in 1973.

The strength of the New Right derives from its organizational structure and its innovative use of political action committees and direct-mail solicitation. As the editors of *Conservative Digest* are quick to point out, the ability to "network" has been key to New Right political mobilization:

Important for the New Right success is its leaders' willingness to work as a team. The New Right network has regular meetings of citizen action groups, political action committees and political strategists, and, while all participants of course maintain autonomy of action, the exchange of viewpoints is smooth and usually results in harmonious activities. [10]

Central to the New Right's ability to mobilize a mass-based constituency has been its use of direct-mail solicitation, which Richard Viguerie has cultivated into something approaching a science.[11] The need to "market" right-wing ideas was one of the lessons learned by the right in the wake of the Goldwater defeat in 1964. What good were "correct ideas," they wondered, if they lacked the power to sell them to the electorate? The problem was compounded by what the New Right perceived as a "liberal bias" in the media.[12] In their view, direct-mail solicitation would overcome the impediments of media distortion of New Right ideas by allowing a clear message to be sent directly to the "political consumer" and by avoiding the complications encountered in channeling funds through traditional party sources. Direct-mail solicitation is a flexible medium which can accommodate a variety of slogans and angles; its impact can be precisely measured by the rate of return; it can target specific sectors of the population; and it generates mailing lists which can be segmented or recombined for future campaigns. But perhaps most importantly for the New Right, it helps tap into the "silent majority" of the populace--those who might not otherwise engage in political action through parties, interest groups, or voluntary organizations.[13]

Peele suggests that there are several features which distinguish the New Right from the orthodox Republican Party, the older conservative movement, and neoconservatism: " . . . its aggressive mood of determination; its hostility to the existing party structure; its special agenda of issues; [and] its populism."[14] By the 1970s, the New Right was a disciplined, well-organized, and well-financed network of "single-issue" affiliates. It displayed an aggressive political style, an outspoken religious and cultural traditionalism, and a fierce populist commitment.

Race and the New Right

Despite continuing problems of discrimination and inequality, a new mood of "social meanness" pervades the United States. At best, many sectors of the American populace are callous about the plight of blacks and other minorities. At worst, many Americans openly resent having to provide for the "underprivileged." Indeed, these people feel that far from being the victims of deprivation, racial minorities are unfairly receiving "preferential treatment" with respect to jobs and educational opportunities.

Operating within this context, New Right populism combines venerable American ideological themes such as respect for authority, mistrust of "big government," and defense of traditional morality, with resistance to racial minority demands for "affirmative action" in education, jobs, and housing. The latter issue has been a crucial feature of the "politics of resentment."

Some analysts view this resentment as a status revolt by those who, according to Ben Wattenberg, are "unyoung, unpoor, and unblack."[15] They resent any mobility on the part of lower-status groups and demand that the political process recognize the traditional values to which they subscribe. Their anger is directed at those who are "not like themselves"; this involves a racial dimension which, as Allen Hunter notes, is experienced as a *cultural* threat as well as an economic one:

> Black demands for racial justice--the Right argues--threaten
> family, community, parental control; they also threaten
> individual rights, liberty, freedom to compete and be
> rewarded for one's own efforts.[16]

Elected officials who have "stood up" to issues which feed on white racial anxieties have become New Right cult heroes. Spiro Agnew's acceptance by the New Right, for example, was based on the way he "talked back" to black leaders. Former Los Angeles Police Chief Ed Davis endeared himself to anti-affirmative action activists with statements such as, "I always felt that the government really was out to force me to hire 4-foot-11 transvestite morons."[17]

The central political cult figure for the New Right with respect to race is undoubtedly Jesse Helms, the Republican Senator from North Carolina. Senator Helms was *the* spokesperson for the New Right at the Republican National Convention in 1980. His influence helped to secure New Right "victories" in key platform battles over Taiwan, opposition to SALT, and the dropping of support for the ERA. Helms gained his political influence from a powerful grass-roots organization built upon direct-mail appeals,[18] from the support of Christian fundamentalist groups, and from a network of conservative think tanks which he and his Senate aides helped to organize.[19]

Helms echoes New Right themes in his critique of New Deal liberalism and the social injustice it has created:

> For forty years an unending barrage of "deals"--the New
> Deal, the Fair Deal, the New Frontier, and the Great Society
> not to mention court decisions tending in the same
> direction--have regimented our people and our economy and
> federalized almost every human enterprise. This onslaught
> has installed a gigantic scheme for redistributing the wealth
> and rewards the indolent and penalizes the hardworking.[20]

While his "America-first," anti-welfare, anti-ERA, anti-abortion politics have
captured national attention, his racial politics have consistently been at the
center of his appeal:

> Race was central to Helms' campaign in 1972 . . . Helms'
> anti-"busing" stance was the core of his campaign . . . As
> recently as his 1978 reelection campaign, Helms told
> reporters that segregation was right "for its time." Unlike
> many "New South" Republicans, who saw an overture to
> Blacks as crucial to the Republican party's future in the
> region, Helms made no special effort to reach Black voters.
> In contrast to Strom Thurmond, also running for reelection
> that year, Helms added no Blacks to his staff and made no
> effort to appear responsive to Black needs.[21]

In 1983 Helms launched a filibuster in the Senate to block legislation
for a Martin Luther King, Jr. national holiday. "The legacy of Dr. King was
really division," Helms declared, "not love." He went on to denounce King for
associating with communists[22] and for his "calculated use of non-violence as a
provocative act." "Dr. King's action-oriented Marxism," Helms argued, " . . . is
not compatible with the concepts of this country."[23] Actions such as these,
coupled with his strong refusal to cater to black voters, have served to define
the "hard-line" New Right position on racial politics.[24]

Code Words and the Rearticulation of Racial Ideology

In the aftermath of the racial upheavals of the 1960s, any effective
challenge to the egalitarian ideals framed by the racial minority movements
could no longer rely on the racism characteristic of Social Darwinist ideologies.
Racial equality had to be acknowledged, at least in the abstract, as a desirable
goal. But the *meaning* of equality, and the proper means for achieving it,

remained open to political contestation. In harnessing the "politics of resentment," the New Right cannot simply defend patterns of racial inequality by demanding a return to segregation or by reviving simplistic notions of biological superiority/inferiority.[25]

The New Right generally does not display *overt* racism. It has gained political currency by *rearticulating* [26] racial ideology--by using "code words" (non-racial rhetoric which disguises racial issues) which mask the explosive racial elements of a range of social issues. Rearticulation does not require an explicitly racial discourse, and would in fact be severely limited by any direct advocacy of racial inequality. While referring indirectly to racial themes, the use of "coded" phrases and symbols does not directly challenge or contradict popular democratic or egalitarian ideals (e.g., "justice" or "equal opportunity").

The use of code words should not, however, be construed as simply a flimsy cover for racist ideas. Most New Right activists do not believe that blacks are innately inferior to whites, but they may associate blacks with a distinct "belief system" in opposition to their own. By such logic, blacks come to symbolize "the crisis of morality," "the disintegration of the family," and "lawlessness and disorder." Racial categories are thus infused with new meaning and manipulated in political discourse.

The New Right's use of "code words" is a classic example of rearticulation, geared to mobilize a mass base threatened by minority gains, but disinclined to embrace overtly racist politics. Beginning with the Wallace campaign of 1968, one can trace the pattern of New Right experimentation with the rearticulation of racial meanings through the use of these code words.

New Right Rumblings and "Coded" Racial Politics

In some respects, the first rumblings of the present-day New Right agenda were heard in George Wallace's 1968 presidential bid. His entry into the presidential race was first seen as a replay of the Dixiecrat strategy which had led to the candidacy of Strom Thurmond twenty years earlier. Few analysts expected Wallace to have mass appeal outside the South, yet in Northern blue-collar strongholds like Milwaukee, Detroit, and Philadelphia, he demonstrated surprising strength.

Although Wallace's image as a racist politician had originally launched him into the national spotlight, the cultivation of such an image was clearly a liability to a legitimate presidential contender in the late-1960s. Wallace was forced to incorporate his racial message as a subtext, implicit but "coded," in a dramatic populist appeal. In doing so, he struck certain chords that anticipated the New Right agenda--defense of traditional values, opposition to "big government," and emotion-laden patriotic and militaristic themes. But the centerpiece of his appeal remained his racial politics,[27] however this time free of the "race baiting" which characterized his previous political incarnations. Wallace presented himself as a "law-and-order" candidate, an anti-statist, an inheritor of classical Southern populist traditions. He advocated the stepped-up use of force to repress ghetto rebellions, derided the black movement and the war on poverty, and attacked the "misguided" efforts of liberal politicians and intellectuals.

During the same campaign, voting-trends analyst and former congressional aide Kevin Phillips submitted a lengthy and scholarly analysis of U.S. voting trends to Nixon headquarters, arguing that a Republican victory and long-term electoral realignment was possible on *racial grounds*. Published the following year as *The Emerging Republican Majority*, Phillips' book assessed the collapse of New Deal liberalism and targeted the racial catalyst for its demise:

> The principal force which broke up the Democratic (New Deal) coalition is the Negro socioeconomic revolution and the liberal Democratic ideological inability to cope with it. . . . The Democratic Party fell victim to the ideological impetus of a liberalism which had carried it beyond the programs taxing the few for the benefit of the many (the New Deal) to programs taxing the many on behalf of the few (the Great Society). [28]

Phillips suggested a turn to the right for Republicans and the use of "coded" anti-black campaign rhetoric (e.g., law and order). Wallace's popular appeal, the disarray in Democratic ranks caused by the "Negro socio-economic revolution," and polling data from blue-collar districts around the country convinced Phillips that a strategic approach of this kind (dubbed the "southern strategy") could fundamentally shift political alignments which had been in effect since 1932. These insights continue to bear rich political fruit in the "Reagan revolution's" attempts to capitalize on the collapse of New Deal liberalism.

The New Right Agenda

Civil liberties are essential to a society which recognizes diversity and values pluralism, but "New Right philosophy rejects pluralism and thus often considers civil liberties as superfluous or dangerous."[29] James McClellan, president of the Center for Judicial Studies (which has been funded in large part by the Moral Majority Foundation) has said that "civil rights has nothing to do with liberty, but is in fact part of the Marxist Agenda."[30] Among a host of other concerns, the New Right would like to see

- The elimination of federal affirmative action programs.

- The gutting of the Voting Act and the Civil Rights Act.

- The reduction of available legal services to the poor by crippling or abolishing the Legal Services Corporation.

- The enactment of legislation stripping federal courts of jurisdiction over constitutional challenges.

- The enactment of a constitutional amendment to abolish the right to choose abortion.

- The enactment of legislation providing federal aid to religious schools or tax breaks to parents paying tuition to such schools.

- The enactment of a restrictive immigration policy coupled with strict enforcement efforts by the Immigration and Naturalization Service to "regain control of our borders."

Many of these issues have racial subtexts. From foreign policy to family politics, the issue of race is implicitly woven into the framing of New Right politics.

New Right foreign policy initiatives are guided by the objective of restoring U.S. hegemony in world affairs. This has meant a refusal to surrender turf (every major New Right organization conducted campaigns in 1977 against ratification of the Panama Canal treaties), a call to restore the balance of trade in America's favor, and an ever-vigilant struggle against communism. Japan receives an inordinate amount of blame for the rising trade deficit, with New Rightists employing racist clichés reminiscent of World War II propaganda in their demands for restrictions on Japanese imports.

The New Right's goal for Latin America is to contain communism (or eradicate it, in Nicaragua's case) and to bolster seemingly eroding support for regimes sympathetic to the United States. But a more immediate concern is fear of the massive immigration to the United States which may result from political destabilization in the region:

> The deep concern of much of Central America is that the dominos are now likely to fall, and that the consequences will be the flooding of the U.S. by immigrants on a scale and of a bent of culture and mind sufficient to terminate the Republic in the Pacific Southwest, in fact if not in law, in behavior if not in formal allegiance, in time if not tomorrow.[31]

On South Africa, the New Right has conceded that apartheid is a morally unacceptable system, but has framed the discussion as a question of the lesser of two evils. The *National Review* suggested to its readers that "before we pressure South Africa into exchanging imperfection for chaos, we should ask ourselves whether we really want to feed it."[32] An article in *Human Events* claimed that what black South African protesters were really after was " . . . the overthrow of South Africa's current pro-western government and its replacement by terrorist groups which are financed by Moscow."[33]

Other examples of the racial subtext to issues abound on the New Right agenda, but the most effective use of "code words" appears in the New Right's treatment of the gnawing issues of affirmative action and equality in education.

Affirmative Action and "Reverse Discrimination"

On the issue of affirmative action, the New Right has made significant advances in rearticulating the meaning of racial equality. The strength of its argument is its specific appeal to equality and "fairness." The New Right suggests that it wants a "colorblind" society--a social order where racial considerations are never entertained in the selection of leaders, in hiring decisions, or in the distribution of goods and services in general. What blocks the attainment of such a good and just society, the New Right argues, is the state's aquiescence to the demands of racial minorities and other "special interests" at the expense of whites.

As the New Right sees it, different forms of racial "injustice" emerged from the political gains of racial minority movements in the 1960s. This new injustice confers "group rights" upon racial minority groups, thus granting the privilege of "preferential treatment" to individuals who "belong" to these groups. The culprit behind this new form of "racism" is seen as the state itself. In attempting to eliminate racial discrimination, the state has gone too far: it legitimized group rights, established affirmative action mandates, and spent money on a range of social programs which, according to the New Right, debilitated, rather than uplifted, its target populations. In this scenario, the victims of racial discrimination have dramatically shifted, due to "reverse discrimination," from racial minorities to whites, particularly white males.

The New Right's ability to mobilize resentment against the "group rights" demands of racial minorities dovetails with the neoconservative argument that only "equality of opportunity" can be a valid objective of state policy. The New Right's mobilization of "grass-roots" opposition to residential and school desegregation, to preferential hiring and school admission schemes, and to minority "set-asides" in government contracting, provides a populist counterpoint to the more abstract and theoretically developed critique developed by neoconservative scholars such as Nathan Glazer and Thomas Sowell. What distinguishes New Right from neoconservative politics on this issue is that the New Right seeks to capitalize on the resentment of whites toward "reverse discrimination" as a basis for political mobilization--something which the neoconservatives find dangerous to the well-being of the nation. Nathan Glazer has warned:

> The demand for special treatment will lead to animus against other groups that already have it, by those who think they should have it and don't. One sees the opportunity for the growth of antagonisms with a potentiality for evil that all such ethnic and group antagonisms possess. And the fact that among the victims might be that old elite that practiced discrimination in the past scarcely reassures us: as in Lebanon today, the former discriminators and the discriminated against would go down together.[34]

Busing

Perhaps the single most important judicial decision to usher in the modern civil rights movement was the U.S. Supreme Court's decision in *Brown v. Board of Education of Topeka*. The attorney for the plaintiff, and later-to-be Supreme Court Justice, Thurgood Marshall, predicted that racially segregated schools would be eliminated within five years.[35]

His optimism proved to be unfounded. Busing has become an explosive issue leading to resentment, anger, and mob violence in cities such as Pontiac, Michigan and Boston, Massachusetts. Many cities experience "white flight" as a political response on the part of whites who opposed busing. But those who could not, or chose not to leave, joined anti-busing organizations. Some of these groups became rallying points for the emerging New Right network.

New Right leaders have helped to coordinate anti-busing mobilization. Howard Phillips worked with anti-busing protesters in Boston, maintaining close ties with the South Boston Information Center. Former Young Americans for Freedom activist Arnold Steinberg organized the BUS-STOP group and raised money for anti-busing activists through a highly successful direct-mail campaign.[36]

In addressing the issue of busing, the New Right has downplayed the unabashedly racist sentiments and ideology which initially characterized anti-busing mobilization. "Power to the people, fuck the niggers" (a slogan used by the anti-busing movement in Pontiac) may be in touch with the populist sentiment which the New Right seeks to exploit, but its angry denunciation of blacks makes for bad politics.

The New Right has opposed busing not as an overt effort to maintain school segregation or racial purity in residential life, but as an assault on those cherished institutions, the "family" and the "community." School integration, New Right activists have argued, means that the state is usurping powers which properly belong to parents, who have the right to decide what kind of communities their children will be raised in and what kind of education their children will receive. The state, through its reckless intervention in the private social affairs of individuals, is bringing about the demise of the family and the collapse of communal identity:

> The anti-busing movement is nourished by . . . fears for the loss of the family. The loss of neighborhood schools is perceived as a threat to community, and therefore family stability by many people, particularly in cities where ethnically homogeneous communites remain.[37]

Formerly progressive themes of "parental involvement" and "community control" are thus harnessed by the New Right in their conservative discourse. The objective result is the prevention of race mixing in the schools, while charges of racism are blunted or avoided altogether. One measure of the success of this strategy is the confusion it engendered in leftist groups during the Boston busing controversy of the mid-1970s. The Socialist Workers Party endorsed the busing plan, criticized the local and national media for downplaying the degree of racial hostility towards blacks in South Boston, and supported the use of federal troops to enforce desegregation efforts.[38] The Revolutionary Union, by contrast, opposed the busing plan, minimized the extent of racial violence, and organized People for a Decent Education, arguing that the question was not one of race, but of quality education.[39]

The Fundamentalist Christian School Movement

The question of racial segregation in schooling was central to the New Right's coup of bringing right-wing Christian fundamentalists into its political orbit. In the late 1950s, in the wake of the *Brown* decision, White Citizens' Councils established segregated schools in the South. These schools formed the core of the fundamentalist Christian school movement of today. Jerry Falwell, in his controversial 1981 *Penthouse* interview, commented on the dramatic growth of this movement: "We've grown from 1,400 schools in 1961 to 16,000. We're adding a new school every seven hours."[40]

Unlike Catholic academies, which have traditionally lobbied for increased public assistance, the Christian schools have adamantly refused to depend on federal monies and have defended their autonomy from state and federal curricular guidelines. By the late 1970s, however, the effects of school desegregation battles brought them under closer federal scrutiny and, somewhat ironically, to the attention of the New Right:

> These schools, though they seek to avoid government regulation . . . are indirectly affected by government policy because they enjoy charitable status, which means that they are exempt from taxation. However, in 1978, under the Carter administration, the Internal Revenue Service tried to implement a policy which would have required all schools founded after 1953 to abide by public policy guidelines on matters of racial integration. Unless schools were willing to do so the tax-exempt status of a school would be removed. The legal source and precise meaning of this initiative were unclear, but the campaign against it brought into political alliance a large number of Baptist pastors and new-right pressure-groups.[41]

Paul Weyrich of the Committee for the Survival of a Free Congress encouraged the New Right to take up the cause of a number of segregated

Christian schools precisely at the time when the Internal Revenue Service was moving against them. This was a crucial connection, and it was in 1979, with the creation of the Christian Voice, Moral Majority, and Religious Roundtable, that Jerry Falwell, Pat Robertson, and other fundamentalist preachers threw their lot in with the New Right.

The religious right and the New Right share a similar distrust of the interventionist state; they harbor a similar contempt for the "secular humanism"[42] which, they argue, pervades public education; and they utilize a common political vocabulary--particularly with regard to code words:

> One longtime observer of North Carolina schools, noting that many of the so-called Christian schools were thrown together in the wake of court-ordered desegregation and are known throughout the South as "seg academies," remarked, "When they said busing," they usually mean "niggers." Nowadays when they say "Christian," they usually mean "white."[43]

Thus, racial meaning is effectively conveyed without resorting to racial categories. Political organizing in such a context allows activists (and their adherents) to disguise any overt racism--they become less susceptible to charges which would "delegitimate" their actions. It is a strategy which the alliance of the New Right and the religious right has effectively exploited.

Textbook Censorship

The New Right has fueled and fed upon a growing movement towards censorship in the United States. According to the American Library Association, censorship incidents have jumped 300 percent since 1980. The public burning of books, records, and posters has become frighteningly commonplace. New Right concerns have centered on school texts which they argue denigrate, and therefore undermine, traditional forms of authority, present "deviant" sexual behavior and alternative lifestyles in a positive manner, and offer evolutionary perspectives on the origins of living things, to the exclusion of creationist explanations.

Interestingly, the monitoring of books for public school adoption is another issue where a "hidden" racial dimension informs New Right politics. The social movements of the 1960s had a profound effect on curriculum development in primary and secondary education. The racial/ethnic, sexual, class, and religious biases of traditional educational materials came under attack from educators, parents, and students alike. As it was, the adventures of "Dick and Jane" effectively marginalized those whose experiences were different. Thus, the demand arose for materials which would reflect the diversity of the nation's peoples and their lives. Efforts in this direction helped to "revolutionize" texts and what was taught in the classroom.

In the wake of what was in some respects a minor "cultural revolution," some analysts began to wonder whether educators had gone too far in accommodating the demands of those who had been previously "marginalized." They feared that we had replaced the traditional educational mission of "assimilating" young people from non-Anglo-American backgrounds into the mainstream of American life, with some form of radical "cultural pluralism."[44] Members of the "silent majority" resented their fall from being portrayed as the "ideal-typical" people. In many local communities, the content of the new textbooks was challenged and the effort to present cultural diversity questioned.

In 1975 the Heritage Foundation formed the National Congress for Educational Excellence to coordinate the activities of roughly 200 textbook-protest organizations nationwide. This effort capitalized on the feelings of many whites that their values and lifestyles were being neglected by "multi-cultural" texts:

> The supplementary books, in particular, play out the alienation felt by urban intellectuals and university militants of the 1960s, who seem to the protesters to have taken over the publishing houses in New York. Some of the selections were unpatriotic, sacrilegious and pro-minorities, and they would, as the parents predicted, legitimize different values and raise heretofore taboo questions. Equally important was the almost total exclusion of people like themselves from the "multi-cultural" texts. . . . Paradoxically, the board's [Kanawha County school board in West Virginia] attempt to broaden the English curriculum had shifted the spectrum away from the majority of citizens in the country.[45]

The New Right, in this instance, can push a racial agenda merely by arguing for "traditional" lifestyles and families, and for the return to a more homogeneous image of everyday life, purged of "secular humanism" and the rest of the unsettling ambiguities generated over the past several decades.

Race and the New Class Alignment

> On one side, threatening traditional values, are the feminists,
> the liberals, the university communities, minorities,
> residents of urban centers, and the media. On the other--the
> side of the angels--are the "pro-family" forces, the leadership
> of the New Right and its disgruntled constituents, plus a
> growing political movement of fundamentalist evangelical
> ministers. . . . Both sides are competing for the soul of
> America.[46]

The New Right's dream is to consolidate a "new majority" which can dismantle the welfare state, legislate a return to "traditional morality," and stem the tide of political and cultural dislocation which the 1960s and 1970s represented.[47] This project links the assault on liberalism and "secular humanism" and the obsession with individual guilt and responsibility where social questions are concerned (crime, sex, education, poverty), with a fierce critique of the liberal state. The Supreme Court is criticized for its liberal bias in matters of race relations. The electoral college system is opposed for restricting third-party efforts and, as Kevin Phillips has suggested, for maximizing the influence of a "Third World state"[48] such as California. The political strategy the New Right advances is populist--use of the initiative process, for example, serves as an "end-run" around the courts, the bureaucracy, the Congress, and state legislatures.

While castigating "big government" in the abstract, the New Right's political perspective reveals a contradictory approach to the state around the question of what is *legitimate* state activity. In the eyes of New Right leaders, affirmative action is not an appropriate form of state intervention but the abolition of abortion or tax credits to segregated "Christian" schools is. While preaching an anti-statism which relentlessly chastises government for meddling in too many places, the New Right nonetheless calls on the state to intervene in issues (e.g. prayer in schools) that advance its concerns. Thus, while calling for a return to the basics of the Constitution, New Right activists also seem intent on revising it through amendments that address their social concerns.

Conclusion

Central to my analysis of New Right racial politics is the belief that race has been, and continues to be, a fundamental *organizing principle* of social relationships in the United States.[49] The organization of the labor market, the distribution of "rights" and "privileges," and the manner in which economic, social, and political "interests" are understood and articulated are all shaped by ever-changing conceptions of race.

Race has been and continues to be a defining issue of political reaction and a key feature of New Right mobilization. The "politics of resentment" has incubated and developed in the political atmosphere created by the racial minority movements of the past several decades; its agenda has been framed in opposition to the politics and ideology of these movements. Through advocacy of the limits of state intervention, the New Right seeks to reinterpret the meaning of race in the United States within a conservative discourse.

Race and class politics interface and overlap in the United States. Individuals and groups interpret the objective conditions of their existence as well as their subjective experiences in ways that draw upon both racially-based and class-based meanings. The New Right has been quite successful in grafting these meanings together. New Right publisher William Rusher provides an apt illustration of the racial dimension "hidden" in much of the "new class" analysis of the right:[50]

> A new economic division pits the producers--businessmen, manufacturers, hard-hats, blue-collar workers, and farmers--against a new and powerful class of non-producers comprised of a liberal verbalist elite (the dominant media, the major foundations and research institutions, the educational establishment, the federal and state bureaucracies) and a semipermanent welfare constituency, all coexisting happily in a state of mutually sustaining symbiosis.[51]

The "semipermanent welfare constituency" is implicitly nonwhite in the popular political imagination. Rusher's approach conjures up anti-big government sentiments by blaming unemployed racial minorities for being parasites at the expense of "productive" workers. (David Edgar, for example, has stated that "California's tax-cutting referendum Prop. 13 was as much a vote against black welfare as it was a vote for lower taxes."[52]) Rusher's *ressentiment* is racial, even though his vocabulary is that of class. This rearticulation of racial ideology has been crucial to recent New Right advances.

Notes

1.   Alan Crawford, *Thunder on the Right: The "New Right" and the Politics of Resentment* (New York: Random House, 1980), 5.

2.   Along with Crawford see, for example, Gillian Peele, *Revival and Reaction: The Right in Contemporary America* (Oxford: Oxford University Press, 1984); and John S. Saloma III, *Ominous Politics: The New Conservative Labyrinth* (New York: Hill and Wang, 1984).

3.   See, for example, Linda Gordon and Allen Hunter, "Sex, Family and the New Right: Anti-Feminism as a Political Force," *Radical America* 11 (1977) and 12 (1978).

4.   Lillian Rubin, *Busing and Backlash* (Berkeley and Los Angeles: University of California Press, 1972).

5.   Allen Hunter, "In the Wings: New Right Ideology and Organization," *Radical America,* Spring 1981, 1. (Page cited refers to a copy of the article in the Data Center Files: Data Center, 464 19th St., Oakland, CA 94612).

6.   The term "new social movements" is employed with reservations to distinguish the popular movements of the postwar period from their earlier antecedents (where applicable), and from movements of class- or status-based groups in the traditional Marxian or Weberian sense. The significance of the new social movements in transforming the political and cultural landscape of the U.S. in the 1960s is discussed at length in Michael Omi and Howard Winant, *Racial Formation in the United States: From the 1960s to the 1980s* (New York and London: Routledge and Kegan Paul, 1986).

7.   Peele, *Revival and Reaction*, 52.

8.   Hunter, *In the Wings,* 3-4.

9.   In addition, certain newspapers express New Right perspectives in their framing of the news and in their editorial observations. These include the

Manchester Union Leader (New Hampshire), the *Richmond News-Leader* (Virginia), the *Arizona Republic*, and the *Santa Ana Register* (California). New Right publishing houses include Arlington House in New Rochelle, New York (which distributes many of its books through the Conservative Book Club) and Green Hill Publications of Ottawa, Illinois.

10. "The New Right: A Special Report," *Conservative Digest*, June 1979, 10.

11. Viguerie comments on how he became the most successful direct-mail fundraiser in America:

> [The New Right] had outstanding writers, debaters and public speakers . . . I could have tried to go that route. And I probably wouldn't have amounted to a hill of beans. I didn't have the educational background, and I was starting too late to catch up with the others . . . But I realized that what we didn't have was someone who could take ideas, the writings and the books and market them to the people (Richard Viguerie, *The New Right: We're Ready to Lead* [Ottawa, Ill: Green Hill Publications, 1981], 27-28).

12. The seriousness of the New Right's crusade to purge the media of its liberal bias can be seen in the activities of Accuracy in Media and the attempt by activists to organize a hostile takeover of CBS in 1985.

13. This "politicization" raises some disturbing questions. Direct mail frequently involves a simplification of political debates and divisions to the point of distortion. On top of this, as Peele warns, "It has been suggested that the creation of single-issue constituencies by direct mail without the need for the normal accommodation demanded by personal encounters within a voluntary association may make politics in the United States less amenable to bargaining and compromise" (Peele, *Revival and Reaction*, 58).

14. Ibid, 54.

15. Crawford, *Thunder on the Right*, 148.

16. Hunter, *In the Wings*, 14.

17. Rowland Evans and Robert Novak, "Ed Davis, Toned-Down Favorite," *Washington Post*, 3 February 1978, cited in Crawford, *Thunder on the Right*, 104.

18. His 1978 reelection campaign was a milestone in contemporary politics; it reached out to a national audience to decide the fate of a state election. Direct mail appeals, orchestrated by Richard Viguerie, brought in 7 million dollars from over 200,000 donors. The Congressional Club, Helms' political organization, emerged from this reelection effort.

19. These include the Institute for American Relations, the Center for a Free Society, the American Family Institute, and the Institute for Money and Inflation.

20. Jesse Helms, *When Free Men Shall Stand* (Grand Rapids, Michigan: Zondervan Publishing House, 1976), 11.

21. Bob McMahon, "Helms: Shining Light of the New Right," *Guardian*, 3 September 1980.

22. Ironically these charges had their origins in the FBI's campaigns to discredit King, in which Robert Kennedy was also involved.

23. "Helms Rips King Holiday," *San Francisco Chronicle*, 4 October 1983.

24. Richard Viguerie and Terry Dolan, by contrast, have argued for making overtures to conservative blacks to get them in the New Right fold.

25. More complex scientistic ideologies of racial inferiority are a different matter, and here the New Right is actively engaged. See L. Kamin, R. Lewontin and Stephen Rose, *Not in Our Genes* (New York: Pantheon Books, 1984) for an excellent account of the modern application of biologism to social and political categories such as race.

26. *Rearticulation* is the process of redefinition of political interests and identities, through the recombination of familiar ideas and values in hitherto unrecognized ways. The role of rearticulation in mobilizing the racial minority movements of the 1960s and the forces on the right which seek to recast the meaning of racial equality in the present period is discussed in Omi and Winant, *Racial Formation*.

27. This observation was not lost by conservative analysts. "American conservatives should make no mistake about it, the only thing Wallace has against Washington is its racial policy. In all his other attitudes he is one of the biggest centralizers of them all" (John Ashbrook, "And Anyway, Is Wallace a Conservative?," *National Review*, 22 November 1968, 1048).

28. Kevin Phillips, *The Emerging Republican Majority* (New Rochelle: Arlington House, 1969), 37.

29. Chip Berlet, "Civil Liberties," *Shmate* 11 and 12 (Summer 1985): 37.

30. Cited in a fundraising letter by Anthony Podesta, president of (the anti-new Right) People for the American Way, 1986.

31. John Hutchinson, *National Review* 24 (1984). Cited in "The U.S. Right-Wing and Latin America," *The Hammer* 7 (Summer 1984), 9.

32. *National Review* 11 (1985).

33. Cited in "The U.S. Right Looks at South Africa," *The Hammer* 9 (Spring 1985): 14.

34. Nathan Glazer, "Liberty, Equality, Fraternity--And Ethnicity," *Ethnic Dilemmas: 1964-1982* (Cambridge, Mass. and London: Harvard University Press, 1983), 229.

35. Richard Kluger, *Simple Justice: The History of Brown v. Board of Education and Black America's Struggle for Equality* (New York: Random House, 1975), 706.

36. Crawford, *Thunder on the Right*, 159.

37. Gordon and Hunter, *Sex, Family and the New Right*, 11.

38. Willie Mae Reid, Peter Camejo, Fred Halstead, Dave Frankel and Elizabeth Stone, *The Racist Offensive Against Busing: The Lessons of Boston and How to Fight Back* (New York: Pathfinder Press, 1974).

39. *Revolutionary Union*, "The Busing Situation and Education: Fight for Equality and Against the Ruling Class' Divide and Conquer Schemes," December 1974.

40. Hunter, *In the Wings*, 14.

41. Peele, *Revival and Reaction*, 96-97.

42. The definition of "secular humanism" is itself a matter of political debate. William Safire notes: "Secular humanism, to the evangelist James Kennedy, is a 'godless, atheistic, evolutionary, amoral, collectivist, socialistic, communistic religion' posing a threat to schoolchildren. To Michael J. Rosenberg, editor of *Near East Report*, 'Secular humanist has become the new label employed to indict anyone who opposes school prayer, believes in evolution or disagrees with the religious right's views on abortion'" (William Safire, "Secs Appeal," *This World, Sunday Magazine, San Francisco Chronicle*, 2 February 1986, 17).

43. Mark Pinsky, "Helmsman of the Right," *The Progressive*, April 1980, 47.

44. Neoconservative scholars such as Nathan Glazer have echoed these fears. Writing on the "strong" cultural pluralist orientation of contemporary "multicultural education," Glazer mourns the manner in which assimilationist perspectives have been discarded and assesses its meaning for racial minorities:

> It is my impression that those who want to teach loyalty to a single nation that has virtues are intimidated and demoralized by the events of 1965-1975 and the ways these have been interpreted in the dominant media and in many scholarly circles. Thus the problem is not that minority groups will be crushed by American culture but that, quite the opposite, they will be taught an unrealistic and unrewarding emphasis on the independence and separate virtue of each group, and the necessity for it to defend itself from the basically corrupt Anglo-American dominated society (Nathan Glazer, "The Problem of Ethnic Studies," *Ethnic Dilemmas*, 118).

45. Curtis Selzer, "A Confusion of Goals," *The Nation*, 2 November 1974, 430.

46. Crawford, *Thunder on the Right*, 145.

47. This paper cannot sufficiently delve into the impact of New Right politics on "mainstream" party politics--and more specifically the Reagan administration. Suffice it to say that while Reagan has incurred the wrath of some New Rightists for his abandonment of, or slow-moving posture towards some social issues (e.g., anti-abortion and prayer in public schools amendments), his scorecard on racial issues remains nearly impeccable.

48. The term "Third World state" is from Phillips, who uses it to describe states which have an increasing racial minority population. Phillips writes, "Retention of the Electoral College would probably guarantee a minority-oriented presidential selection process for the 1980s" (Kevin Phillips, "Abolish the Electoral College!" *Morgantown Dominion-Post*, 15 July 1977 cited in Crawford, *Thunder on the Right*, 324).

50. The presumed failure of the Great Society and other liberal experiments has focused attention on members of the "new class" (educators, administrators, planners, consultants, network journalists, etc.). The New Right believes that these "pointy-heads" (a New Right characterization) control much of the state apparatus and are responsible for the current political, economic, and cultural malaise. During the 1960s and 1970s, according to the New Right, the state was recklessly allowed to expand and intervene in every aspect of social life; it now continues to dictate policy with disastrous results. In particular, it has acceded to racial minority demands and now gives minorities privileged access to jobs and social services.

51. William Rusher, *The Making of a New Majority Party* (Ottawa, Ill.: Greenhill Publications, 1975), 31.

52. David Edgar, "Reagan's Hidden Agenda: Racism and the New American Right," *Race & Class* 22 (1981): 231.

Reaganomics and
Latino Organizational Strategies

Isidro D. Ortiz and Marguerite V. Marin

At the beginning of the 1980s, a major American corporation declared that the decade was to be the "Decade of the Hispanics," during which Latinos would make unprecedented socioeconomic and political strides. As the decade unfolded, however, any strides made by Latinos were quickly eclipsed by actions taken by the new presidential administration. Declaring that it possessed a mandate to reshape the federal programmatic landscape, the Reagan administration quickly moved to reduce or terminate many federal programs, including some which Latinos had used to gain socioeconomic and political toeholds during the 1960s and 1970s.

Various predictions about the significance and political consequences of the Reagan administration's initiatives have been articulated since 1981. In 1982, according to Dolbeare, the cutbacks had been characterized by Piven and Cloward as "a class war of the rich against the poor, intended to reduce workers' bargaining power, improve businesses' profit margins and thus restore general prosperity."[1] The two writers predicted that the Reagan administration's policies would precipitate a resistance movement to be led by organized labor, environmentalists, the elderly, the poor, and women, joined by social service and state workers. Loosely constituting a "class," this alliance would be "called into political efforts by Reagan's policies, and ultimately would triumph in the name of democracy."[2] The corporate sector and its government allies would lose strength in the face of such resistance.

Dolbeare concluded that some of the major aspects of the Piven and Cloward prediction had emerged clearly by 1984. In his view, Latinos, especially urban Latinos, are in a position to play a decisive role in the outcome of the current political struggle. Given this assessment of the pivotal role of Latinos, which we believe to be accurate, an examination of the Latino response to the budgetary cutbacks is in order. We shall focus on the reaction of Latino political organizations and their leaders to the Reagan initiatives and highlight the responses of two of the major Latino organizations--The Mexican-American Legal Defense and Educational Fund (MALDEF) and the National Council of La Raza (NCLR). Piven and Cloward predicted that Latino organizations would articulate and mobilize opposition to the Reagan programmatic cutbacks and coalesce with other organizations which are also opposed to the Reagan initiatives. We will document the course of action that these two organizations have actually taken.

Organizations are critical institutions in the Latino community. In the past they have shaped and at present they continue to influence political life among Latinos. Most of them have been negatively affected by the federal budgetary cutbacks: for example, as a result of the cutbacks from 1981 to 1983, Latino organizations in cities across the country lost over 4,000 staff positions.[3] Moreover, the loss of funding precipitated the demise of some organizations and created pessimism over the federal funding of organizational endeavors in general.

An emphasis on the activities of MALDEF and NCLR is warranted for several reasons: they have played a significant advocacy role in national policymaking and have established programs and services for indigent Latinos in communities throughout the United States.[4] Both organizations were created in the late 1960s with the assistance of the Ford Foundation.[5] Thereafter, they grew rapidly and have been recognized as influential organizations in the Latino community by the mass media, the philanthropic foundations, government officials, and Latinos themselves. Both have suffered from the recent federal budgetary cutbacks. In 1981, for example, MALDEF lost $600,000 in federal grants which amounted to 20 percent of its 1981-82 budget. As a result of the loss, MALDEF's leadership found it necessary to undertake a "painful staff reduction" that resulted in the elimination of about one-fourth of MALDEF's staff positions in 1982-83.[6] The reductions disrupted MALDEF's activities in the areas of urban crime prevention, equal employment, and immigration.[7] In light of the organizations' roles and the impact of the federal budget cuts on them, an examination of their behavior is crucial if we are to assess accurately the prospects for the emergence of a class-based resistance movement involving Latinos.

We shall look first at the responses of these organizations to the Reagan Administration's budgetary cutbacks. We will demonstrate that while MALDEF and NCLR have reacted generally in a manner anticipated by Piven and Cloward, they have also reacted in an unanticipated way. Specifically, they have managed to secure resources from corporations and have formed new partnerships with the corporate sector, although this sector's interests are in conflict with the interests of the "new" class coalition conceived by Piven and

Cloward, particularly its poor and disadvantaged racial-minority segments.[8] In addition, the organizations have cultivated a positive image of corporations that may obscure the negative political consequences of federal supported policies for Latinos. We will discuss the implications of this development and predict future organizational activities vis-a-vis corporations.

Organizational Responses

The Articulation and Mobilization of Opposition

In response to the Reagan Administration's initiatives, MALDEF and NCLR articulated and mobilized opposition to them and selectively coalesced with other groups, as Piven and Cloward had anticipated. Their efforts aimed to preserve programmatic gains important to Latinos (such as bilingual education programs in local school districts), to prevent violations of civil rights and other forms of discrimination against Latinos, and to enhance Latino participation in the electoral process. As Charts 1 and 2 indicate, MALDEF and NCLR conducted a diverse repertoire of activities against the Reagan initiatives. However, the actions taken were not their only responses.

The Development of the Corporate Grantsmanship and Articulation Strategy [9]

Throughout the twentieth century, Latino political organizations have developed new strategies in response to changes in their environment, as Marin and Sierra have documented.[10] The corporate grantsmanship and articulation strategy represents yet another adaptation. This strategic innovation, which makes use of the desire of corporations to capitalize on the growing Latino consumer market, was not anticipated in the scenario painted by Piven and Cloward.

In 1981, MALDEF and NCLR joined more than 15 Latino organizations to submit grant proposals to 135 corporations, including 59 among the Fortune 500.[11] Fifty-eight percent of the organizations succeeded in getting one or more of their grant proposals funded.[12] The support received by MALDEF and NCLR reflects the type of assistance gained through the grantsmanship effort.

MALDEF obtained approximately $460,000 from a range of corporations, as Table 1 indicates. Large portions of the funding were unrestricted and made it possible for MALDEF to pay basic operating costs and to launch new projects. MALDEF also obtained "in-kind" contributions. In

Chart I

MALDEF
Resistance Activities
1983-84

Protecting civil rights

1. Testified orally and in writing against provisions of Simpson-Mazzoli immigration legislation in Congress.

2. Sponsored conference on Simpson-Mazzoli legislation in Southern California and formed national coalition to seek modification of provisions of Simpson-Mazzoli legislation.

3. In conjunction with the Leadership Conference on Civil Rights' Access to Justice Task Force developed campaign against Reagan administration legislative proposal prohibiting non-profit organizations from recovering fees in litigation against governmental agencies.

Preserving programmatic gains

1. Developed and implemented a two-year strategy to prevent passage of Reagan amendments to Bilingual Education Act in conjunction with the National Association of Bilingual Education.

2. Conducted information campaign on proposed amendments to the Bilingual Education Act to congressional and educational supporters of bilingual education.

3. In coalition with groups such as the American Civil Liberties Union, lobbied against Reagan administration proposals limiting access of poor people to courts as part of re-authorization of Legal Services Corporation Act.

4. Coordinated efforts of national civil rights organizations to remove rider on Legal Services Corporation Act prohibiting Legal Services Corporation attorneys from representing undocumented workers.

5. With fifty-four groups conducted study and submitted report to Congress documenting and criticizing the impact of the Reagan administration's

proposed 1983-84 budget.

6. Publicized anticipated negative impact on Latinos and poor of budgetary proposals.

Chart 2

NCLR Resistance Activities
1983-84

Preserving programmatic gains

1. With National Association for Bilingual Education and other minority organizations drafted legislation to reauthorize and strengthen existing federal bilingual education; legislation introduced by Latino congressmen.

2. Lobbied against Reagan administration proposed bilingual education measures.

Enhancing participation in the political process

1. Co-sponsored National Hispanic Voter Registration Campaign, bringing together the major Latino voter registration and education drives.

2. Registered Latino voters in drive to register one million new Latino voters by November 1984.

3. Created Civil Rights Network to provide community organizations with information on civil rights enforcement topics in order to enhance ability of Latino groups to participate in governmental hearings and complaints process as part of effort to impede perceived Reagan administration relaxation of enforcement of civil rights legislation.

Sources: Chart 1: Avila (1983); MALDEF (1983)
        Chart 2: NCLR (1984a, b; 1985b).
Charts 1 and 2 specify the organizations for 1983 and 1984. For a delineation of 1981 and 1982 organizational actions, particularly MALDEF's, see Martinez (1981, 1982).

Table 1
Corporate Supporters
MALDEF and NCLR
1982-83

MALDEF

Aerospace Corporation
Aetna Life and Casualty
American Telegraph & Telephone
   Company
American Toyota
Anheuser-Busch, Inc.
Avon Products
Bank of America
Chevron USA
Columbia Broadcasting System, Inc.
Continental Bank Foundation
Control Data Corporation
Cummins Engine
Dayton Hudson Corp.
Equitable Life Assurance Society
Exxon Corporation
Foremost Mc Keesm, Inc.
General Electric Corp.
General Mills, Inc.
Grace W.R.
Hunt-Wesson
IBM Corporation
Illinois Bell
Kaiser Aluminum
Kraft Co., Inc.
Lever Brothers
Levi Strauss Corp.
Lockheed Corp.
Manfacturers Hanover Trust Co.
McGraw-Hill, Inc.
Mobil Oil Corp.
Montegomery Ward
Pacific Mutual

Penny, J.C. Co., Inc.
Prudential Insurance Co.
Revlon
Rockwell International
   Corp.
S. Mark Corp.
Sears Roebuck and Co.
Spanish International
   Network
Standard Oil of Indiana
Stauffer Chemical Co.
Syntex Corp.
Twentieth-Century Fox
United Vinters
Wells Fargo Bank
Xerox Corp.

NCLR

Aetna Life and Casualty
Atlantic Richfield Co.
Chevron USA
Citibank/Citicorp.
Coca-Cola
Columbia Broadcasting
   System, Inc.
Conoco, Inc.
Control Data Corp.
Equitable Life Assurance
Society
Exxon Corp.
Levi Strauss Corp.
Standard Oil of Ohio
Tenneco Oil
Westinghouse

Source: Nuestro, 1982

1982, for example, MALDEF acquired access to the results of Levi-Strauss and Company's minority recruitment and employment efforts. The data "added ammunition to MALDEF's testimony on affirmative action before the U.S. Congress."[13] MALDEF's pamphlets were printed by Chevron, and MALDEF also received critiques on public relations matters from Anheuser-Busch, Inc. Moreover, corporate executives, such as Walter Haas, Jr. of Levi-Strauss, recruited "influential leaders" to appear at MALDEF's fund-raising dinners. These executives also hosted luncheons for their peers, enabling MALDEF to solicit additional corporate support. MALDEF's staff was encouraged by the support, as the vice president for development noted in 1982: "Each contribution is enormously helpful and it's encouraging to know we have many friends to rely on."[14]

NCLR's efforts to gain corporate support also proved productive, as Table 1 indicates. In 1982 NCLR obtained support for its technical assistance project, "Project RAICES (roots),"[15] from the Atlantic Richfield Foundation, Chevron USA, Levi-Strauss Foundation, Conoco, Inc., Standard Oil of Ohio, Aetna Life and Casualty Foundation, Coca-Cola Co., Citibank/Citicorp., Westinghouse, and Tenneco Oil. With the help of these corporations, NCLR developed accounting systems and provided formal training to the staff of urban and rural community-based organizations. The RAICES staff also helped to package proposals for housing and for infrastructure or industrial development projects and helped the recipients to conduct research on grant or investment fund sources.[16]

Corporate Articulation

While engaging in corporate grantsmanship, MALDEF and NCLR also laid the foundation for a collaborative definition of urban Latino problems, needs, and ameliorative approaches with the corporate sector. The first major step taken was the planning and sponsorship of the "First Corporate/Hispanic Partnership Summit" in San Francisco, California on October 23, 1982. This day-long conference brought together the leadership of major national Latino organizations and representatives from the corporate sector. Attended by approximately 125 persons, the meeting was sponsored by the Forum of National Hispanic Organizations and the Independent Sector. The former is an advocacy coalition of thirty-two Latino organizations with national programs and constituencies. Established in 1975, its objective is to increase Latino participation at all levels of the public and private sectors through a unified approach. The Independent Sector is an umbrella organization of more than 400 voluntary organizations, corporations, and foundations with national interests and a substantial impact in philanthropy and volunteer action.[17]

Several months after the summit, the president of NCLR, Raul Yzaguirre, promoted the "new partnerships" between Latinos and corporations at the fifth annual affiliates conference of NCLR. The private sector, he noted in his annual speech to the affiliates, was "realizing the importance of Latinos." Private sector executives believed that they had an obligation to offset the federal cutbacks, he said; moreover, the corporate sector had demonstrated a willingness to provide support to Latino organizations, as evidenced by its participation in the "summit meeting" in San Francisco. Both the corporate sector and Latinos had a "lot to gain" if a "partnership" between them succeeded. Therefore, he concluded, Latinos should work to make the partnership successful.[18]

Shortly thereafter, NCLR, under Raul Yzaguirre's direction, took a formal step to create the partnerships. NCLR formed a Corporate Advisory Council (CAC), composed of top-level officials of Gulf Oil Corporation, G.D. Searle & Company, the Equitable Life Assurance Society of the United States, Coca-Cola USA, Time, Inc., Johnson and Johnson, Rockwell International Corporation and General Motors Corporation. Its mission was to advise and assist NCLR in obtaining foundation and corporate funding and increased access to financal resources for NCLR-assisted projects. The CAC also served as a source of technical consultation on the improvement of NCLR operations, as well as projects and products, such as its publications.

In 1984, NCLR and CAC jointly planned NCLR's Seventh Annual Conference. The theme of the conference was "Hispanic Leadership: Impact, Influence and Involvement." The conference provided a "showcase for the concerns and accomplishments of NCLR and its network of Hispanic community-based organizations and its corporate and public sponsors." NCLR's president envisioned it as

> . . . a perfect opportunity to bring together and highlight Hispanic leaders, both for the Hispanic community and the nation, and to present them to corporate leaders. This stimulates the sharing of ideas and information, and a more productive cooperation within the community and potential private-sector funding sources.[19]

As a result of NCLR's and CAC's efforts, over thirty-five companies agreed to participate through financial contributions, exhibit booths, and sponsorship of special events at the conference. NCLR obtained financial support for the conference from Sears, Roebuck and Company, the Nestle

Company, Coca-Cola U.S.A., and General Motors Corporation.[20] The conference highlight was a speech by Vice-President George Bush, who cited opportunities afforded Latinos by the Reagan administration.[21]

On October 29, 1984, NCLR and five other national Latino organizations signed a multimillion dollar agreement with the Adolph Coors Company in Los Angeles, whose terms were intended to surpass the agreement reached by Coors and black organizations.[22] The Coors company agreed to hire more Latinos and to donate a minimum of $2.5 million to Latinos and Latino organizations between 1985 and 1990, provided that sales of its products increased among Latinos. The immediate objective was to increase the percentage of Latinos in the 9,000-member Coors company labor force from 8.5 percent to 12 percent. To achieve this objective, Coors would utilize Latino employment agencies. In return, the Latino organizations called off a boycott of Coors' products aimed at changing Coors' discriminatory hiring practices.

Coors also agreed to appoint a Latino vice president, increase the number of Hispanic-owned distributorships, and donate at least $500,000 a year to Latino projects in the succeeding five years. One-third of the money was designated for educational programs. The agreement was signed by representatives of NCLR, National Image, United States Hispanic Chamber of Commerce, American G.I. Forum, National Puerto Rican Coalition, and the Cuban National Planning Council. In accordance with the agreement, the organizations and the Coors Company formed a committee to monitor the progress of the Coor's commitment by meeting on a quarterly basis in 1985 and semi-annually every year thereafter.[23]

The Function: Amplification

It is tempting to regard corporations as omnipotent bodies which need not cultivate contacts and relationships with organizations in racial minority communities. Such a view, Orren has pointed out, is not appropriate, for urban-oriented minority organizations can perform functions vital to the achievement of corporate objectives. These functions are: orientation, protection, auxiliary services, non-profit sponsorship, and amplification.[24] Since 1981, MALDEF and NCLR have performed the latter function for their corporate supporters.

Amplification refers to the articulation within the minority community "of the good will and material achievements of the corporation."[25] Amplification may occur in written form through organizational publications or orally at organizational events such as annual conferences, fund raisers, and banquets. As Orren has noted, the "function is crucial to business aims, not only because the goal of ghettto projects is heightened legitimacy, but also simply because of the small scale of the individual projects."[26]

After garnering corporate support, MALDEF amplified corporate endeavors in its annual reports, newsletters, and events. In its 1981, 1982, 1983 and 1984 annual reports, MALDEF listed its corporate supporters for the preceding program year. MALDEF amplified corporate endeavors in its newsletter as early as 1982 through articles describing corporate deeds on behalf of MALDEF and Latinos and/or photographs of corporate officials providing support to MALDEF or being honored for their corporations' assistance to MALDEF. Three examples reveal how the amplification function has been performed. The first is an article entitled "Some Corporate Friends" which begins as follows:

> Do corporations owe it to society to pursue anything other than the almighty dollar? Some companies say "no." But a growing number believe it's not only good citizenship, but also good business to help minority communities. That turn of mind often means useful advice, lively printed work, cooperative allies and dependable financial support for MALDEF's work.[27]

The article then delineates the level of corporate support received by MALDEF, the nature of the support, and the corporations whose support had been exceptional. Lastly, it details the diversity of support and notes that each contribution facilitated MALDEF's efforts on behalf of Chicanos.

The second example is entitled "Anheuser-Busch Grant Spurs Leadership, Citizenship." As indicated by its title, this article publicizes the receipt of a grant from Anheuser-Busch for the operation of leadership development and citizenship programs. The article begins as follows: "Advancement for Hispanics nation-wide through three innovative programs will be the product of a major $200,000 grant to MALDEF from Anheuser-Busch, Inc."[28]

The third article illustrates the public recognition and articulation of corporate contributions. Entitled "Benefit MALDEF Dinners: Success in Los Angeles," it reports the results and proceedings of a MALDEF fund-raising dinner and graphically documents MALDEF's amplification of corporate support.[29]

NCLR also amplified corporate efforts in this manner, particularly in 1984. At its National Conference Awards Banquet, NCLR honored John

McNulty, Vice President for Public Relations, General Motors Corporation. One of the original members of CAC, McNulty was awarded NCLR's "President Award" for contributions to the philosophy, goals, and mission of NCLR. According to NCLR's president, McNulty had "played a key role in improving NCLR visibility in the corporate sector." He deserved the award because "he had demonstrated an understanding concern, and willingness to take action in support of Hispanics and Hispanic issues."[30]

In addition, NCLR formally acknowledged its appreciation of corporate support by listing its corporate supporters on a page of its convention program. It also encouraged its members to review the list and express their appreciation to the representatives of the corporations who were attending the conference and expressed its hope that when members of NCLR were purchasing goods or services, they would "remember--and buy from--these friends of the Council."[31] (The page is reproduced in Appendix A.)

In its second 1984 newsletter, *El Noticiario*, NCLR also publicized the donation of computer equipment and software by TRW, Inc. for the development of a Job Fair at its 1984 NCLR affiliates conference. The computerization, NCLR noted, promised to enhance the employment prospects for Hispanics in cities throughout the country. In an article entitled, "New Computerized Job Fair Offers Link with Success," NCLR noted that TRW, Inc. had promised to give NCLR the software developed for the Job Fair, thus making possible additional Job Fairs and other Hispanic events.[32]

Although amplification was not required for the receipt of corporate support, it is now anticipated by some corporate patrons. If the function is not performed, an organization's prospects of corporate support may be diminished. As a corporate official in the alcohol brewing industry noted:

> It's understood that if I'm making a major contribution at a banquet, you will ask me to say a few words. It's like routine now, that is, "it's my pleasure to present $55,000 for a scholarship" . . . Latino organizational leadership is becoming very professional--they know they have to stroke their sponsors. It's nice when you get it, in fact the wiser organizations will publish our contributions. When you see that sort of thank you note, I circulate it because it means we are appreciated. I may not remember if I don't receive this kind of thank you. But I'll remember when the organization approaches again for contributions. If I can't remember any follow up on our contribution, like a thank you note in our files or some sort of publicity, then it will probably

influence me later on.[33]

Discussion

Although in some ways Latino organizations have reacted to the Reagan administration's initiatives in a manner suggested by Piven and Cloward, they have simultaneously reacted in an unanticipated way. Corporations have acquired allies among Latinos who are encouraging political support for corporate-endorsed programs of economic renewal--programs that Dolbeare has said are antithetical to democracy. Such support, as Dolbeare has noted, has been conspicuous by its relative absence but this will probably change as a result of the continued amplification by Latino organizations.[34]

Our findings are consistent with recent theories about the role of the middle class in social change, particularly the "contradictory locations" theory developed by Eric Wright which asserts that the middle class engages in "ambiguous politics," assuming postures supportive of as well as challenging the status quo.[35] Our findings do not support the theories that hold that the middle class is likely to be exclusively a revolutionary vanguard or exclusively a reactionary force. Rather, our data demonstrate, as Wright would predict, that the Latino middle class, to which the leadership of NCLR and MALDEF belongs, practices the politics of resistance *and* the politics of accommodation. If unequivocal, vigorous resistance against corporate-supported federal initiatives is to develop further among Latinos, it will have to be spearheaded by other sectors of the population. At certain historical junctures, intellectuals have played this role. Although there are many Latino intellectuals, they appear, as Acuna has suggested, to lack the inclination to engage in political mobilization.[36]

What about the future? Will organizations such as MALDEF and NCLR continue to pursue the corporate grantsmanship and articulation strategy? We hypothesize that they will. The reasons can be delineated by using the framework developed by Freeman for the analysis of social-movement organizational decision-making.[37] In this framework, organizational actions are a function of four factors: (1) mobilizable resources possessed by the organizations; (2) constraints on the organizations' resources; (3) the structure and internal environment of the organizations; and (4) the organizations' expectations about their potential targets.

One major reason that Latino organizations will continue their corporate grantsmanship and articulation strategy is that they lack sufficiently large independent funding bases to sustain their operations. Since 1973, MALDEF has unsuccessfully tried to create such a base. Thus, entering the 1980s it found itself still having to seek funding from foundations and corporations. As its former president and general counsel, Vilma Martinez, observed:

> My big dream was that we'd have enough money to just live off the interest. But we've never been able to do that. So, basically MALDEF has to go out there every year and raise money.[38]

Additionally, the organizations do not have a membership base from which to generate funding. They lack this base, in part, because they were created as national professional social-movement organizations, or they have pursued strategies that have increasingly led them to become such organizations.[39] NCLR has become such an organization largely as a result of abandoning the strategy of community organization, as Sierra has shown.[40]

MALDEF's leadership believes that Latinos could be a source of funding for their organization. As the president and general counsel noted after being asked whether she felt that Latinos could underwrite organizations such as MALDEF:

> One thing we haven't done, which we are starting to do now is keep a central file. We have helped thousands of people in our lawsuits and advocacy efforts, and yet we have never kept a central file of these people, so that we could at some future date cultivate them, and get them to donate $25.00 a year.[41]

On the basis of this belief, MALDEF has taken steps to create a base of support through a special project--"The Hispanic Strategic Initiative Fund." The project will serve as a vehicle for "countering the attack" on the rights of Latinos by the Reagan administration's initiatives. It is to be MALDEF's *"strategic offensive tool to take back the initiative* by advocating positive solutions to the problems confronting Latinos."[42] Ultimately the project may generate the desired base of support. However, it is of such recent origin that Latinos are unlikely to serve as the exclusive source of support desired and required by the organizations in the immediate future.

At the same time, MALDEF's and NCLR's "development" units

possess the expertise necessary if the strategy is to succeed. MALDEF's "development and public relations" department is perhaps the most sophisticated among all Latino organizations. It is directed by a Vice President for Development and staffed by six professionals whose primary responsibility is the development and implementation of fund-raising as well as public relations strategies which enhance MALDEF's image and visibility. In addition to possessing grantsmanship expertise, the organizations have access to the networks and decision-makers of the corporate philanthropic sector. The organizations are valued by corporations for their visibility and influence among Latinos. Their prominence has been documented by Coca-Cola in a "visibility poll" conducted as part of a large study with the objective of ascertaining Latino attitudes and priorities.[43] The organizations' high profile has facilitated their ability to acquire support from corporations. As the MALDEF president and general counsel noted,

> We have been successful again because of the high visibility
> that we have in our community. Thus an investment in our
> organization is sending out a message.[44]

This visibility facilitates MALDEF's support from some corporations. For example, when officials of one of the major corporations in Southern California receive a MALDEF proposal, it is "immediately channeled through."[45]

The organizational leadership is highly optimistic that the corporations will respond to the grantsmanship and articulation strategy. This optimism is due in part to the findings of a survey by the Council of Foundations which sought to determine the "corporate"-giving attitudes of the chief executive officers of major corporations. As the president of NCLR maintains, the results were "very promising."[46]

The leadership recognizes that there is no guarantee Latinos "will receive a fair share" of corporate funds. But the leadership is optimistic that the potential can become a reality through work and cooperation. It treats past corporate support as evidence of corporate willingnness to provide assistance. To quote NCLR's president,

> Making the potential become reality will require persistence
> and skill on our part and good will and a sense of fair play
> on the part of chief executives.
>
> The support *we* received at our conference from the

corporate community is evidence that this sector *does* care about Hispanics. We will build on that foundation. (Emphasis in original.)[47]

The optimism is also rooted in a perception that the orientation of corporations toward Latinos is undergoing change. As the former president and general counsel of MALDEF noted:

Corporations are changing themselves. They are also undergoing change. They are becoming more sensitive to the issues presented by the Hispanic community. They are trying to improve their standing within the community. They are making very positive efforts in their minority representation at all levels. Those kinds of corporations really are, in essence, investing in themselves--which is good. Part of that investment is to the benefit of the Hispanic community.[48]

We hypothesize that the continued pursuit of corporate grantsmanship and articulation will have two major consequences. First, it will enable the organizations to continue on the road towards institutionalization and a permanent role in society.[49] It will secure for the organizations the kind of resources vital to their institutionalization, in particular, funding for the continued employment of professional staff. Institutionalization in the short-run will afford selected sectors of the Latino population discrete services and advocacy, such as the referral and technical services and assistance provided under NCLR's RAICES project. In light of the need for such services, assistance, and advocacy, their continued availability is quite significant.

Second, the pursuit of the corporate grantsmanship and articulation strategy will lead to a Latino presence in urban institutions. Some of the organizations are conducting projects which will develop such a presence; perhaps the most notable example is the MALDEF leadership development and advocacy program.[50] The development of representation, networks, and presence as new citizens through such projects is important, it goes without saying, in terms of the political strength of the Latino population. When portrayed as benefits made possible through corporate beneficence, however, the benefits obscure the negative consequences for Latinos of corporate-supported policies. We predict that a consciousness of these negative consequences is unlikely to develop in the face of continued amplification of corporate deeds by organizations such as MALDEF and NCLR. Without such a consciousness,

Latinos may not contribute to coalitions supporting governmental control of corporate interests. This probably will not disappoint corporate leaders, for, as Orren has noted, to minimize censure and control has been an objective of the corporate sector.[51] However, the failure of opposition to corporate dominance will threaten to circumscribe democracy in the United States.[52]

Lastly, we also predict that, for several reasons, the "partnerships," which the corporate grantsmanship and articulation strategy is producing, will not benefit all Latinos, as some of their proponents claim.[53] One reason is that the development of the partnerships places a high premium on the capacity of organizations to engage in grantsmanship and on organizational visibility, but as the demise of several hundred organizations testifies, not all organizations possess a similar capacity or visibility.

Corporate support is unlikely to continue indefinitely because such support is only feasible when corporations are economically successful. The overwhelming majority of current corporate supporters is successful; they will continue to provide support so long as their economic health is good. As an official of one of the major corporate contributors noted:

> . . . We are very lucky in that year after year we have seen increases in sales. We have not had a negative sales trend. If things were to slow down and we actually saw a retreat in sales we may see a reversal in the funding of projects. Services come from the profits we make and as profits decline so do our other activities. So we have been very lucky. Until the economy picks up and strengthens, we're picking up where the government is leaving off in a lot of cases and we just can't continue to do it. I visualize in the future that I will get a memo that says reject eighty percent of the proposals.[54]

The pursuit of the corporate grantsmanship and articulation strategy indicates that Latino organizations are serious about providing services to Latinos. However, we believe that if the unequal status of the Latino population is to be remedied, the strategy must be supplemented with, if not replaced by, a strategy of garnering corporate support for policies such as vigorous affirmative action or guaranteed annual income. The latter has a greater potential to diminish inequality than does service provision, because it is less dependent on corporate economic success for its effectiveness. It remains to be seen whether such a course of action will be pursued.

Appendix A

About one-third of the National Council of La Raza's funding comes from corporations and corporate foundations. Their support enables the Council to maintain field offices which provide capacity-building technical assistance to the NCLR network, pays a considerable proportion of the organization's administrative costs, and makes possible the annual conference.

Listed below are the corporations and corporate foundations which have contributed at least $2,500 annually to NCLR during Fiscal Year 1983 or thus far in 1984. The Council hopes that members of the NCLR network will review this list and express their appreciation to the representatives of these corporations who are attending the conference.

NCLR also hopes that when members of the NCLR network are purchasing goods or services, they will remember--and buy from--these friends of the Council.

ABC, Inc.
Aetna Life and Casualty Foundation
Alcoa Foundation
Allied Corporation
Allstate Insurance Company and Foundation
American Can Company and Foundation
American Express Foundation
Foundation
American Gas Association
American Petroleum Institute
American Telephone and Telegraph Co.
Anheuser-Busch, Inc.
Arizona Public Service
Atlantic Richfield Company and Foundation
Avon Products, Inc.
Bell Atlantic
Burger King Corporation
Carnation Company
CBS, Inc.
Chevron U.S.A., Inc., and the Chevron Fund

Cigna Corporation
Citibank, N.A.
Clairol, Inc.
Coca-Cola, U.S.A.
Conoco, Inc.
Adolph Coors Company
Cummins Engine

Dayton Hudson Corporation
    and Foundation
Digital Equipment Corp.
Eastern Airlines
Edison Electric Institute
Equitable Life Assurance
    Society
Exxon Company, U.S.A.
Ford Motor Company
Gannett Company, Inc., and
    Foundation
General Motors Corporation

Grumman Aerospace Corporation
GTE Corporation and Foundation
Gulf Oil Corporation
Hewlett Packard Company
Hiram Walker Corporation
IBM Corporation
Johnson & Johnson Family of Companies
 and Contribution Fund
Kraft, Inc.
Levi Strauss Foundation
Litton Industries, Inc.
McDonald's Corporation
McGraw-Hill, Inc.
Metropolitan Life Insurance Company
 and Foundation
Miller Brewing Company
Monsanto Corporation
NBC, Inc.
Nestle Company
New York Life Foundation
Prudential Insurance Company of America
 and Foundation
Rockwell International Corporation
 and Trust
Joseph E. Seagram and Sons, Inc.
G. D. Searle and Company
Sears, Roebuck and Company
Seven-Up Company
Shell Companies Foundation
State Farm Insurance Company
Sun Company
Tenneco, Inc.
Time, Inc.
United Parcel Service of America, Inc. (UPS)
Wang Laboratories, Inc.
Warner-Lambert, Inc.
Westinghouse Electric Corporation
Xerox Foundation

Notes

1.   K. Dolbeare, *Democracy at Risk*   (Chatham: Chatham House Publishers, 1984); F. F. Piven and R. Cloward, *The New Class War: Reagan's Attack on the Welfare State and its Consequences* (New York: Pantheon Books, 1982).

2.   Dolbeare, *Democracy at Risk*, 215.

3.   K. Whisler, "How Hispanic Organizations Have Fared with the Cutbacks: A Survey," *Caminos* 3 (April 1983): 54-55.

4.   R. de la Garza, "And Then There Were Some . . . Chicanos as National Political Actors, 1967-1980," *Aztlan* 15 (Spring 1984): 1-24.

5.   C. M. Sierra, "The Political Transformation of a Minority Organization: The Council of La Raza, 1965-1980" (Ph.D. diss., Stanford University, 1982).

6.   J. Avila, *Report to the MALDEF Board of Directors* (San Francisco: Mexican-American Legal Defense and Education Fund, 1983).

7.   V. Martinez, *Report to the MALDEF Board of Directors* (San Francisco: Mexican-American Legal Defense and Education Fund, 1981); V. Martinez, *Report to the MALDEF Board of Directors* (San Francisco: Mexican-American Legal Defense and Education Fund, 1982); J. Avila, *Report to the MALDEF Board of Directors* (San Francisco: Mexican-American Legal Defense and Education Fund, 1983).

8.   Piven and Cloward, *The New Class War;* Dolbeare, *Democracy at Risk.*

9.   As used here, the term "corporate grantsmanship and articulation strategy" refers to efforts to secure corporate funds for organizational operations and activities, the definition of issues, and the development of strategies.

10.   M. V. Marin, "Protest in an Urban Barrio: The Chicano Movement in East Los Angeles" (Ph.D. diss., University of California, Santa Barbara, 1980);

C. M. Sierra, "The Political Transformation of a Minority Organization: The Council of La Raza, 1965-1980" (Ph.D. diss., Stanford University, 1982).

11.   "Corporate Money for Organizations . . . Who Gives It? . . . Where Does It Go?" *Nuestro* 6 (March 1982): 27-31.

12.   Whisler, "Hispanic Organizations."

13.   Mexican American Legal Defense and Education Fund, "Some Corporate Friends," *MALDEF* 12 (Spring/Summer1982): 8.

14.   Ibid.

15.   Project *Raices* is a project through which NCLR provides technical assistance of various kinds to community organizations. The technical assistance ranges from fiscal expertise to advice on grant research and writing. The assistance is intended to facilitate the organizations' ability to survive and to provide services to Latinos.

16.   National Council of La Raza, "Policy Analysis Update," *El Noticiario* 4 (First Quarter 1985): 2.

17.   H. Gallegos, "Making a Dent in the Corporate Sector," *Nuestro* 6 (November 1982): 49-51.

18.   "Hispanics and the Private Sector: New Partnerships," *Caminos*, April, 1983, 42-43, 66.

19.   National Council of La Raza, "Seventh Annual NCLR Conference to Focus on Hispanic Leadership," *El Noticiario* 3 (First Quarter 1984): 1-3.

20.   Ibid.

21.   National Council of La Raza, "NCLR Conference Focus: Hispanic Groups/Private Sector Cooperation," *El Noticiario* 4 (First Quarter 1985): 2.

22.   The signing of the agreement evoked criticism from several sectors of the Latino population. The signees acknowledged that the support of Coors and other corporations amounted to "corporate paternalism" (A. Jaramillo, "Coors & Hispanics--Time Now to Show Some Good Faith," *Hispanic Link,*

3 March 1985). However, they justified the agreement either by demonstrating that its terms were superior to the terms of the agreement signed by Coors and black organizations (Jaramillo, *Hispanic Link*) or by dismissing the criticism as sour grapes on the part of malcontents among Latinos.

23. T. Diaz, "Coors and Hispanics: A New Business Partnership," *Hispanic Business Review*, January/February 1985, 16-21.

24. K. Orren, "Corporate Power and the Slums: Is Big Business a Paper Tiger?" *Theoretical Perspectives on Urban Politics*, ed. D. Willis, et al. (Englewood Cliffs, N.J.: Prentice-Hall, 1976), 46-47.

25. Ibid., 58.

26. Ibid.

27. Mexican American Legal Defense and Education Fund, "Some Corporate Friends," *MALDEF* 12 (Spring/Summer1982): 8.

28. MALDEF, "Anheuser-Busch Grant Spurs Leadership, Citizenship," *MALDEF* 12 (Fall/Winter 1982): 1.

29. MALDEF, "MALDEF Dinners: Success in Los Angeles," *MALDEF* 12 (Fall/Winter 1982): 5.

30. National Council of La Raza, "Seventh Annual NCLR Conference to Focus on Hispanic Leadership," *El Noticiario* 3 (First Quarter 1984): 1-3.

31. NCLR, "Council Appreciates Corporate Assistance," *Seventh Annual Conference Program*, 1984.

32. NCLR, "GM's John McNulty, Cong. Garcia Among Those to be Honored at 1984 National Conference," *El Noticiario* (Second Quarter 1984): 1-2.

33. Interview, anonymous, 16 March 1985.

34. Dolbeare, *Democracy at Risk*.

35.   E. Wright, "Intellectuals and the Working Class," *Insurgent Sociologist* 3 (Fall 1978): 5-17.

36.   R. Acuna, "La Generacion de 1968: Unfulfilled Dreams," *Caminos,* 1982.

37.   Jo Freeman, "Resource Mobilization and Strategy: A Model for Analyzing Social Movement Organization Actions," *The Dynamics of Social Movements,* ed. J. D. Zald and M. N. McCarthy (Cambridge; Mass: Winthrop Publishers, Inc., 1979).

38.   Interview, Vilma Martinez, 16 March 84. The interviews with the officials of MALDEF were conducted by Alma Candelaria, an undergraduate student at the University of California, Santa Barbara, at the time.

39.   The term "professional social movement organization" was initially used by J. D. McCarthy and M. N. Zald, *The Trend of Social Movements in America: Professionalization and Resource Mobilization* (Morristown, N.J.: General Learning Press, 1973). It refers to an organization that seeks to bring about social change through activities conducted by professionals, such as lawyers, who earn their living through full-time employment in the organization; K. O'Connor and L. Epstein, "A Legal Voice for the Chicano Community: The Activities of the Mexican-American Legal and Educational Fund," *Social Science Quarterly* 15 (1984): 245-67.

40.   C. M. Sierra, "The Political Transformation of a Minority Organization: The Council of La Raza, 1965-1980" (Ph.D. diss., Stanford University, 1982).

41.   Interview, Joaquin Avila, 22 March 1984.

42.   Avila to *Friend of MALDEF,* 1985.

43.   Coca-Cola, 1984.

44.   Interview, Joaquin Avila, 22 March 1984.

45.   Interview, anonymous, 16 March 1985.

46.   "Hispanics and the Private Sector: New Partnerships," *Caminos,* April, 1983, 43.

47.   Ibid.

48.   Interview, Joaquin Avila, 22 March 1984.

49.   The term "institutionalization" refers to the achievement of stable enduring operations and a distinctive role played by an organization within the social structure.

50.   This program was initiated in 1980 by MALDEF as a vehicle for overcoming the pattern of underrepresentation or nonrepresentation of Latinos on public boards and commissions at the local level. The program provides training to qualify them for appointment to relevant boards. Funded primarily by a grant from Anheuser-Busch, Inc., the program has contributed to the representation of Latinos on local boards and commissions and the establishment of networks of professionals in selected parts of California and Colorado. It has been complemented with a legislative internship program in Washington D.C. and in California, as well as a citizenship program designed to facilitate the naturalization of Mexican nationals, a group regarded by MALDEF as a potentially potent political force.

51.   Orren, "Corporate Power and the Slums."

52.   Dolbeare, *Democracy at Risk;* Piven and Cloward, *The New Class War.*

53.   Jaramillo, "Coors & Hispanics."

54.   Interview, anonymous, 16 March 1985.

References

Acuna, R. "La Generacion de 1968: Unfulfilled Dreams." *Caminos* (1982).

Avila, J. *Report to the MALDEF Board of Directors*. San Francisco: Mexican-American Legal Defense and Education Fund, 1983.

"Corporate Money for Organizations . . . Who Gives It? . . . Where Does It Go?" *Nuestro* 6 (1982).

de la Garza, R. "And Then There Were Some...Chicanos as National Political Actors, 1967-1980." *Aztlan* 15 (1984).

Diaz, T. "Coors and Hispanics: A New Business Partnership." *Hispanic Business Review* (1985).

Dolbeare, K. *Democracy at Risk*. Chatham: Chatham House Publishers, 1984.

Freeman, Jo. "Resource Mobilization and Strategy: A Model for Analyzing Social Movement Organization Actions." *The Dynamics of Social Movements*. Edited by J. D. Zald and M. N. McCarthy. Cambridge, Mass: Winthrop Publishers, Inc., 1979.

Gallegos, H. "Making a Dent in the Corporate Sector." *Nuestro* 6 (1982).

"Hispanics and the Private Sector: New Partnerships." *Caminos*. April 1983.

Jaramillo, A. "Coors & Hispanics--Time Now to Show Some Good Faith." *Hispanic Link,* 3 March 1985.

Martinez, V. *Report to the MALDEF Board of Directors*. San Francisco: Mexican-American Legal Defense and Education Fund, 1981.

-----. *Report to the MALDEF Board of Directors*. San Francisco: Mexican-American Legal Defense and Education Fund, 1982.

McCarthy, J. D., and Zald, M. N. *The Trend of Social Movements in America: Professionalization and Resource Mobilization.* Morristown, N.J.: General Learning Press, 1973.

Mexican American Legal Defense and Education Fund. "Some Corporate Friends." *MALDEF* 12 (Spring/Summer 1982).

-----. "Anheuser-Busch Grant Spurs Leadership, Citizenship." *MALDEF* 12 (Fall/Winter 1982).

-----. "Federal Budget Unfair to Latinas." *MALDEF* 12 (Spring/Summer 1983).

"The Movement's Organization Man." *Nuestro* 6 (March 1982).

National Council of La Raza. "Seventh Annual NCLR Conference to Focus on Hispanic Leadership." *El Noticiario* 3 (First Quarter 1984).

-----. "GM's John McNulty, Cong. Garcia Among Those to be Honored at 1984 National Conference." *El Noticiario* 3 (Second Quarter 1984).

-----. "Council Appreciates Corporate Assistance." *Seventh Annual Conference Program* (1984).

-----. "Policy Analysis Update." *El Noticiario* 4 (First Quarter 1985).

O'Connor, K., and Epstein, L. "A Legal Voice for the Chicano Community: The Activities of the Mexican-American Legal and Educational Fund." *Social Science Quarterly* 15 (1984).

Orren, K. "Corporate Power and the Slums: Is Big Business a Paper Tiger?" *Theoretical Perspectives on Urban Politics.* Edited by D. Willis, et al., pp. 46-47. Englewood Cliffs, N.J.: Prentice-Hall, 1976.

Piven, F. F., and R. Cloward. *The New Class War: Reagan's Attack on the Welfare State and its Consequences.* New York: Pantheon Books, 1982.

Sierra, C. M. "The Political Transformation of a Minority Organization: The Council of La Raza, 1965-1980." Ph.D. Dissertation, Stanford University, 1982.

Tybout, R. A. "Cooperation, Not Confrontation." *Sierra* 70 (1985).

Whisler, K. "How Hispanic Organizations Have Fared with the Cutbacks: A Survey." *Caminos* 3 (1983).

Wright, E. "Intellectuals and the Working Class." *Insurgent Sociologist* 3 (1978).

Notes on Contributors

Sucheng Chan is Professor of History at the University of California, Santa Barbara. She received her Ph.D. in 1973 from the University of California, Berkeley. She specializes in the comparative study of Asian international migrations and the economic history of Asian Americans. She has published "Overseas Sikhs in the Context of International Migrations," in *Sikh Studies: Comparative Perspectives on a Changing Tradition*, ed. Mark Juergensmeyer and N. Gerald Barrier (Berkeley: Graduate Theological Union, 1979), 191-206; "Public Policy, U.S.–China Relations, and the Chinese American Experience: An Interpretive Essay" in *Pluralism, Racism, and Public Policy: The Search for Equality*, ed. Edwin G. Clausen and Jack Bermingham (Boston: G.K. Hall and Co., 1981), 5-38; "Chinese Livelihood in Rural California: The Impact of Economic Change, 1860-1880," *Pacific Historical Review* 53 (1984): 273-307; *This Bittersweet Soil: The Chinese in California Agriculture, 1860-1910* (Berkeley and Los Angeles: University of California Press, 1986); *Asians in California History* (San Francisco: Boyd and Fraser Publishing Co., 1988); and "Chinese American Entrepreneur: The California Career of Chin Lung," in *Chinese America: History and Perspectives, 1987*, 73-86.

Jenni Currie is a graduate student in Teaching English as a Foreign/Second Language at San Francisco State University.

Michael W. Fitzgerald is Assistant Professor of History at St. Olaf College, Northfield, MN. He received his Ph.D. in 1986 from the University of California, Los Angeles. He specializes in the study of Afro-American and southern U.S. history. He has published *The Union League Movement in Alabama and Mississippi: Politics and Agricultural Change in the Deep South During Reconstruction* (Baton Rouge: Louisiana State University Press, 1988); and "Radical Republicanism and the White Yeomanry during Alabama Reconstruction, 1865-1868," *Journal of Southern History*, forthcoming.

Gilbert G. Gonzalez is Associate Professor of Comparative Cultures at the University of California, Irvine. He received his Ph.D. in 1974 from the University of California, Los Angeles. He specializes in the study of Chicanos/Latinos in the U.S., U.S. educational history, and Chicano community development in the Southwest. He has published "Racism, Education, and the Mexican Community in Los Angeles, 1920-1930," *Societas* 4 (Autumn 1974): 287-300; *Progressive Education: A Marxist Interpretation* (Minneapolis: Marxist Education Press, 1982); and "Segregation of Mexican

Children in a Southern California City: The Legacy of Expansionism and the American Southwest," *The Western Historical Quarterly* 16 (1985): 55-76.

Ramón A. Gutiérrez is Assistant Professor of History at the University of California, San Diego. He received his Ph.D. in 1980 from the University of Wisconsin, Madison. He specializes in the study of the cultural history of the Hispanic Southwest, with particular interest in religion, gender ideology, and the history of sexuality. He has published "El Problema Chicano," *Historia* 16 (June 1977): 104-09; "From Honor to Love: Transformation of the Meaning of Sexuality in Colonial New Mexico," *Interpreting Kinship Ideology and Practice in Latin America,* ed. Raymond T. Smith (Chapel Hill: University of North Carolina Press, 1984), 237-63; and "Honor Ideology, Marriage Negotiation, and Class-Gender Domination in New Mexico, 1690-1846," *Latin American Perspectives* 44 (Winter 1985): 81-104.

Aida Hurtado is Assistant Professor of Psychology at the University of California, Santa Cruz. She received her Ph.D. in 1982 from the University of Michigan. She specializes in the study of social identity, language attitudes, and political consciousness. She has published (with P. Garcia), "Joblessness Among Hispanic Youth: 1973-1981," *Aztlan: Chicano Journal of the Social Sciences and Arts* 15 (1984): 243-61; and (with P. Gurin), "Ethnic Identity and Attitudes Towards Bilingualism," *Hispanic Journal of Behavioral Sciences* 9 (1987): 1-18.

Karen Leonard is Professor of Social Relations at the University of California, Irvine. She received her Ph.D. in 1969 from the University of Wisconsin, Madison. She specializes in the study of caste, family, ethnicity, and social history of India and of Asian Americans in rural California. She has published *Social History of an Indian Caste: The Kayasths of Hyderabad* (Berkeley and Los Angeles: University of California Press, 1978; Indian edition, Delhi: Oxford University Press, 1978); "The Hyderabad Political System and its Participants," *Journal of Asian Studies* 30 (1971): 569-82; "The 'Great Firm' Theory of Mughal Decline," *Comparative Studies in Society and History* 21 (1979): 151-67; (with John Leonard), "Social Reform and Women's Participation in Political Culture: Andhra and Madras," *The Extended Family: Women and Political Participation in India and Pakistan,* ed. Gail Minault (Columbus, Mo.: South Asia Books and Delhi: Chanakhya Publications, 1981); (with Bruce LaBrack), "Conflict and Compatibility in Punjabi-Mexican Immigrant Families in Rural California: 1915-1965," *Journal of Marriage and the Family* 46 (1984): 527-37; "Punjabi Farmers and California's Alien Land Law," *Agricultural History* 59 (1985): 549-62.

Gene N. Levine is Professor of Sociology at the University of California, Los Angeles. He received his Ph.D. in 1959 from Columbia University. He specializes in the study of ethnic, racial, and religious minority groups. He has published *Workers Vote* (Totowa, N.J.: Bedminster Press, 1963); *Inducing Social Change in Developing Communities* (N.Y. and Geneva: United Nations, 1967); *Confronting New Ways* (Geneva: U.N. Research Institute for Social Development, 1975); (Ed.), "Research on Racial and Cultural Minorities" *Journal of Social Issues* 33 (1977): 175-78; (with C. Rhodes), *The Japanese American Community* (N.Y.: Praeger Publishers, 1981); (with J. Modell), *Public Opinion on the Fallout Shelter Issue* (N.Y.: Clearwater Publishing Co., 1981).

Marguerite V. Marin is Assistant Professor of Sociology at Gonzaga University, Spokane, Washington, and formerly research sociologist at the Social Process Research Institute, University of California, Santa Barbara. She received her Ph.D. in 1980 from the University of California, Santa Barbara. She specializes in the study of social movements, stratification, and political sociology. She has recently completed a book-length manuscript on Chicano protest organizations in the Los Angeles area during 1966-1974 and is presently working on an article on race and class as feminist issues.

Maria Eugenia Matute-Bianchi is Associate Professor of Education at the University of California, Santa Cruz. She received her Ph.D. in 1979 from Stanford University. She specializes in the study of minority group education, bilingual education, and cross-cultural education. She has published (with John Ogbu), "Understanding Sociocultural Factors: Knowledge, Identity and Adjustment,"*Beyond Language* (Los Angeles: Evaluation, Dissemination, and Assessment Center, California State University, Los Angeles,1986); "Ethnic Identities and Patterns of School Success and Failure Among Mexican-Descent and Japanese American Students in a California High School: An Ethnographic Analysis," *American Journal of Education* 95 (1986): 233-55.

Michael Omi is Lecturer in Asian American Studies at the University of California, Berkeley. He received his Ph.D. in Sociology from the University of California, Santa Cruz in 1987. He has published (with Howard Winant) *Racial Formation in the United States: From the 1960s to the 1980s* (New York and London: Routledge & Kegan Paul, 1986).

Isidro D. Ortiz is Assistant Professor of Mexican American Studies at San Diego State University and formerly research political scientist at the Social Process Research Institute, University of California, Santa Barbara. He received his Ph.D. in 1978 from Stanford University. He specializes in the study of

Chicano/Latino politics with an emphasis on organizational politics. He has published "Chicano Urban Politics and the Politics of Reform in the Seventies," *Western Political Quarterly* 37 (1984): 564-77; "The Political Economy of Chicano Urban Politics," *Plural Societies* 11 (1980): 41-54; (co-edited with Eugene E. Garcia and Francisco Lomeli), *Chicano Studies: A Multidisciplinary Approach* (New York: Teachers College Press, Columbia University, 1984).

Alvina Quintana is a doctoral candidate in the History of Consciousness program at the University of California, Santa Cruz. She will receive her Ph.D. in 1988. She specializes in the study of feminist theory, literary criticism, cultural theory, and Marxist theory and semiotics. She has published "Language, Power & Women," *Critical Perspectives* (University of California, Berkeley: Ethnic Studies Dept., 1984), 10-20; "Prisoners of the Word," *Chicana Voices: Intersections of Race, Class & Gender* (Austin: Center for Mexican-American Studies. 1986), 208-18; "Expanding a Feminist View: Challenge & Counter-Challenge," *Revista Mujeres* 2 (1985): 11-20. "Being-Not Being: Reflections on Questions Regarding the Self," *Tecolote*, Dec. 1985, 4; "O Mama, With What's Inside of Me," *Revista Mujeres* 3 (1986): 38-40; "Contemporary Chicana Poetry: a Review," *Third Woman* (Bloomington: Third Woman Press, 1986), 144-46.

Mary Stephanie Reynolds is a doctoral candidate in the Comparative Cultures program at the University of California, Irvine. She will receive her Ph.D. in 1988. She specializes in the study of cross-cultural dance, philosophy, religion, and the visual arts. She has published "Concepts of Nature and Power: Environmental Ethics of the Northern Ute," *Environomental Review* 9 (1985): 150-70; "Imperatives and Persuasion in the Conservation of Culture: Gender Constraints in Tongan Dance," *Proceedings of the Third International Symposium of the Pacific Arts Association, September 1984* (New York: Metropolitan Museum of Art, forthcoming).